THE HARMONIZED

GOSPEL

Apocalyptic Version

by
Pallant Ramsundar

602 apokalupsis (ap-ok-al'-oop-sis);
from 601; disclosure: (Strong's Greek/Hebrew dictionary)
- appearing, coming, lighten, manifestation, be revealed, revelation.

Dan 12:9 And he said, Go your way, Daniel:
for the words are closed up and sealed till the time of the end. (NKJV)

The Harmonized Gospel

Apocalyptic Version

Copyright © 2023 Pallant Ramsundar

All rights reserved. No part of this publication may be reproduced, distributed, or transmitted in any form or by any means, including photocopying, recording, or other electronic or mechanical methods, without the prior written permission of the publisher, except in the case of brief quotations embodied in critical reviews and certain other noncommercial uses permitted by copyright law.

ISBN-13: 978-0-9860958-0-1

4th Edition—October 2023

Book abbreviations used are:
Matthew - Matt; Mt
Mark - Mark; Mk
Luke - Luke; Lk
John - John; Jn

ACKNOWLEDGEMENTS

We owe a debt of gratitude to those, throughout the ages, who assiduously studied and offered comments and analyses on various aspects of the Bible.

A special thanks to
Mr. Herbert Armstrong
for his work in unveiling many biblical truths that were lost over the centuries, and the ministers, teachers and writers of the Churches of God, who propagated his work.

Foremost, we give thanks and praise to the Eternal God for preserving His word and inspiring its revelation to many along the way, as part of His continuing creative work.

FOREWORD

This Book began as a straightforward paraphrase of the Gospels of Matthew, Mark, Luke and John in the pattern of my previous book 'The Apocalyptic Version of the Books of Genesis and Revelation with Commentary'. The intention was to present the Gospels in modern day language and especially to provide a commentary covering some new insights into the Bible.

However, in analyzing the Gospel accounts, I found that the Synoptic Gospels (Matthew, Mark and Luke) largely focus on the closing ministry of Christ lasting five to six months. The Gospel of John, on the other hand, focused on filling some gaps in Christ's life prior to and during that period and did so non-sequentially.

Since existing works on the Harmony of the Gospels generally do not consider these factors, I felt that readers would be better served by a Gospel account that integrates the four Gospels into a chronological biography of Jesus Christ. This book is the result.

The Gospel of Matthew was chosen as the backbone for this publication, not only because of his apostolic credentials, but also since he had a background as a tax collector and is likely to be more precise in his record. For the most part, this work presents events in the life of Jesus chronologically, except for some subject matter agglomeration and juxtaposition of similar statements made by Jesus at different times. Examples of these are the discussions on the Sabbath (Matt 12, Mark 2 & 3, Luke 6, 12 &13) and the parables.

My sincere hope is that this work will bring more clarity to the life and teachings of Jesus Christ and also help readers to strengthen their faith in God and in His divine inspiration of the Bible.

Pallant Ramsundar

October 2023

CONTENTS

Foreword	v
The Harmonized Gospels	1
Unassigned Scriptures	175
Chapter Listing (Numeric)	176
Chapter Listing (Alphabetic)	181
Verse Finder Index	187

The Harmonized Gospels — Apocalyptic Version

CHAPTER I
The origin of Jesus Christ

A From eternity, a being called 'the Word' existed. This 'Word' always was a God and he was with another God being[1].	Jn1:1
B From eternity, these two were together.	Jn1:2
C The 'Word' was involved in everything that was done and nothing was made without his participation[2].	Jn1:3
D He too possessed eternal life and his manifestation was a light to mankind.	Jn1:4
E This light shone in darkness of *this world* and the world did not understand it.	Jn1:5
F His was the true Light, which shows the way to everyone born into the world.	Jn1:9
G He was in the world, which was made by him, but the world did not know him.	Jn1:10
H He came to his creation and they did not receive him.	Jn1:11
I But to those who will receive him, he makes them into the very sons of God. This he does to all who come to believe in him.	Jn1:12
J He was made flesh and blood, not by any human means, but by the power of God.	Jn1:13
K This 'Word' was made flesh and walked among us. We did witness his excellence as the only one sired of the Father, full of grace and truth,	Jn1:14
L and of this fullness and abounding grace we have all partook.	Jn1:16
M For the law was given through Moses, *while* forgiveness truly came by Jesus Christ[3].	Jn1:17
N Here then is the gospel of Jesus Christ[4], the Son of God.	Mk1:1

---

1 This is the first time in the Bible that God has clearly revealed himself to be two entities working in consort. The old testament merely hinted at the true nature of God in Gen 1:26, where God said 'Let **us** make man in **our** image ...', while prophesying of Christ's future role in Dan 7:9 ~14; Ps 110:1 and Is 9:6 . The entity that John calls 'The Word' in John 1:1 gave up his immortality and became Jesus Christ (John 1:14; Phil 2:6 ~ 8) while the other God entity was referred to as 'The Father' by Christ (Matt 11:28). Christ's prior existence as a God being is reinforced in Matt 1:23 and John 17:5.
2 'The Word' was involved in all creation (John 1:3, 10) and he was the God being that directly communicated with mankind prior to his manifestation as Jesus Christ (John 1:18; Gen 3:9; Gen 18:13; Gen 32:30; Jos 5:14-15; ICor 10:4; Heb 7:1-3).
3 Though Moses wrote down the law, statutes and judgments, it was the pre-incarnate Christ who gave them to him (Ex 34:1; Lev 26:46; Num 30:16).
4 The Books of Matthew, Mark, Luke and John have come to be known as the Gospels and are historical accounts of the life, work and teachings of Jesus Christ. The word 'gospel' is derived from the Greek 'euaggelion' (Strong's 2098) meaning good news or good message. The good news that Christ delivered was about a new and perfect government to be set up by God, and that all humans could be eventually reborn as immortals because Christ would die to clear their sins.

CHAPTER 2

The miraculous conception of John the Baptist

A During the reign of Herod, king of Judaea, there was a priest named Zacharias, of the course of Abia[1]. His wife, Elisabeth, was also from the line of Aaron.	Lk1:5
B Both of them were righteous, walking faithfully before God in all the commandments and ordinances of the Lord.	Lk1:6
C However, they were childless, because Elisabeth was barren, and they were now in their old age.	Lk1:7
D One day, Zacharias was carrying out his duties as a priest in the temple according to the schedule of his course.	Lk1:8
E By tradition, his assigned job as a priest was to burn incense in the temple of the Lord,	Lk1:9
F and he was carrying out this task at the appointed time, while a sizable number of people were praying before the altar.	Lk1:10
G Then, on the right side of the altar, an angel of the Lord appeared and stood before him.	Lk1:11
H Zacharias looked at the angel with some trepidation,	Lk1:12
I but the angel said to him 'Do not be afraid , Zacharias, for your prayer has been heard. Your wife Elisabeth shall give birth to your son, and you shall name him John.	Lk1:13
J 'You shall rejoice and be happy and many others shall rejoice at his birth,	Lk1:14
K 'for he shall be great in the sight of the Lord. He shall drink neither wine nor strong drink and he shall be led by God, even from his mother's womb.	Lk1:15
K 'He shall turn many of the children of Israel to the Lord their God,	Lk1:16
L 'and he shall go before him in the spirit and power of Elias, to turn the hearts of the fathers to the children, and the disobedient to righteousness, and so make ready a people prepared for the Lord[2]'.	Lk1:17
M Zacharias then said to the angel 'How can I believe this, seeing that I am an old man and my wife is quite old also?'	Lk1:18
N The angel answering 'I am Gabriel, who stands in the presence of God. I have been sent to speak to you of this wonderful news.	Lk1:19
O 'But because you do not believe me, you shall be dumb and unable to speak, until the day that this event is fulfilled in its due time'.	Lk1:20
P The people were waiting for Zacharias to come out to them from the temple altar and were wondering why he was taking so long.	Lk1:21
Q When he did eventually come out, he could not speak, but he gestic-	Lk1:22

---

1 The priests were rostered for duty at the temple according to their lineage. This arrangement was formalized in the days of king David (IChron 24:10).
2 Mal 4:5-6

ulated to the people and they understood that he had seen a vision in the temple and had become speechless.
R As soon as his schedule of service in the temple was accomplished, he went to his own house. | Lk1:23
S As prophesied, his wife Elisabeth conceived. She kept the news to herself for five months, and then said | Lk1:24
T 'The Lord has done good to me at this time and has looked with kindness on me to take away my childlessness'. | Lk1:25

CHAPTER 3
Gabriel visits Mary

A In the sixth month, the angel Gabriel was sent by God to a town of Galilee, called Nazareth, | Lk1:26
B to speak to Mary. She was a virgin betrothed to a man named Joseph, of the house of David. | Lk1:27
C The angel greeted her and said 'You are greatly blessed for the Lord is with you. Of all women, you have been singularly blessed'. | Lk1:28
D Mary looked at the angel with some puzzlement, wondering about his salutation. | Lk1:29
E The angel then said to her 'Do not be afraid Mary, for you have been favored by God. | Lk1:30
F 'You will shortly conceive a child and bear a son, whom you shall call "Jesus". | Lk1:31
G 'He shall be great, and he shall be called the Son of the Highest. To him will the Lord God give the throne of his fore-father David, | Lk1:32
H 'and he shall reign over the house of Jacob forever. His kingdom will have no end'. | Lk1:33
I Mary said to the angel 'How can this be, seeing that I have not been with a man?' | Lk1:34
J The angel replied 'God shall reach out to you and His power will work in you, so that the child you bear shall be called the Son of God[1]. | Lk1:35
K 'Know this too, that your cousin Elisabeth has also conceived a son in her old age, and this is the sixth month of her pregnancy, though she was barren. | Lk1:36
L 'With God nothing shall be impossible'. | Lk1:37
M Then Mary said 'I am the handmaid of the Lord. Let it be to me as you have said' and the angel departed. | Lk1:38

---

1 The Holy Spirit carries the mind and character of God, Presently the Holy Spirit fills the Father and Jesus Christ, and fractionally guides the members of the true church (John 1:1, 14:7; 2 Cor 5:5), with the intention to eventually extend it fully to mankind (Joel 2:28). God created Adam and all creation (Gen 2:19). Causing Mary's ovum to divide and form Jesus Christ is much less complex than the original creative work described in the book of Genesis. (Gen 2:7, 21-22; Luke 1:35)

CHAPTER 4
Mary visits Elizabeth

A Mary right away set out for a town in the highlands of Judah, — *Lk1:39*
B and coming to the house of Zacharias she greeted Elisabeth. — *Lk1:40*
C As soon as Elisabeth heard Mary's words, the baby leapt in her womb and the power of God stirred up Elisabeth. — *Lk1:41*
D Under inspiration she said 'You are singularly blessed among women and blessed also is the fruit of your womb. — *Lk1:42*
E 'For even the mother of my Lord has come to me. — *Lk1:43*
F 'As soon as I heard your greeting, the baby leapt in my womb for joy. — *Lk1:44*
G 'Blessed is she that believed, for all the things told to her by the Lord will come to pass'. — *Lk1:45*
H Mary replied 'My heart gives glory to the Lord — *Lk1:46*
I 'and all my being rejoices in God my Savior. — *Lk1:47*
J 'For he has looked on this insignificant handmaiden and from now onwards, all generations shall call me blessed. — *Lk1:48*
K 'He that is mighty has done great things to me. Holy is his name, — *Lk1:49*
L 'and his mercy is on those that fear him from generation to generation. — *Lk1:50*
M 'By the strength of his arm he has scattered the proud in the imaginings of their hearts. — *Lk1:51*
N 'He has put down the mighty from their exalted place and raised up those of low estate. — *Lk1:52*
O 'He has filled the hungry with good things and sent the rich away with nothing. — *Lk1:53*
P 'He has lifted up his servant Israel, who He looks on with his tender mercy, — *Lk1:54*
Q 'as He promised to our father Abraham and to his seed for ever'. — *Lk1:55*
R Mary stayed with Elizabeth for about three months and then returned to her own house. — *Lk1:56*

CHAPTER 5
Joseph marries Mary

A Mary was betrothed to Joseph, but before they had any sexual activity, she was found to be pregnant with the child created in her by God. — *Mt1:18*
B Joseph, her betrothed husband, was a god-fearing man and did not want to humiliate her in public, so he sought to quietly terminate their relationship. — *Mt1:19*
C As he considered what to do, he had a dream, in which an angel of the Lord appeared to him and said 'Joseph, offspring of David, do not be afraid to take Mary as your wife, for the child she carries is created in her by God. — *Mt1:20*

The Harmonized Gospels — Apocalyptic Version

D She shall bear a son, and you shall call his name "JESUS", for he shall save his people from their sins'.	Mt1:21
E All of these events fulfilled the prophecy of the Lord, which says,	Mt1:22
F 'It will come to pass that a virgin shall be with child, and shall bring forth a son, who they shall call "Emmanuel", which means, "God with us[1]"'.	Mt1:23
G Joseph awoke and did as the angel of the Lord had instructed him, by making Mary his wife.	Mt1:24
H Joseph did not have sexual relations with her until after she had borne her firstborn son, who he named 'Jesus'[2].	Mt1:25

CHAPTER 6
The birth of John the Baptist

A Elisabeth's pregnancy came to term and she delivered a son.	Lk1:57
B Her neighbors and her relations heard of how the Lord in His great mercy had blessed her and they all rejoiced with her.	Lk1:58
C On the eighth day, as they circumcised the child[3], they expected to call him Zacharias, after his father,	Lk1:59
D but his mother said to them 'No. He shall be called John'.	Lk1:60
E Those with her said 'But you have no kindred that is called by that name'.	Lk1:61
F They called his father and asked him what to name the child.	Lk1:62
G *Zacharias* signaled for a writing tablet and wrote, 'His name is John'. At this the people were all amazed.	Lk1:63
H Zacharias immediately recovered his voice, so he spoke praising God.	Lk1:64
I Under the inspiration of God, Zacharias prophesied,	Lk1:67
J 'Blessed be the Lord God of Israel, who has visited and redeemed his people.	Lk1:68
K 'He has raised up a horn of salvation for us from the house of his servant David,	Lk1:69
L 'as He has spoken by the mouth of His holy prophets, from the very beginning.	Lk1:70
M 'That we should be delivered from our enemies and from the hand of those that hate us.	Lk1:71
N 'So that He may extend the mercy promised to our fathers, by his holy covenant	Lk1:72
O 'which he swore to our father Abraham,	Lk1:73
P 'to grant us deliverance from the hand of our enemies so that we might serve him without fear,	Lk1:74

---

1 Is 7:14
2 Mt12:47; Mt13:55 ~ 56; Gal 1:19—Mary had children with Joseph after Christ was born.
3 Gen 17:12

The Harmonized Gospels — Apocalyptic Version

Q 'even in holiness and righteousness before him, all the days of our life.	Lk1:75
R 'As for you child, you shall be called the prophet of the Highest, for you shall go before the face of the Lord to prepare the way for him[1],	Lk1:76 Jn1:6,7
S 'by preaching salvation to his people and the remission of their sins.	Lk1:77
T 'By the tender mercy of our God, light has come to us,	
U 'To show the way to those that sit in the darkness of the shadow of death, and to guide our feet into the way of peace'.	Lk1:78 Lk1:79
V Fear fell on the people that lived nearby and all these events were repeated throughout the hill country of Judaea.	Lk1:65
W The people that heard the news were sobered by it and they wondered what kind of child shall this be, who had the hand of the Lord on him.	Lk1:66
X As for the child, he grew in godliness, and was in the desert till the day of his unveiling to Israel.	Lk1:80

CHAPTER 7
The birth of Jesus

A At that time, a decree sent out by Caesar Augustus to tax all his territories was being enforced.	Lk2:1
B This taxing was done prior to the one done by Cyrenius, governor of Syria[2],	Lk2:2
C and everyone had to go to their own city to be taxed.	Lk2:3
D Being of the house and lineage of David[3], Joseph journeyed from Nazareth in Galilee and went to the city of David called Bethlehem, which was in Judaea.	Lk2:4
E Mary his wife accompanied him. She was pregnant and near term	Lk2:5
F and while they were there, she went into labor	Lk2:6
G and delivered her firstborn son. He was wrapped up in warm blankets and laid in a manger, because there was no room for them in the inn.	Lk2:7
H At the time this occurred, some shepherds were in the fields nearby, watching over their flocks during the night.	Lk2:8
I The angel of the Lord came to them and a brightness from him shone about them. The *shepherds* were fearful,	Lk2:9
J but the angel said to them 'Do not be afraid, for I bring you wonderful and joyful news for all people.	Lk2:10
K 'For today in the city of David, the Savior is born, who is Christ the	Lk2:11

---

1 Mal 3:1
2 P. Ramsundar, 'Dating Christ's Crucifixion' American Journal of Biblical Theology 2010, 9(52); section 5.3.5.
3 Matt 1:1 ~16

The Harmonized Gospels — Apocalyptic Version

Lord.
L 'You will identify the child as the one wrapped up and lying in a manger'. | Lk2:12
M The angel was joined by others from heaven, all praising God saying, | Lk2:13
N 'Glory to the great God. Peace on earth and good will to all men'. | Lk2:14
O Then as the angels disappeared back up in the sky, the shepherds said 'Let us go to Bethlehem and see this thing, which the Lord has just revealed to us'. | Lk2:15
P They left immediately and found Mary, Joseph and the babe lying in a manger. | Lk2:16
Q After they saw them, they told all they met about what had transpired concerning this child. | Lk2:17
R The people that heard them considered what the shepherds had told them and kept it in mind. | Lk2:18
S Mary too took to heart at all that happened and wondered what it will lead to. | Lk2:19
T The shepherds returned to their flocks, glorifying and praising God for all the things that they had heard and seen, and which were revealed to them. | Lk2:20
U On the eight day at his circumcision[1], the child was named 'Jesus'[2] according to the instruction given by the angel before *the child* was conceived. | Lk2:21
V After the days of her purification as prescribed by the law of Moses[3], they brought the child to Jerusalem to present him to the Lord, | Lk2:22
W according to the instruction that every firstborn male child was to be set apart to the Lord, | Lk2:23
X and redeemed by a sacrifice stipulated by the law of the Lord, of either a pair of turtledoves or two young pigeons[4]. | Lk2:24
Y At that time there was a man in Jerusalem, named Simeon, who was just and devout. He was waiting for the savior of Israel, for God had previously revealed to him | Lk2:25
Z that he should not see death, before he had seen the Christ of the Lord. | Lk2:26
AA Under the inspiration of God, he was directed to the temple and when the parents brought the child Jesus to him, as was the custom, | Lk2:27
AB he took him up in his arms and praised God saying | Lk2:28
AC 'Lord, you have granted that your servant may now die in peace, as you have said, | Lk2:29
AD 'For mine eyes have seen your salvation, | Lk2:30
AE 'which you have prepared for all peoples. | Lk2:31

---

1 Gen 17:12
2 Luke 1:31
3 Lev 12:2 ~ 6
4 Lev 1:5 ~ 8—That Mary offered two birds rather than a lamb and a bird is an indication that they were not wealthy.

The Harmonized Gospels — Apocalyptic Version

AF 'A light to the Gentiles and the glory of your people Israel[1]'.	Lk2:32
AG Joseph and the child's mother wondered at the things that were being said about him.	Lk2:33
AH Then Simeon blessed them and said unto Mary his mother 'Know that this confirms the death and resurrection of many in Israel and for a sign against it.	Lk2:34
AI 'A sword shall pierce through your own soul also, and the inner thoughts of many shall be revealed'.	Lk2:35
AJ Also there was a prophetess named Anna, the daughter of Phanuel, of the tribe of Aser. She was very old and had a husband for seven years after puberty,	Lk2:36
AK before becoming widowed. She was now about eighty four years old and did not leave the temple, but worshipped God night and day with fasting and prayer.	Lk2:37
AL She came in at that moment and also gave thanks to the Lord, praising him for all who waited for redemption in Jerusalem.	Lk2:38
AM When *Joseph and Mary* had performed all their duty according to the law of the Lord, they returned to Galilee to their own city of Nazareth.	Lk2:39
AN The child grew and blossomed in character, filled with wisdom, for the grace of God was upon him.	Lk2:40

CHAPTER 8
The Genealogies

A Jesus Christ was a descendant of Abraham through the lineage of David.	Mt1:1
B Abraham fathered Isaac who fathered Jacob. Jacob fathered Judas and other children.	Mt1:2
C Judas fathered Phares and Zara by Thamar. Phares fathered Esrom and Esrom fathered Aram.	Mt1:3
D Aram fathered Aminadab and Aminadab fathered Naasson, who fathered Salmon.	Mt1:4
E Salmon fathered Booz by Rachab. Booz fathered Obed by Ruth and Obed fathered Jesse.	Mt1:5
F Jesse fathered David the king, who fathered Solomon by the woman who had been the wife of Urias.	Mt1:6
G Solomon fathered Roboam and Roboam fathered Abia who fathered Asa.	Mt1:7
H Asa fathered Josaphat[2] and Josaphat fathered Joram[3] who *was an*	Mt1:8

---

1 Gen 22:16 ~ 18—God promised Abraham that the savior of the world would be his descendant.
2 Jehoshaphat (IChron 3:10).
3 Jehoram (IChron 3:11; IKings 22:50; IIChron 21:1; IIChron 22:1, 2).

The Harmonized Gospels — Apocalyptic Version

ancestor[1] of Ozias[2].

I Ozias fathered Joatham, father of Achaz[3] who fathered Ezekias[4].	*Mt1:9*
J Ezekias fathered Manasses and Manasses fathered Amon who fathered Josias.	*Mt1:10*
K Josias *was the grandfather*[5] *of* Jechonias[6], who was carried away to Babylon with his brethren.	*Mt1:11*
L After they were brought to Babylon, Jechonias fathered Salathiel and Salathiel fathered Zorobabel.	*Mt1:12*
M Zorobabel fathered Abiud and Abiud fathered Eliakim who fathered Azor.	*Mt1:13*
N Azor fathered Sadoc and Sadoc fathered Achim who fathered Eliud.	*Mt1:14*
O Eliud fathered Eleazar and Eleazar fathered Matthan who fathered Jacob.	*Mt1:15*
P Jacob fathered Joseph the husband of Mary, who bore Jesus, called the Christ.	*Mt1:16*
Q So from Abraham to David were fourteen generations. From David to the deportation to Babylon were fourteen generations and fourteen generations afterwards came the Christ[7].	*Mt1:17*
R Jesus was regarded as the son of Joseph, who was the *son-in-law*[8] of Heli,	*Lk3:23*
S *Heli* was the son of Matthat, whose father Levi was the son of Melchi, who was the son of Janna, the son of Joseph.	*Lk3:24*
T *Joseph* was the son of Mattathias, whose father Amos was the son of Naum, who was the son of Esli, the son of Nagge.	*Lk3:25*
U *Nagge* was the son of Maath, whose father Mattathias was the son	*Lk3:26*

---

1 Matthew omits here three names in the lineage viz. Ahaziah, Joash and Amaziah. Joram fathered Jehoahaz (also called Ahaziah) who fathered Joash who fathered Amaziah who fathered Azariah (also called Uzziah) (IChrin 3:11,12; IIChron 21:1, 17; 22:1, 2; 24:1, 25; 25:1, 28; 26:1). The three kings not included in the genealogy were all killed in office.

2 Uzziah or Azariah (IChron 3:12; IIChron 26:1; IIKings 15:1,2))

3 Ahaz (IChron 3:13)

4 Hezekiah (IChron 3:13)

5 Matthew omits here the name of Jehoiakim (also called Eliakim) in the lineage. Josias fathered Jehoiakim who fathered Jeconias (IChron 3:15; IIChron 36:1, 4, 6). Jehoiakim was removed from office and taken captive by Nebuchadnezzar to Babylon.

6 In Jer 22:30 Jeconiah was cursed as not having a descendant to sit on the throne of David. It should be noted that though Jesus' legal status is traced through Joseph, Joseph is not his blood Father. Thus Jesus is not of the seed of Jeconiah.

7 Matthew lists fourteen names from Abraham to David, thirteen names from Solomon to Josias, whose son Jehoiakim, also known as Eliakim, was taken into captivity (IIChron 35:15; IIChron 36:1,4,6) and fourteen names from Jehoikim's son, Jeconias, who was born in captivity, to Jesus, citing generations and not Kings. Jehoahaz was replaced by his brother Eliakim (renamed Jehoiakim) who was taken captive to Babylon by Nebuchadnezzar. Jehoiakim's son Jehoiachin, was then made King but only lasted three months before being replaced by his brother Zedekiah. (2Chron 36: 2, 4, 8, 10)

of Semei, who was the son of Joseph, the son of Juda.
V Juda was the son of Joanna, whose father Rhesa was the son of Zorobabel, who was the son of Salathiel, the son of Neri. | *Lk3:27*
W Neri was the son of Melchi, whose father Addi was the son of Cosam, who was the son of Elmodam, the son of Er. | *Lk3:28*
X Er was the son of Jose, whose father Eliezer was the son of Jorim, who was the son of Matthat, the son of Levi. | *Lk3:29*
Y Levi was the son of Simeon, whose father Juda was the son of Joseph, who was the son of Jonan, the son of Eliakim. | *Lk3:30*
Z Eliakim was the son of Melea, whose father Menan was the son of Mattatha, who was the son of Nathan, the son of David[1]. | *Lk3:31*
AA David was the son of Jesse, whose father Obed was the son of Booz, who was the son of Salmon, the son of Naasson. | *Lk3:32*
AB Naasson was the son of Aminadab, whose father Aram was the son of Esrom, who was the son of Phares, the son of Juda. | *Lk3:33*
AC Juda was the son of Jacob, whose father Isaac was the son of Abraham, who was the son of Thara, the son of Nachor, | *Lk3:34*
AD Nachor was the son of Saruch, whose father Ragau was the son of Phalec, who was the son of Heber, the son of Sala. | *Lk3:35*
AE Sala was the son of Cainan, whose father Arphaxad was the son of Sem, who was the son of Noe, the son of Lamech. | *Lk3:36*
AF Lamech was the son of Mathusala, whose father Enoch was the son of Jared, who was the son of Maleleel, the son of Cainan. | *Lk3:37*
AG Cainan was the son of Enos, whose father Seth was the son of Adam, the son of God. | *Lk3:38*

CHAPTER 9
Visit of the men from the East and the sojourn in Egypt

A Jesus was born in Bethlehem of Judaea at the time when Herod was the king. Sometime after his birth, devout men from the east came to Jerusalem[2], | *Mt2:1*
B asking 'Where is he that is born to be the King of the Jews? We know this from an angel who appeared to us in the east and we have come to worship him[3]'. | *Mt2:2*
C When Herod the king heard these things, he was troubled, and all | *Mt2:3*

---

1 By Is 11:1, the messiah was prophesied to be a descendant of Jesse. The genealogies of Jesus on both his mother and step-father's side lead back to David by different routes.
2 The coming of the Messiah was long prophesied by Daniel (Dan 9:25). To understand the message about the birth of this King and make a long two year (Matt 2:7, 16) journey from the East would require a level of religious awareness and devotion likely only from the Jewish priests.
3 The Greek 'στήρ' translated 'star' in many versions is a common symbol for an 'angel' (Rev 1:20). That the 'star' reappeared in Matt 2:9 and led them to the child confirms that an angel is intended meaning.

The Harmonized Gospels — Apocalyptic Version

Jerusalem was astir with the news.

D Herod assembled all the chief priests and scribes, and he demanded that they tell him where Christ was to be born. | *Mt2:4*

E They replied to him 'In Bethlehem of Judaea. For it is written by the prophet, | *Mt2:5*

F "And you Bethlehem, in the land of Juda, shall not be least among the provinces of Juda, for out of you shall come the one to rule my people Israel[1]".' | *Mt2:6*

G Herod privately called the men *from the east* and carefully examined them as to the time that the angel appeared to them. | *Mt2:7*

H Herod then sent them on to Bethlehem saying 'Go and search diligently for the child. When you find him, come back and tell me, that I may also come and worship him'. | *Mt2:8*

I After speaking with the king, the men *from the east* continued on their journey and the angel, which they had seen in the east, met them and led them to the place where the young child was. | *Mt2:9*

J When the men *from the east* saw the angel, they were exceedingly joyful, | *Mt2:10*

K and when they entered the house and saw the child with Mary his mother, they fell on their faces and worshipped him. Then *they arose* and presented him with valuable gifts of gold, frankincense and myrrh that they had brought[2]. | *Mt2:11*

L The men from the East then journeyed to their country by another route, because God had warned them in a dream, not to return to Herod. | *Mt2:12*

M Soon after the men *from the east* departed, the angel of the Lord appeared to Joseph in a dream, saying 'Arise, take the child with his mother and flee into Egypt. Stay there till I tell you, for Herod will seek to destroy the young child'. | *Mt2:13*

N Joseph awoke, and taking the child with his mother, they hurriedly left during that night for Egypt, | *Mt2:14*

O where they stayed until the death of Herod. This fulfilled the prophecy of the Lord saying 'Out of Egypt have I called my son[3]'. | *Mt2:15*

P When Herod saw that his instructions were disregarded by the devout men from the east, he was furious. He commanded that all the children in Bethlehem and the surrounding districts that were two years old and under, be slain[4]. Herod did this based on the time he obtained from the faithful men *of the east*. | *Mt2:16*

---

1 Micah 5:2
2 The number of men who came from the east is not specified. Gifts of gold, frankincense and myrrh were valuable commodities of the time and appropriate offerings to a king. The mythology of 'the three wise men' may be derived from the mention of these three kinds of gifts and belies the fact that anyone could give multiple gifts.
3 Hos 11:1
4 Though Christ was born in Bethlehem of Judea when his parents came to be taxed, they actually lived in Nazareth of Galilee (Luke 2:4).

Q This fulfilled the words of Jeremy the prophet, which says	Mt2:17
R 'In Rama there were heard voices of lamentation, weeping and great mourning. Rachel weeps for her children, and would not be comforted, because they are no more[1]'.	Mt2:18
S Sometime afterwards, when Herod was dead, an angel of the Lord appeared in a dream to Joseph while he was in Egypt,	Mt2:19
T and said to him 'Arise, take the child and his mother, and return to the land of Israel, for they which sought his life are dead'.	Mt2:20
U *Joseph* departed with the young child and his mother, and came into the borders of Israel,	Mt2:21
V but when he heard that Archelaus reigned in Judaea after his father Herod, he was afraid to go there. He was guided by God, in a dream, to go into the region of Galilee.	Mt2:22
W So *Joseph* came and dwelt in the city of Nazareth. This fulfilled the prophecy which says, 'He shall be called a Nazarene'.	Mt2:23

CHAPTER 10

Jesus at twelve in the temple

A The parents *of Jesus* went to Jerusalem every year at the feast of the Passover[2].	Lk2:41
B When *Jesus* was twelve years old, they went up to Jerusalem as they were accustomed to.	Lk2:42
C After the celebration had come to an end, *Joseph and Mary* started on the journey home, but Jesus stayed behind in Jerusalem, unbeknown to his parents,	Lk2:43
D who thought *Jesus* was among the company. After they had travelled for the day they looked for him among their kinfolk and friends.	Lk2:44
E When they did not find him, they went back to Jerusalem looking for him.	Lk2:45
F After three days, they found him in the temple sitting with the religious scholars, listening to them and asking them questions.	Lk2:46
G Those speaking with him were astonished at his understanding and the things he spoke.	Lk2:47
H When his parents found him, they too were amazed. His mother said to him 'Son, what have you been doing? Your father and I have been looking for you all this time and worrying'.	Lk2:48
I He replied 'Where were you looking for me? Did you not know that I	Lk2:49

---

1 Jer 31:15

2 The Passover commemorated the saving of the firstborn of the Israelites from death when the Lord slew all the firstborn of Egypt (Ex 12:27). The Passover is the first in a series of religious observances that were to be kept by Israel (Lev 23). In time, the Passover, Days of Unleavened Bread and the Wave Sheaf offering which occurred in the first month of Abib (Nissan) were grouped together and collectively referred to as the Passover (Ezek 45:21).

must be about my Father's business?'
J They did not fully understand what he said. | *Lk2:50*
K He went back with them to Nazareth, and was subject to them. His mother however, reflected on all these things that transpired. | *Lk2:51*
L Jesus increased in wisdom and stature, and grew in favor with God and man. | *Lk2:52*

CHAPTER I I

The ministry of John the Baptist and his Baptism of Christ

A While John the Baptist, the son of Zacharias was in the wilderness, the word of God came to him. | *Mt3:1; Mk1:4* *Lk3:2*
B This was during the fifteenth year of the reign of Tiberius Caesar, when Pontius Pilate was the governor of Judaea. Herod was the tetrarch of Galilee and his brother Philip was the tetrarch of Ituraea and the region of Trachonitis. Lysanias was the tetrarch of Abilene, and Annas and Caiaphas were the high priests. | *Lk3:1, 2*
C John moved to the regions bordering the Jordan river preaching repentance and immersion in water (baptism) for the washing away of sins, | *Lk3:3; Mk1:4*
D saying 'Repent, for God is about to inaugurate his government over the earth[1]'. | *Mt3:2*
E This same John wore clothing of camel's hair, with a leather girdle about his waist, and he ate locusts and wild honey. | *Mt3:4; Mk1:6*
F Many went out to him from Jerusalem and Judaea, and from all the regions about the Jordan. | *Mt3:5*
G They were baptized by him in the Jordan, confessing their sins. | *Mt3:6; Mk1:5*
H When *John* saw many of the Pharisees and Sadducees coming to be baptized, he said to them 'You generation of vipers, who has warned you to flee from the coming retribution? | *Mt3:7; Lk3:7*
I 'Now show the fruits of repentance | *Mt3:8; Lk3:8*
J 'and do not say to yourselves "Our father is Abraham", for I tell you, God is able to raise up children of Abraham from these stones. | *Mt3:9; Lk3:8*
K 'The axe is about to be brought down on the roots of the trees. | *Mt3:10; Lk3:9*

---

1 Ever since Adam and Eve disobeyed God, their descendants have suffered the consequences of sinful behavior. God has promised to restore the utopian conditions of the Garden of Eden (Is 2:1~4; Micah 4:1~4). The coming of John the Baptist and Christ were the reassurances from God that not only was He committed to fulfilling that promise but also to inaugurate Christ as the King of that new world government under God (Matt 19:29; Rev 2:26 ~27). The fulfillment of that prophesied kingdom will occur at Christ's return to earth (Acts 1:10 ~ 11; Rev 11:15).

The Harmonized Gospels — Apocalyptic Version

Every tree which does not produce good fruit is to be cut down and cast into the fire'.
L The people asked of him 'What shall we do then?' | Lk3:10
M He said to them 'He who has two coats should give to those who lack and he who has food should likewise share it'. | Lk3:11
N When the government agents who came to be baptized asked him 'Master, what shall we do?', | Lk3:12
O he said 'Extort no more than that which is legally due'. | Lk3:13
P To the soldiers who likewise inquired of him, he said 'Do not mistreat anyone, nor accuse anyone falsely. Also, be content with your wages'. | Lk3:14
Q It was the time when people were expecting the Christ to appear and they wondered whether John was the Christ or not. | Lk3:15
R The Jews also sent priests and Levites from Jerusalem to ask him 'Who are you?' | Jn1:19
S John emphasized to them 'I am not the Christ'. | Jn1:20
T They pressed him asking 'Who then? Are you Elias?' | Jn1:21
U To this John said 'I am not'. | Jn1:21
V 'Are you a prophet?' they asked him again, and he confirmed 'No'. | Jn1:21
W Then said they to him 'Tell us who you are so that we may give an answer to those that sent us. What can you tell us of yourself?' | Jn1:22
X John said 'I am the voice of one crying in the wilderness "Make straight the way of the Lord" as was said by the prophet Esaias. | Jn1:23
Y (This is the fulfillment of the words of the prophet Esaias, saying 'A voice cries out in the wilderness, to prepare the way of the Lord and make his paths straight. Every valley shall be filled, and every mountain and hill shall be brought low. The crooked shall be made straight, the rough ways shall be made smooth and all flesh shall see the salvation of God[1]'. | Mt3:3; Mk 1:3 Lk3:4 ~ 6
Z It is also written by the prophets 'Behold, I send my messenger before you, to prepare the way for you[2]'.) | Mk 1:2
AA Those who were sent were Pharisees, | Jn1:24
AB and they asked 'Why do you baptize then, if you are not the Christ, nor Elias, nor a prophet? | Jn1:25
AC John said to them 'My baptism of repentance is with water, but he that comes after me is greater than me for he was before me. I am not worthy to carry his shoes, much | Mt3:11; Mk1:7,8 Lk3:16; Jn1:8, 15; Jn1:26 ~ 28

---

1 Is 40:3,4; 49:6; 52:10
2 Mal 3:1

The Harmonized Gospels — Apocalyptic Version

less untie them. He will cleanse you with the very nature of God and with fire[1].

AD 'He comes with a winnow in his hand, with which he will thoroughly sort his threshing-floor. He will gather his wheat into his granary, but he will utterly destroy the chaff with a consuming fire'. — *Mt3:12; Lk3:17*

AE John likewise preached many other things to the people. — *Lk3:18*

AF Then Jesus came from Galilee to the Jordan to be baptized by John. — *Mt3:13; Mk1:9; Lk3:21*

AG But John tried to stop him, saying 'It is I who should be baptized by you. Why do you come to me?' — *Mt3:14*

AH Jesus answered 'Let it be this way, for it is appropriate to show what is right'. — *Mt3:15*

AI John therefore accommodated him, — *Mt3:15*

AJ and as Jesus was baptized and came out of the water, *John* saw the Spirit of God alight on him from above, like a dove, — *Mt3:16; Mk1:10; Lk3:22; Jn1:32*

AK and heard a voice from on high announcing 'This is my beloved Son, in whom I am well pleased'. — *Mt3:17; Mk1:11; Lk3:22*

AL This occurred just before Jesus was thirty years of age, in Bethabara beyond Jordan, where John was baptizing. — *Lk3:23; Jn1:28*

CHAPTER 12
The temptation of Jesus[2]

A Soon after this God put it into Jesus' mind to go into the wilderness to be tempted of the devil[3]. — *Mt4:1; Mk1:12; Lk4:1*

B There Jesus fasted for forty days and forty nights, after which he ached for sustenance. — *Mt4:2; Mk1:12; Lk4:2*

C Then the tempter put into his mind[4] 'If you are the Son of God, command these stones to be turned into bread'. — *Mt4:3; Lk4:3*

D But Jesus responded 'It is written, Man shall not live by — *Mt4:4; Lk4:4*

---

1 The cleansing of humans can only be accomplished by God's Nature working in man to create a new creature. (Rom 8:7; Ezek 11:19~20; Gal 2:20).

2 The sequence of the temptations in Matthew is different from that in Luke, which indicates that at least one is not chronological.

3 Satan instigated Eve and Adam to reject God's authority in the garden of Eden (Gen 3:1~6). Jesus, born with the nature of God, was a new quality of being and he proved to be of sterner stuff than Adam, for he withstood far more serious attempts by Satan to get him to reject God the Father (Rom 8:29).

4 Satan influences us by stirring up thoughts, feelings and passions in us, not specifically by conversation. Satan's question "If you are the son of God' is an attempt to stir up doubts in Christ's mind as to his authenticity and sanity. Christ, though born of God was subject to human frailty (Heb 4:15; Luke 22:42~44; John 8:41; Mark 6:4~5).

bread alone, but by every word that comes out of the mouth of God[1]'.

E Jesus then had a vision[2] of the devil taking him into the holy city, to the highest point of the temple, | Mt4:5; Lk4:9

F and putting into His mind 'If you are the Son of God, throw yourself down, for it is written "He shall command his angels concerning you, that they hold you up in their hands to keep you from knocking your foot against a stone[3]".' | Mt4:6; Lk4:9~11

G Jesus responded 'It is also written "You shall not tempt the Lord your God[4]".' | Mt4:7; Lk4:12

H Again in vision, the devil took him up to an exceeding height, and showed him all the kingdoms of the world, with all their glory in an instant of time, | Mt4:8; Lk4:5

I and said to him 'All this power and glory I can give to you, for it has been given to me, and I can give it to whoever I choose. | Mt4:9; Lk4:6

J 'If you will worship me, all shall be yours[5]'. | Mt4:9; Lk4:7

K To this Jesus responded 'Get away from me Satan, for it is written "You shall worship the Lord your God, and serve none but him[6]".' | Mt4:10; Lk4:8; Lk4:13

L At this the devil left him, and angels came and tended to him. | Mt4:11; Mk1:13

CHAPTER 13
Jesus' first disciples

A Some time after this, John *the Baptist* saw Jesus walking towards him and said 'There goes the Lamb of God, who takes away the sin of the world. | Jn1:29

B 'This is one I was talking about when I said 'A man is coming after me who is greater than me, for he existed before me. | Jn1:30

C 'I did not know him previously, but he is the one who shall be revealed to Israel. He is the reason that I am baptizing with water'. | Jn1:31

D John also witnessed 'I saw the Spirit of God coming down from above and alighting on him like a dove. | Jn1:32

E 'I never saw him before, but the one who sent me to bap- | Jn1:33

---

1 Deut 8:3.
2 Matt 4:5 and 8 are likely scenarios communicated by visions. Matt 4:8 for instance occurred in an instant of time.
3 Ps 91:11.   *4* Deut 6:16.
5 Though Satan influences the world, God keeps him in check (John 8:44; Rom 13:1~2; Dan 4:25; 10:13,20; Acts 17:24~25). Satan is a liar (John 8:44). Christ did not fall for this lie as Eve fell for another lie of Satan (Gen 3:4).   *6* Deut 6:13; Jas 4:7.

The Harmonized Gospels — Apocalyptic Version

tize with water said to me "When you see the Spirit of God come down and resting on someone, know that he is the one who will baptize with God's very nature[1]".

F 'This I did see and now witness that this is the Son of God'. — Jn1:34

G Later, John was standing with two of his disciples. — Jn1:35

H Seeing Jesus walking by he said 'There goes the Lamb of God!' — Jn1:36

I The two disciples who heard him left and went after Jesus. — Jn1:37

J Jesus seeing them walking after him asked 'What do you want?' They said 'Rabbi, (which means Master,) where do you live?' — Jn1:38

K Jesus replied 'Come and see'. They went with him to his dwelling and stayed with him that day till about the tenth hour. — Jn1:39

L One of the disciples who heard John speak and who followed *Jesus* was Andrew, Simon Peter's brother. — Jn1:40

M After leaving *Jesus* he went straightaway to his brother Simon, and said to him 'We have found the Messias', (which is another name for the Christ.) — Jn1:41

N *Andrew* took *Simon Peter* to see Jesus and when Jesus saw Simon he said 'You are Simon the son of Jona. You shall be called Cephas', (which means, "a stone"). — Jn1:42

O The next day Jesus went to Galilee and seeing Philip he said to him 'Be my disciple'[2]. — Jn1:43

P Philip lived in Bethsaida, which was also the town of Andrew and Peter. — Jn1:44

Q Philip went and found Nathanael and said to him 'We have found the one who Moses wrote about in the law[3], and who the prophets also wrote about. He is Jesus of Nazareth, the son of Joseph'. — Jn1:45

R Nathanael asked 'Can any good thing come out of Nazareth?' Philip replied 'Come and see'. — Jn1:46

S When Nathanael came to Jesus, Jesus said to him 'Ah, an true Israelite, in whom there is no guile!' — Jn1:47

T Nathanael asked 'Do you know me?' Jesus replied 'Before Philip came to you, while you were yet under the fig tree, I saw you'. — Jn1:48

U Nathanael said 'Rabbi, you are indeed the Son of God, the King of Israel'. — Jn1:49

V Jesus said to him 'Do you believe because I told you that I saw you under the fig tree? you shall see even greater things than this'. — Jn1:50

W Jesus continued 'I tell you with certainty that from now onwards, you shall see the heavens open, and the angels of God ascending and descending upon me[4]. — Jn1:51

---

1 The Greek 'πνεῦμα' translated as 'Spirit' is imprecise and refers to diverse things. In this verse the word is also translated 'nature' to reflect Jesus' shared characteristics with God the Father.
2 'Follow me' is intended to be a spiritual allegiance.
3 Deut 18:15
4 Here and in a number of instances subsequently, Jesus used the phrase 'Son of man' to refer to himself. (Dan 7:13)

CHAPTER 14
Jesus' first public miracle

A A marriage was taking place in Cana of Galilee. Jesus' mother,	Jn2:1
B as well as Jesus and his disciples all attended because they were invited to the marriage.	Jn2:2
C On the third day the wine ran out and Jesus' mother told him 'They have no wine'.	Jn2:3
D Jesus said to mother 'Mother, why are you telling me this. It is not yet time for my revealing'.	Jn2:4
E Nevertheless his mother said to the servants 'Whatsoever he tells you to do, do it'.	Jn2:5
F There were six stone jars at hand, with a capacity of twenty to thirty gallons of water, which was used by the Jews for their ceremonial washings.	Jn2:6
G Jesus said to the servants 'Fill the jars with water' and they did so, filling the jars to the brim.	Jn2:7
H Then Jesus told them 'Draw out some and take it to the chief guest', which they did.	Jn2:8
I The chief guest at the marriage feast, tasted the water that was made wine, not knowing what had transpired, but the servants which drew out the water knew. The chief guest at the feast then called the bridegroom,	Jn2:9
J and said to him 'Every man brings out the best wine first and when the men have been satiated they bring out the inferior, but you have kept the best wine for last'.	Jn2:10
K This was the first miracle that Jesus did and it was done in Cana of Galilee. By this and other signs, his disciples came to believe him.	Jn2:11

CHAPTER 15
Jesus' second significant encounter with Peter, Andrew, James and John

A *Jesus* was at Gennesaret by the Sea of Galilee and the people pressed upon him to hear the word of God,.	Lk5:1
B There were two fishing boats moored at the shore of the lake and the fishermen were outside washing their nets.	Lk5:2
C *Jesus* entered into one of the boats, which belonged to Simon, and asked him to cast off a short distance from the land. There he sat down and taught the people from on the boat.	Lk5:3
D After he finished speaking, Jesus said unto Simon 'Launch out into the deep waters and let down your nets for a catch'.	Lk5:4

The Harmonized Gospels — Apocalyptic Version

E Simon replied 'Master, we have been casting all night, and have taken nothing. Nevertheless, at your word, I will let down the net'. | Lk5:5

F When they had done this, they netted a catch of fish, so huge that their net broke. | Lk5:6

G They beckoned to their partners, which were in the other boat to come and help them. So they came and filled both the boats till they were in danger of being swamped. | Lk5:7

H When Simon Peter saw this, he fell on his knees at Jesus' feet and said 'Depart from me, for I am a sinful man, O Lord,' | Lk5:8

I for he was astonished at the catch of the fishes which they had taken. | Lk5:9

J So too were James and John, the sons of Zebedee, who were partners with Simon. Jesus said to Simon 'Do not be afraid. From now on, you shall catch men'. | Lk5:10

K They brought their boats to land, and from then they looked to no other but him[1]. | Lk5:11

CHAPTER 16

Jesus heals at the sheep market pool in Jerusalem

A There was a feast of the Jews and Jesus went up to Jerusalem. | Jn5:1

B At Jerusalem there is a pool by the sheep *gate*[2], which is called Bethesda in the Hebrew tongue. This pool had five covered porches, | Jn5:2

C which were filled by a great multitude of sick people. Some were blind, others lame, and others had various infirmities. They all waited for the water to be disturbed, | Jn5:3

D by an angel who went down from time to time into the pool and stirred up the water. Whoever first entered afterwards was healed of whatever disease he had. | Jn5:4

E There was a certain man there, who had an infirmity for thirty eight years. | Jn5:5

F Jesus saw him lying down and knew that he had been in that circumstance for a long time and he said to the man 'Would you like to be healed?' | Jn5:6

G The crippled man answered 'Sir, when the water is disturbed there is no one with me to put me into the pool. While I am struggling to go, someone else goes ahead of me'. | Jn5:7

H Jesus then said to him 'Rise up, take up your bed, and go on your way'. | Jn5:8

I Immediately the man was healed. He then took up his bed, and went | Jn5:9

---

1 The Jews were on the lookout for a Messiah about this time (John 1:41; Acts 5:36 ~39) based on Daniel's prophecy (Dan 9:25 ~26). This incident served to make Peter, Andrew, James and John aware that Jesus was special and like no other claimant to the messiah-ship. They did not at this time become full-time disciples but continued working as fishermen (See Matt 4:19,20).
2 Neh 3:1

The Harmonized Gospels — Apocalyptic Version

on his way. That day was the Sabbath.

J When the Jews saw the man who was cured they said to him 'It is the Sabbath day. It is not lawful for you to carry your bed'. — Jn5:10

K The man answered and said 'The one that healed me said to me 'Take up your bed and go on your way'. — Jn5:11

L So they asked 'Who is this man who told "Take up your bed, and go on your way?"' — Jn5:12

M The man who was healed did not know who it was, for Jesus had left and the place was crowded with people. — Jn5:13

N Afterward Jesus found the man in the temple and said told him 'Listen to me. You have been healed. Do not sin again or something worse may befall you'. — Jn5:14

O The man left and told the Jews that it was Jesus who had healed him. — Jn5:15

P The Jews then turned on Jesus and wanted to kill him because of his actions on the Sabbath day. — Jn5:16

Q But Jesus said to them 'My Father is working and I too work'. — Jn5:17

R The Jews were all the more anxious to kill him, because he had not only broken the Sabbath, but also claimed that God was his Father, putting himself on the same level with God. — Jn5:18

S Then Jesus said to them 'I tell you with certainty that the Son can do nothing of himself, but what is revealed from the Father. For whatsoever the Father does, the Son does likewise. — Jn5:19

T 'The Father loves the Son and reveals to him all that he is doing and he will work in him even greater works than these, so that you will be astounded. — Jn5:20

U 'Just as the Father resurrects the dead and give them life, so too the Son gives life to whom he will. — Jn5:21

V 'For the Father judges no man, but has handed all judgment to the Son, — Jn5:22

W 'so that all men should honor the Son, just as they honor the Father. He that does not honor the Son does not honor the Father, who sent him. — Jn5:23

X 'With certainty I say to you that he that hears my word and believes him that sent me, has everlasting life, and shall not be condemned *to death*, but is rehabilitated from death to life. — Jn5:24

Y 'With certainty I tell you that the time is soon coming, when the dead shall hear the voice of the Son of God, and all those that hear shall live. — Jn5:25

Z 'For as the Father is the source of life, he has given authority to the Son to be the source of life. — Jn5:26

AA 'He has also given him the authority to judge also because he is a man. — Jn5:27

AB 'Do not wonder at this, for the time is coming when all those who are in the grave shall hear his voice, — Jn5:28

AC 'and shall awake. Those that have done good, to the resurrection — Jn5:29

The Harmonized Gospels — Apocalyptic Version

of eternal life, and they that have done evil, to the resurrection of judgment[1].

AD 'I do nothing on my own, but what is revealed to me, I judge. My judgment is just because I am not acting on my own, but do the will of the Father who has sent me. *Jn5:30*

AE 'If I bear witness of myself, my witness may not be true, *Jn5:31*

AF 'but there is another that bears witness of me and I know that the sign which he saw of me is true. *Jn5:32*

AG 'You asked John and he bore witness of the truth. *Jn5:33*

AH 'But I do not need a testimonial from man, but these things I tell you that you might be saved. *Jn5:34*

AI 'He was a bright and a shining light and you were happy for a while to rejoice in his light. *Jn5:35*

AJ 'I have a greater witness than that of John, for the works which the Father has given me to finish, these very works that I do bear witness of me, that the Father has sent me. *Jn5:36*

AK 'The Father himself also, who sent me, has borne witness of me. You have neither heard his voice at any time nor seen his form. *Jn5:37*

AL 'You also do not have his word abiding in you, for you do not believe he who was sent by him. *Jn5:38*

AM 'Search the scriptures, for you think that you obtain eternal life from it, but it testifies of me. *Jn5:39*

AN 'But you will not come to me, so that you might have eternal life. *Jn5:40*

AO 'I do not get honor from men. *Jn5:41*

AP 'But I know you, that you do not have the love of God in you. *Jn5:42*

AQ 'I have come in my Father's name, and you do not receive me, yet if another comes in his own name, you receive him. *Jn5:43*

AR 'How can you believe, when you seek honor of one another, but do not seek the honor that comes from God alone? *Jn5:44*

AS 'Do not think that I will bring a charge against you to the Father, but there is one that will bring a charge against you, and that is Moses, in whom you trust. *Jn5:45*

AT 'For if you had believed Moses, you would have believed me, for he wrote of me. *Jn5:46*

AU 'But if you do not believe what he wrote, how shall you believe my words?' *Jn5:47*

---

1 Christ here speaks of two resurrections. One of the resurrections is at his return when the converted will be raised to eternal life (ICor 15:22 ~ 23, 51 ~ 54; IThess 4:13 ~ 17). The other, called the resurrection of judgment, takes place a thousand years afterwards (Rev 20:5) when the rest of humanity will be raised to physical life and tested for a further period to determine whether they shall be granted eternal life, or be forever terminated (Is 65:20; Ezek 37:12; John 6:44; Rev 20:12).

CHAPTER 17
Mary and Martha

A At one time Jesus came to a village, where a certain woman named Martha invited him to her house. — Lk10:38

B Her sister Mary, sat at Jesus' feet and listen to all that he was saying, — Lk10:39

C but Martha was busy serving. Martha came to Jesus and said 'Lord, do you not care that my sister has left me to serve alone? Tell her to come and help me'. — Lk10:40

D Jesus replied 'Martha, Martha, you concern yourself with many things, — Lk10:41

E 'but one thing is paramount and Mary has chosen that good thing, which shall not be taken away from her'. — Lk10:42

CHAPTER 18
Jesus heals the man who was blind from birth

A Jesus was going on his way when he saw a man who was blind from his birth. — Jn9:1

B His disciples asked him 'Master, who committed sin that this man was born blind? Was it this man or his parents?' — Jn9:2

C Jesus replied 'Neither this man has sinned, nor his parents. This is so that the works of God should be manifested in him. — Jn9:3

D 'I must do the work of him that sent me, while it is still day, for the night is coming when no man can work. — Jn9:4

E 'As long as I am in the world, I am the light of the world'. — Jn9:5

F After he said these things, he spat on the ground and made a clay paste with the spittle. With this he anointed the eyes of the blind man. — Jn9:6

G Then he said to him 'Go, wash in the pool of Siloam', which means "Sent". The blind man went and washed, as Jesus told him to do, and came out *of the pool* seeing. — Jn9:7

H The neighbors who knew that he was blind before said 'Is not this the man that sat and begged?' — Jn9:8

I Some said 'It is he'. Others said 'He resembles him'. But the man who was blind said 'I am he'. — Jn9:9

J They asked him 'How were you eyes healed?' — Jn9:10

K He said 'A man who is called Jesus made clay and anointed mine eyes. He then told me 'Go to the pool of Siloam and wash'. So I went and washed and I received my sight'. — Jn9:11

L They asked him 'Where is he?' and he replied 'I do not know'. — Jn9:12

M The people brought him to the Pharisees. — Jn9:13

N Now it was on the Sabbath that Jesus made the clay and opened — Jn9:14

The Harmonized Gospels — Apocalyptic Version

the man's eyes.

O The Pharisees also asked him how he had received his sight. He said 'He put clay upon mine eyes and when I washed I was able to see'. | *Jn9:15*

P Some of the Pharisees said 'This man is not of God because he does not keep the Sabbath. Others said 'How can a man who is a sinner do such miracles?' Thus there was a division among them. | *Jn9:16*

Q They asked the one who was blind 'What do you think of the one who opened your eyes?' He replied 'He is a prophet'. | *Jn9:17*

R The Jews doubted that he had been blind and had his sight restored, so they called the parents of the one who had gained his sight. | *Jn9:18*

S They asked them 'Is this your son who was born blind? How is it that he can see?' | *Jn9:19*

T His parents said 'We know that this is our son and that he was born blind. | *Jn9:20*

U 'But as to how he now sees, we do not know. We do not know who opened his eyes. Look, he is of age. Ask him and he shall speak for himself'. | *Jn9:21*

V His parents also said this because they feared the Jews. For the Jews had decided that if any man professed that Jesus was Christ, he should be put out of the synagogue. | *Jn9:22*

W This was why his parents said 'He is of age, so ask him'. | *Jn9:23*

X Then they again called the man who was blind and told him 'Give God the praise. We know that this man is a sinner'. | *Jn9:24*

Y He answered 'Whether he be a sinner or not, I cannot say, but one thing I know. I was blind and now I see'. | *Jn9:25*

Z Then asked him again 'What did he do to you? How did he open your eyes?' | *Jn9:26*

AA He replied 'I have told you already, and you did not hear. Why do you want to hear it again? Do you also want to be his disciples?' | *Jn9:27*

AB Then they turned on him and said 'You are his disciple, but we are Moses' disciples. | *Jn9:28*

AC 'We know that God spoke by Moses, but as for this fellow we do not know where he came from'. | *Jn9:29*

AD The man said to them 'Why this is indeed a marvelous thing. You do not know from where he came and yet he has opened mine eyes. | *Jn9:30*

AE 'Now we know that God does not answer sinners, but if anyone worships God and does his will, God hears him. | *Jn9:31*

AF 'Since the world began it was never heard that any man opened the eyes of one that was born blind. | *Jn9:32*

AG 'If this man was not of God he could do nothing'. | *Jn9:33*

AH The Pharisees replied 'You were undoubtedly born in sin and you dare to teach us?' So they expelled him. | *Jn9:34*

AI Jesus heard that they had put him out, so he searched for the man and when he found him he said 'Do you believe in the Son of God?' | *Jn9:35*

AJ The man answered 'Who is he, Lord, that I might believe on him?' | *Jn9:36*

AK Jesus said to him 'You have both seen and heard him, for it is he | *Jn9:37*

The Harmonized Gospels — Apocalyptic Version

who is now speaking to you'.
AL The man said 'Lord, I believe'. And he worshipped him. *Jn9:38*
AM Jesus said 'For righteousness I have come into this world that they who do not see might see, and that they who do see might be made blind'. *Jn9:39*
AN Some Pharisees close by heard these words, and said to him 'Are we blind also?' *Jn9:40*
AO Jesus replied 'If you were blind you would have no sin, but you say "We see", therefore your sin remains'. *Jn9:41*

CHAPTER 19
Parable of the true shepherd

A 'I tell you the truth, that he that does not enter the sheepfold by the door, but climbs in by some other way, is a thief and a robber. *Jn10:1*
B 'He that enters in by the door is the shepherd of the sheep. *Jn10:2*
C 'The porter will open the door to him. The sheep hear his voice and he calls his own sheep by name. He is the one who leads them out. *Jn10:3*
D 'When he takes the sheep out, he goes before them, and the sheep follow him, for they know his voice. *Jn10:4*
E 'They will not follow a stranger, but they will flee from such, for they do not know the voice of strangers'. *Jn10:5*
F Jesus gave them this parable but they did not understand what he was talking about. *Jn10:6*
G So Jesus explained 'I tell you in truth that I am the door of the sheep. *Jn10:7*
H 'All who came before me were thieves and robbers, which is why the sheep did not hear them. *Jn10:8*
I 'I am the door. If any man enters by me, he shall be saved and shall go in and out and find pasture. *Jn10:9*
J 'The thief does not come unless it is to steal, or to kill, or to destroy. But I am come that they might not only live, but live more abundantly. *Jn10:10*
K 'I am the good shepherd. The good shepherd gives his life for the sheep. *Jn10:11*
L 'The one who is an hireling and not the shepherd, does not own the sheep, so when he sees the wolf coming, he abandons the sheep and runs away, leaving the wolf to catch them and scatter the sheep. *Jn10:12*
M 'The hireling flees because he is an hireling and does not care for the sheep. *Jn10:13*
N 'I am the good shepherd who knows my sheep, just as I am known of mine. *Jn10:14*
O 'Just as the Father knows me, even so I know the Father, and I lay down my life for the sheep. *Jn10:15*
P 'There are other sheep that I have, which are not of this fold. They *Jn10:16*

too I must bring and they shall hear my voice, and there shall altogether be one fold, and one shepherd.
Q 'Because of this my Father loves me, because I lay down my life, so that I might take it up again. | Jn10:17
R 'No man takes it from me, but I lay it down of my own will. I have the power to lay it down, and I have the power to take it again. This guarantee I have received of my Father'. | Jn10:18
S There was a difference in opinion about him among the Jews because of what he said. | Jn10:19
T Many of them said 'He has a devil, and is mad. Why do you listen to him?' | Jn10:20
U Others said 'These are not the words of a man who has a devil. Can a devil open the eyes of the blind?' | Jn10:21

CHAPTER 20
Incident at the Feast of Dedication

A It was winter and the feast of the dedication was being observed in Jerusalem. | Jn10:22
B Jesus was in the temple in Solomon's porch, | Jn10:23
C and the Jews came round about him and said 'How long will you keep us in doubt? If you are the Christ, tell us plainly'. | Jn10:24
D Jesus replied 'I told you and you do not believe. The works that I do in my Father's name, these bear witness of me. | Jn10:25
E 'But you do not believe because you are not of my sheep, as I said unto you. | Jn10:26
F 'My sheep hear my voice. I know them and they follow me' | Jn10:27
G 'I give to them eternal life and they shall never perish, neither shall any man pluck them out of my hand. | Jn10:28
H 'My Father, who gave them me, is greater than all, and no man is able to pluck them out of my Father's hand. | Jn10:29
I 'I and my Father are one'. | Jn10:30
J Then the Jews took up stones to stone him. | Jn10:31
K Jesus said 'Many good works have I shown you from my Father. For which of those works do you stone me?' | Jn10:32
L The Jews replied 'For a good work we do not stone you, but for blasphemy and because you, being a man, make yourself God'. | Jn10:33
M Jesus asked 'Is it not written in your law "I said, You are gods[1]?" | Jn10:34
N 'If he, to whom the word of God came, called them gods, and since the scripture cannot be broken, | Jn10:35
O 'how can you say of him whom the Father has sanctified and sent | Jn10:36

---

1 Ps 82:6

into the world "You blaspheme" because I said "I am the Son of God?"
Q 'If I do not do the works of my Father, do not believe me, *Jn10:37*
R 'but if I do, even though you do not believe me, believe because of the works. By them you can be sure. Believe that the Father is in me and I in him'. *Jn10:38*
S At this they again sought to seize him, but he escaped out of their hand. *Jn10:39*
T Jesus and his disciples went to the region beyond the Jordan, to the place where John first baptized, and stayed there for some time. *Jn10:40*
U Many came to him and it was said 'John did no miracle, but all that John said about this man was true'. *Jn10:41*
V Many believed on him there. *Jn10:42*

CHAPTER 21
The visit of Nicodemus

A A Pharisee called Nicodemus was of the religious leadership of the Jews. *Jn3:1*
B This same one came to Jesus at night, and said 'Rabbi, we know that you are a teacher sent by God, for no man can do the miracles that you have done unless God is with him. *Jn3:2*
C Jesus said 'With absolute certainty I tell you that except a man be reborn, he cannot be in God's new world order[1]'. *Jn3:3*
D Nicodemus said 'How can a man be reborn when he is old? Can he go back a second time into his mother's womb, and be born again?' *Jn3:4*
E Jesus replied 'I tell you with absolute certainty that unless a man be born of water and of the nature of God, he cannot enter into the God's new world order[2]'. *Jn3:5*
F That which is born of the flesh is fleshly and that which is born of spiritual constitution is of non-physical constitution. *Jn3:6*
G 'Do not be puzzled that I told you "You must be reborn". *Jn3:7*
H 'The wind blows where it does and you hear the sound of it but you cannot tell where it comes from and where it goes to. So to is every one that is born of spiritual constitution'. *Jn3:8*
I Nicodemus asked 'How can these things be?' *Jn3:9*

---

1 One of Christ's mission was to preach the 'kingdom of God' (Mark 1:14). What Christ was talking about was a future time when he was going to take over all the governments of the world (Rev 11:15; Matt 19:28). This message has somehow being obscured over the centuries hence the use of the phrase 'God's new world order' which conveys in modern parlance, a dramatic change to the governance of the world.

2 Here Christ explains that when he is talking about a rebirth, the stages are baptism and the receiving of the nature of God, which comes by the laying on of hands of a true servant of God, and which is a prelude to a future resurrection from death to a non-physical and immortal being. (Heb 6:1~2; II Cor 5:5; I Cor 15:53).

The Harmonized Gospels — Apocalyptic Version

J Jesus said to him 'Are you a religious leader of Israel. How is it that you do not know these things? | *Jn3:10*

K 'I tell you with absolute certainty, that I speak of what I do know and testify of what I have seen, yet you do not believe me. | *Jn3:11*

l 'If I told you earthly things and you do not believe me, how can you believe if I tell you about heavenly things? | *Jn3:12*

M 'No man can go up to the heavens, except he that came down from heaven, even *I* who came from the heavens. | *Jn3:13*

N 'Just as Moses lifted up the serpent in the wilderness, even so must *I* be lifted up, | *Jn3:14*

O 'so that whosoever believes in *me* should not perish, but have eternal life. | *Jn3:15*

P 'God so loves the world, that he gave his only begotten Son, so that whosoever believes in him should not perish, but have everlasting life. | *Jn3:16*

Q 'God did not send his Son into the world to condemn the world, but to save the world through him. | *Jn3:17*

R 'Anyone that believes him is not condemned, but he that does not believe stays condemned, because he does not believe in the one who is the only begotten Son of God. | *Jn3:18*

S 'And their condemnation is that though light has come into the world, yet men loved the darkness rather than light, because their deeds were evil. | *Jn3:19*

T 'For every one that does evil, hates the light and will not come to the light, because his deeds will be condemned. | *Jn3:20*

U 'On the other hand, he that does the truth comes to the light, so that his deeds may be made manifest, because they are done to please God'. | *Jn3:21*

CHAPTER 22
Jesus' disciples baptize

A Jesus came with his disciples into the land of Judaea, where they stayed for a while and baptized. | *Jn3:22*

B John was also baptizing in Aenon near to Salim, because there was much water there, and all that came to him were baptized. | *Jn3:23*

C This was before John was cast into prison. | *Jn3:24*

D Then a question came up between some of John's disciples and the Jews about purification. | *Jn3:25*

E So they came to John and said 'Rabbi, the one that came to you beyond Jordan, and who you bore witness of, he also is baptizing and the multitude is coming to him'. | *Jn3:26*

F John replied 'A man can accomplish nothing, except it be granted to him from heaven. | *Jn3:27*

G 'You yourselves are my witnesses that I said "I am not the Christ, | *Jn3:28*

and that I was sent to herald him".
H 'The one that weds the bride is the bridegroom. The friend of the bridegroom, who stands with him and supports him, rejoices greatly at the bridegroom's voice. So it is that my joy is fulfilled. *Jn3:29*
I 'He must increase but I must decrease. *Jn3:30*
J 'He that comes from above is above all, but he that is of the earth is earthly and can witness of earthly things. Now he that comes from heaven is above all, *Jn3:31*
K 'and that which he has seen and heard, he testifies of, yet no one believes his testimony. *Jn3:32*
L 'He that believes his testimony certifies that God is true. *Jn3:33*
M 'For he who is sent by God speaks the words of God, and God did not limit the amount of his nature given to him. *Jn3:34*
N 'The Father loves the Son and has given all things into his hand. *Jn3:35*
O 'He that believes the Son receives eternal life, but he that does not believe the Son shall not see eternal life, but the sentence of God on him stays in effect'[1]. *Jn3:36*

CHAPTER 23
Jesus preaches to the Samaritans

A When Jesus learned that the Pharisees knew that he had baptized more disciples than John, *Jn4:1*
B he left Judaea, and departed for Galilee. *Jn4:2*
C (Jesus himself did not baptize, but his disciples did.) *Jn4:3*
D His route back took him through Samaria. *Jn4:4*
E and he came to a city of Samaria, called Sychar, near to the parcel of ground that Jacob gave to his son Joseph. *Jn4:5*
F Jacob's well was located there and Jesus, being wearied with his journey, sat by the well. It was about noon *Jn4:6*
G and a woman of Samaria came to draw water. Jesus said to her 'Give me some water to drink'. *Jn4:7*
H This took place while some of his disciples had gone to the city to buy food to eat. *Jn4:8*
I The woman of Samaria replied 'How is it that you, a Jew, ask me for water to drink when I am a woman of Samaria?' (In those days the Jews had no dealings with the Samaritans.) *Jn4:9*
J Jesus answered 'If you knew the gift of God, and who it is that said to you "Give me some water to drink", you would have asked of him, and he would have given you living water'. *Jn4:10*
K The woman said 'Sir, you have nothing to draw with and the well is *Jn4:11*

---

1 Gen 2:17; Ezek 18:4, 20.

The Harmonized Gospels — Apocalyptic Version

deep. Where will you get living water?
L 'Are you greater than our father Jacob, who gave us this well, and who drank of it himself, together with his children and his cattle?' | Jn4:12
M Jesus answered 'Whosoever drinks of this water shall become thirsty again, | Jn4:13
N 'But whosoever drinks of the water that I shall give him shall never thirst. Furthermore, the water that I give him shall be as a well of water in him springing up into eternal life'. | Jn4:14
O The woman said 'Sir, give me this water, so that I thirst no more nor need to come back to draw'. | Jn4:15
P Jesus responded 'Go, call your husband and come back'. | Jn4:16
Q The woman answered 'I have no husband'.
Jesus replied 'You are correct when you said "I have no husband", | Jn4:17
R 'for you have had five husbands and the one that you are now with is not your husband. So what you said is the truth'. | Jn4:18
S The woman said 'Sir, I perceive that you are a prophet. | Jn4:19
T 'Our fathers worshipped in this mountain. Do you say that Jerusalem is the place where men ought to worship?' | Jn4:20
U Jesus replied 'Woman, believe me when I tell you that the time is coming when you shall not worship the Father in this mountain nor even at Jerusalem. | Jn4:21
V 'You worship what you do not know. We know what we worship, for salvation is of the Jews. | Jn4:22
W 'But the time is coming, and now at hand, when the true worshippers shall worship the Father in spirit and in truth, for the Father seeks such to worship him. | Jn4:23
X 'God is a spirit and they that worship him must worship him in spirit and in truth'. | Jn4:24
Y The woman said 'I know that Messias is coming, who is called Christ. When he is here he will tell us all things'. | Jn4:25
Z Jesus then said to her 'I am he'. | Jn4:26
AA At this time his disciples returned and marveled that he was talking with the woman, but none of them asked 'What are you trying to find out?' or, 'Why are you speaking with her?' | Jn4:27
AB The woman then left her water-pot, and went back to the city, and said to the men, | Jn4:28
AC 'Come, see a man who told me all things that I ever did. Is not this the Christ?' | Jn4:29
AD The people from the city then came out to see him. | Jn4:30
AE Meanwhile his disciples said 'Master, eat'. | Jn4:31
AF But Jesus replied 'I have food to eat that you do not know of'. | Jn4:32
AG The disciples said to one another 'Has any man brought him stuff to eat?' | Jn4:33
AH Jesus said 'My food is to do the will of him that sent me, and to finish his work. | Jn4:34
AI 'Do you not say that there are four months still before the har- | Jn4:35

vest? Look I tell you. Open your eyes and look on the fields, for they are white already to harvest.
AJ 'He that reaps receives wages and gathers fruit for an eternal life, so that both he that sows and he that reaps may rejoice together. *Jn4:36*
AK 'Here is a true saying 'One sows and another reaps. *Jn4:37*
AL 'I sent you to reap that which you did nor labor for. Other men labored, and you have joined them in their labor'. *Jn4:38*
AM Many of the Samaritans of that city believed him because of the woman who said 'He told me all that I ever did'. *Jn4:39*
AN When the Samaritans came to him they implored him to stay with them, and he stayed there two days. *Jn4:40*
AO Many of them believed when they themselves heard him speak. *Jn4:41*
AP They said to the woman 'Now we believe, not because of what you said, but because we have heard him ourselves, and know that this is indeed the Christ, the Savior of the world'. *Jn4:42*
AQ After the two days Jesus departed and went into Galilee. *Jn4:43*

CHAPTER 24
Jesus heals the nobleman's son at Cana

A When Jesus came back to Galilee, the inhabitants welcomed him, for they had witnessed all the things that he did at Jerusalem, while they were at the feast. *Jn4:45*
B Jesus went to Cana, where he had made the water into wine. While he was there, the son of a certain nobleman lay sick at Capernaum. *Jn4:46*
C On hearing that Jesus had left Judaea and was in Galilee, the nobleman went to him, and besought him to come and heal his son, who was at the point of death. *Jn4:47*
D Jesus said to him 'Except you see signs and wonders, you will not believe'. *Jn4:48*
E But the nobleman pleaded 'Sir, please come or my child will die'. *Jn4:49*
F Jesus told him 'Go back home, for your son lives'. The man believed what Jesus had told him, and he went on his way. *Jn4:50*
G Before he had reached his house, his servants met him and told him 'Your son lives'. *Jn4:51*
H He then asked them when exactly did his son begin to get better and they said 'Yesterday, at the seventh hour, the fever left him'. *Jn4:52*
I The father knew that it was at that same time Jesus had said to him 'Your son lives'. So the nobleman believed Jesus together with all his household. *Jn4:53*
J This is the second miracle that Jesus did at Galilee and it took place on his return from a trip to Judaea. *Jn4:54*

CHAPTER 25
The forgiveness of the sinful woman

A One of the Pharisees invited Jesus to dine with him. Jesus accepted and went to his house, where they sat down to eat. | *Lk7:36*

B A woman of the town who was a sinner, found out that Jesus was having a meal at the Pharisee's house. She took with her an alabaster jar with a pound of ointment of spikenard, which was very costly | *Lk7:37*

C and came and sat behind Jesus' feet. She was weeping and began to wash his feet with her tears, and wiped them with the hairs of her head. She also kissed his feet and anointed them with the ointment she had brought. | *Lk7:38*

D When the Pharisee who had invited Jesus saw this, he thought to himself 'If this man was a prophet, he would know what kind of woman is touching him, for she is a sinner'. | *Lk7:39*

E Jesus then said to him 'Simon, I have something to ask you'. Simon replied 'What is it, Master'. | *Lk7:40*

F Jesus continued 'There was a certain creditor who had two debtors. One of them owed five hundred pence, and the other fifty. | *Lk7:41*

G 'Both of them could not repay him, so he unconditionally released them both from their debt. Tell me therefore, which of them will love him the most?' | *Lk7:42*

H Simon answered 'I suppose, the one to whom he forgave most'. Jesus said to him 'You have judged correctly'. | *Lk7:43*

I Gesturing to the woman, Jesus said to Simon 'Do you see this woman? When I entered your house, you did not give me any water for my feet, but she has washed my feet with tears, and wiped them with the hairs of her head. | *Lk7:44*

J 'You did not give me a welcome kiss, but this woman has not ceased to kiss my feet from the time she came. | *Lk7:45*

K 'You did not anoint my head with oil, but this woman has anointed my feet with precious ointment. | *Lk7:46*

L 'Therefore I say to you that her sins, which are many, are forgiven, for she loved much. He to whom little is forgiven, will love a little'. | *Lk7:47*

M Then Jesus said to the woman 'Your sins are forgiven'. | *Lk7:48*

N Those that were eating at the table thought 'Who is this that can forgive sins?' | *Lk7:49*

O To the woman he said 'Because of your belief, you have been delivered. Go in peace'. | *Lk7:50*

The Harmonized Gospels — Apocalyptic Version

CHAPTER 26
Jesus attends the Feast of Tabernacles

A After these things had taken place Jesus remained in Galilee. He kept away from Judea because the Jews wanted to kill him.	Jn7:1
B At the time that the Jewish feast of tabernacles was approaching and	Jn7:2
C his brothers said to him 'Why don't you go to Judaea, and show your good works to your disciples?	Jn7:3
D 'No man who does any thing in secret can expect others to know what he is doing. Since you are doing good works, go and show yourself to the world'.	Jn7:4
E At that time, even his brothers did not believe in him[1].	Jn7:5
F Jesus said to them 'This is not my time but any time is good for you.	Jn7:6
G 'The world may not hate you, but it hates me because I attest to the fact that its works are evil.	Jn7:7
H 'You go up to this feast. I will not go as yet to this feast, for it is not yet the time for me'.	Jn7:8
I When he said these things to them, he was still in Galilee.	Jn7:9
J After his brothers had left for Judea, he also left to go to the feast. He did not publicize his journey but kept it a secret.	Jn7:10
K The Jews were on the lookout for him at the feast and were asking 'Where is he?'	Jn7:11
L There was a lot of discussions among the people about him. Some said 'He is a good man' while others said 'That's not so, for he deceives the people'.	Jn7:12
M However, no one spoke publicly of him because they were afraid of the Jews.	Jn7:13
N Some days after the feast had started, Jesus went to the temple and began to teach.	Jn7:14
O The Jews were taken aback and said 'How does this man know the scriptures without being schooled?'	Jn7:15
P Jesus explained 'My doctrine did not originate from me but from him that sent me.	Jn7:16
Q 'If any man does his will, he shall recognize whether this doctrine is of God, or whether I speak of myself.	Jn7:17
R 'He that speaks of himself seeks his own glory, but he that seeks the glory of the one that sent him, is indeed true and there is no unrighteousness in him.	Jn7:18
S 'Did not Moses give you the law, and yet none of you keep the	Jn7:19

---

1 After Jesus' death some of his brothers were converted. James is referenced in Gal 1:19 and Jude (Jude 1:1) may also be Jesus' brother.

The Harmonized Gospels — Apocalyptic Version

law? Why do you want to kill me?'

T The people replied 'You have a devil. Who is trying to kill you? — Jn7:20

U Jesus then said to them 'I have done one work and you are all perplexed by it. — Jn7:21

V 'Moses taught you circumcision, though it did not start with Moses, but with the fathers. Yet on the Sabbath day you circumcise a man. — Jn7:22

W 'If a man can be circumcised on the Sabbath day and that does not break the law of Moses, why are you angry with me because I made all of a man clean on the Sabbath day? — Jn7:23

X 'Do not judge according to the appearance, but judge righteous judgment'. — Jn7:24

Y Then some who lived in Jerusalem said 'Is this not the one that they were seeking to kill? — Jn7:25

Z 'But look! He is speaking openly and they can say nothing to him. Do the rulers know if this is really the Christ? — Jn7:26

AA 'How is it we know where this man came from? When Christ comes, surely no man would know where he came from'. — Jn7:27

AB Jesus said to them in the temple 'You both know me, and you know where I came from, but I am not here for myself. The one that sent me is true, but you do not know him. — Jn7:28

AC 'I know him, for I came from him and he has sent me'. — Jn7:29

AD They wanted to seize him then, but no one acted because it was not yet time. — Jn7:30

AE Many people did believe him and said 'When Christ comes, will he do more miracles than what this man has done?' — Jn7:31

AF The Pharisees and the chief priests heard what the people were saying about him and they sent officers to take him. — Jn7:32

AG Jesus said to them 'For a little while longer, I shall be with you and then I will return to the one that sent me. — Jn7:33

AH 'You will seek me but will not find me, for where I am going you cannot come'. — Jn7:34

AI The Jews said among themselves 'Where will he go so that we can't find him? Will he go to the dispersed among the Gentiles or teach the Gentiles? — Jn7:35

AJ 'What is he talking about when he says "You shall seek me, but will not find me, and where I am going you cannot come?"' — Jn7:36

AK On the last day, the great day of the feast, Jesus stood and spoke aloud saying 'If any man thirst, let him come to me, and drink. — Jn7:37

AL 'He that believes on me, as the scripture has said, out of his belly shall flow rivers of living water'. — Jn7:38

AM (He was speaking of the nature of God, which they that believe on him should receive, for the nature of God was not yet given, because Jesus was not yet glorified.) — Jn7:39

AN Many of the people who heard this said 'In truth this is a prophet'. — Jn7:40

AO Some said 'This is the Christ'. But others said 'Shall Christ come out of Galilee? — Jn7:41

AP 'Does not the scripture say that Christ comes of the seed of David and from the town of Bethlehem, where David came from?'	Jn7:42
AQ So there was disagreement among the people about him.	Jn7:43
AR Some would have liked to arrest him but no man laid hands on him.	Jn7:44
AS The officers of the chief priests and Pharisees returned and were asked 'Why have you not brought him?'	Jn7:45
AT They replied 'Never has anyone spoken like this man'.	Jn7:46
AU The Pharisees said 'Are you also deceived?	Jn7:47
AV 'Have any of the rulers or the Pharisees believed on him?	Jn7:48
AW 'But this people who do not know the law are cursed'.	Jn7:49
AX One of their number, Nicodemus, who was the one who came to Jesus by night, said,	Jn7:50
AY 'Does our law judge any man, before it gives him opportunity to speak and ascertains what he did?'	Jn7:51
AZ They replied 'Are you also from Galilee? Search and see, for no prophet comes out of Galilee'.	Jn7:52
BA After this every one went to their home.	Jn7:53

CHAPTER 27

The woman taken in adultery

A Jesus left and went to the mount of Olives.	Jn8:1
B Early in the morning he returned to the temple, where the people there congregated around him. So he sat down and began to teach them.	Jn8:2
C There the Scribes and Pharisees brought to him a woman caught in adultery and set her before the crowd.	Jn8:3
D They said 'Master, this woman was committing adultery and was caught in the very act.	Jn8:4
E 'Moses, in the law, commanded that such a one should be stoned. What do you think should be done to her?'	Jn8:5
F They had come deceitfully hoping to find some reason to accuse him, but Jesus looked down and using his finger, he wrote on the ground as though he did not hear them.	Jn8:6
G They continued to press him for an answer, so finally he straightened himself and said to them 'He that is without sin among you, let him be the first to cast a stone at her'.	Jn8:7
H Jesus then bent down again and continued writing on the ground.	Jn8:8
I The people who heard him were convicted by their own conscience, so they left one by one, from the eldest to the youngest till Jesus was left alone with the woman they had brought.	Jn8:9
J Jesus looked up and saw no one except the woman, so he asked her 'Woman, where are all your accusers? Has no man condemned you?'	Jn8:10
K She replied 'No man, Lord'. Then Jesus said 'Neither do I condemn you. Go, and sin no more'.	Jn8:11

CHAPTER 28
Jesus — the light of the world

A Jesus said to the gathering 'I am the light of the world. He that follows me shall not walk in darkness but shall have light to walk in the way of life'. — Jn8:12

B The Pharisees said 'You endorse yourself so you are not to be believed'. — Jn8:13

C Jesus replied 'Though I speak of myself, it is true, for I know where I came from and where I am going. You, on the other hand, do not know where I came from or where I am going. — Jn8:14

D 'You judge people but I judge no man. — Jn8:15

E 'But if I judge, my judgment is true, for I am not on my own, but the Father that sent me is with me. — Jn8:16

F 'It is also written in your law that the testimony of two men is true. — Jn8:17

G 'I speak of myself and the Father that sent me, he also bears witness of me'. — Jn8:18

H They said to him 'Where is your Father?' Jesus replied 'You do not know me nor my Father. If you knew me, you would have known my Father also'. — Jn8:19

I Jesus spoke these words in the treasury of the temple, but no one tried to stop him, for his time had not yet come. — Jn8:20

J Jesus continued 'I will go my way and you will look for me till you die in your sins, but where I am going you cannot come'. — Jn8:21

K The Jews said 'Is he going to kill himself?' This was because he said 'Where I am going, you cannot come'. — Jn8:22

L He explained 'You are from here, but I am from above. You are of this world, but I am not of this world. — Jn8:23

M 'This is why I say to you that you shall die in your sins. For if you do not believe that I am the one, you shall die in your sins'. — Jn8:24

N They asked 'Who are you?' Jesus replied 'I told you from the beginning. — Jn8:25

O 'I have many things to say for you to understand, but he that sent me is true and I speak to the world of those things which have been revealed by him'. — Jn8:26

P They did not understand that he spoke to them of the Father. — Jn8:27

Q Jesus continued 'When you have lifted me up, then you shall know that I am the one and that I do nothing by myself, but what my Father reveals to me, these things I speak. — Jn8:28

R 'He that sent me is with me. The Father has not left me alone, for I always do those things that please him'. — Jn8:29

S When he spoke these words many believed him. — Jn8:30

T Addressing the Jews who believed him, he said 'If you live as I have told you, then you will truly be my disciples. — Jn8:31

The Harmonized Gospels — Apocalyptic Version

U 'You shall come to know the truth and the truth shall make you free'.	Jn8:32
V They asked 'We are Abraham's descendants and have never been bonded to any man. How then you say that you will make us free?'	Jn8:33
W Jesus replied 'I tell you the truth that whosoever commits sin is the servant of sin.	Jn8:34
X 'The servant does not remain in the house. The Son on the other hand, he lives in it forever.	Jn8:35
Y 'If the Son makes you free, then only can you be free.	Jn8:36
Z 'I know that you are Abraham's children, but you want to kill me, because you cannot accept my word.	Jn8:37
AA 'I speak of what I have seen with my Father. You also do that which you have seen with your father'.	Jn8:38
AB They said again 'Abraham is our father'. But Jesus told them 'If you were Abraham's children, you would do the things that Abraham would do.	Jn8:39
AC 'But you seek to kill me, even though I have told you the truth, which I have heard of God. This is not how Abraham behaved.	Jn8:40
AD 'You indeed do the things that your father would do'. They replied 'We are not illegitimate and we have one Father, even God'.	Jn8:41
AE Jesus said 'If God were your Father, you would love me, for I was sent by God and came from him. I did not come on my own, but he sent me.	Jn8:42
AF 'Why is it that you do not understand my speech? It is because you cannot receive my word.	Jn8:43
AG 'You are of your father the devil, and the lusts of your father you will carry out. He was a murderer from the beginning, and strayed from the truth, because there is no truth in him. When he speaks a lie, it is his own concoction, for he is a liar, and the originator of lies.	Jn8:44
AH 'Now I tell you the truth and you do not believe me.	Jn8:45
AI 'Which of you can accuse me of sin? Yet when I speak the truth, why do you not believe me?	Jn8:46
AJ 'He that is of God hears God's words. You cannot hear them because you are not of God'.	Jn8:47
AK The Jews then said 'Were we not correct to say that you are a Samaritan and have a devil?'	Jn8:48
AL Jesus answered 'I do not have a devil, but I honor my Father, yet you dishonor me.	Jn8:49
AM 'I am not seeking mine own glory, but there is one who looks and judges.	Jn8:50
AN 'I tell you the truth, that if a man does what I say, he shall never see death'.	Jn8:51
AO The Jews replied 'Now we know for sure that you have a devil. Abraham is dead, as are the prophets. Yet you say "If a man does what I say he shall never taste of death.	Jn8:52
AP 'Are you greater than our father Abraham, who is dead or the prophets who are also dead. Who do you think you are?'	Jn8:53

The Harmonized Gospels — Apocalyptic Version

AQ Jesus answered 'If I honor myself, my honor is vain. But it is my Father who honors me. He is the one who you say is your God.	Jn8:54
AR 'You have not known him, but I know him. If I should say I do not know him, then I shall be a liar like you. But I do know him and does what He says.	Jn8:55
AS 'Your father Abraham rejoiced when he came to know of my future revealing and when he found out, he was glad'.	Jn8:56
AT Then the Jews said 'You are not yet fifty years old, yet you claim to have seen Abraham?'	Jn8:57
AU Jesus answered 'I tell you the truth. Before Abraham was born, I existed'.	Jn8:58
AV The people then took up stones to throw at him, but Jesus hid amongst the crowd and went out of the temple, passing through the midst of them.	Jn8:59

CHAPTER 29

The resurrection of Lazarus

A A certain man named Lazarus was sick. He was from Bethany, the town of Mary, who's sister was Martha.	Jn11:1
B This was the same Mary who *later* anointed the Lord with ointment and wiped his feet with her hair, and it was her brother Lazarus who was sick[1].	Jn11:2
C The sisters sent a message to Jesus saying 'Lord, the one whom you love is sick'.	Jn11:3
D When Jesus heard this he said 'This sickness will not result in his death, but it is to the glory of God, so that the Son of God might be magnified.	Jn11:4
E Now Jesus had deep affection for Martha, her sister and Lazarus.	Jn11:5
F Yet when he was told that Lazarus was sick, he stayed where he was for two more days.	Jn11:6
G After that time Jesus said to his disciples 'Let us return to Judaea'.	Jn11:7
H His disciples said 'Master, the Jews there sought to stone you not long ago. Do you still want to return there?'	Jn11:8
I Jesus replied 'Are there not twelve hours in the day? If any man walks in the day, he does not stumble, because he sees the light of this world.	Jn11:9
J 'But if a man walks in the night, he will stumble because there is no light in him'.	Jn11:10
K After he said this he continued 'Our friend Lazarus sleeps, but I go that I may awake him out of sleep'.	Jn11:11

---

1 The anointing by Mary (John 12:3) occurred later than the anointing by the sinful woman Luke (7:37 ~ 38).

The Harmonized Gospels — Apocalyptic Version

L His disciples said 'Lord, if he sleeps, then he must be well'. — *Jn11:12*

M Jesus though, was speaking of his death, but they thought that he was speaking of sleep. — *Jn11:13*

N Then Jesus told them plainly 'Lazarus is dead. — *Jn11:14*

O 'I am glad for your sakes that I was not there, that your belief may be strengthened. Now let us go to him'. — *Jn11:15*

P Thomas, who is also called Didymus, said to his fellow disciples 'Let us go also that we may die with him'. — *Jn11:16*

Q When Jesus came he found that Lazarus had been in the grave for over four days. — *Jn11:17*

R Bethany was not far from Jerusalem, being about three kilometers away, — *Jn11:18*

S and many of the Jews came to Martha and Mary, to comfort them for their brother. — *Jn11:19*

T As soon as Martha heard that Jesus was approaching, she went and met him, but Mary stayed in the house. — *Jn11:20*

U Martha said to Jesus 'Lord, if you had been here, my brother would not have died. — *Jn11:21*

V 'But I know, that even now, whatsoever you ask of God, He will give it to you'. — *Jn11:22*

W Jesus replied 'Your brother shall rise again'. — *Jn11:23*

X Martha said 'I know that he shall rise again in the resurrection at the last day'. — *Jn11:24*

Y Jesus said 'I am the resurrection and the life. He that believes in me, even though he is dead, he shall yet live. — *Jn11:25*

Z 'And anyone alive who believes in me shall by no means endure in death. Do you believe this?' — *Jn11:26*

AA She said 'Yes, Lord. I believe that you are the Christ, the Son of God, who was prophesied to come into the world'. — *Jn11:27*

AB Martha then left to call Mary her sister, saying to her in secret 'The Master is come, and sent for you'. — *Jn11:28*

AC As soon as she heard this, Mary immediately got up and went to Jesus, — *Jn11:29*

AD who had not yet come into the town, but was in the place where Martha had met him. — *Jn11:30*

AE When the Jews who were with Mary in the house consoling her, saw that she got up and quickly went out, they followed her saying 'She goes to the grave to weep there'. — *Jn11:31*

AF When Mary came to the place where Jesus was, she fell down at his feet and said 'Lord, if you were here, my brother would not have died'. — *Jn11:32*

AG When Jesus saw her weeping, as well as the Jews who came with her, he was moved in his heart — *Jn11:33*

AH and said 'Where have you laid him?' They said 'Lord, come and see'. — *Jn11:34*

AI Jesus too wept. — *Jn11:35*

The Harmonized Gospels — Apocalyptic Version

AJ The Jews seeing him said 'Look how much he loved him!' — *Jn11:36*

AK Some of them said 'Could not this man, who opened the eyes of the blind, prevent this man from dying?' — *Jn11:37*

AL Jesus touched by their mourning came to the grave, which was a cave with a stone at the entrance. — *Jn11:38*

AM Jesus said 'Take away the stone'. Martha, the sister of the one who died, said to him 'Lord, by this time he stinks, for he has been dead for four days'[1]. — *Jn11:39*

AN Jesus said to her 'Did I not say to you that, if you would believe, you shall see the glory of God?' — *Jn11:40*

AO So they took away the stone from the entrance of the place where the dead was laid, and Jesus lifted up his eyes and said 'Father, I thank you that you have heard me. — *Jn11:41*

AP 'I know that you hear me always, but because of the people who are standing here, I said it, so that they may believe that you have sent me'. — *Jn11:42*

AQ Then he said in a loud voice 'Lazarus, come forth'. — *Jn11:43*

AR Then he that was dead came out, still wrapped hand and foot with grave-clothes, with his face wrapped with a napkin. Jesus said to them 'Loose him, and let him go'. — *Jn11:44*

AS After this many of the Jews who had come to Mary, and saw the things which Jesus did, believed him. — *Jn11:45*

AT Some of them went back to the Pharisees and told them what Jesus had done. — *Jn11:46*

AU The chief priests and the Pharisees held a council, and said 'What shall we do for this man does many miracles?' — *Jn11:47*

AV 'If we let him alone, everyone will believe in him and the Romans will come and take away both our place and our nation'. — *Jn11:48*

AW Then one of them named Caiaphas, who was the high priest that year, said to them 'You know nothing at all, — *Jn11:49*

AX 'nor consider that it is expedient for us, that one man should die so that the whole nation does not perish'. — *Jn11:50*

AY The words he spoke were not of himself, but being the high priest that year, he prophesied that Jesus should die for that nation, — *Jn11:51*

AZ and not for that nation only, but also that he should gather together the children of God that were scattered abroad. — *Jn11:52*

BA From that day onwards they consulted among themselves on how to put him to death. — *Jn11:53*

BB Jesus therefore did not stay among the Jews but went to a remote area, in a town called Ephraim, and stayed there with his disciples. — *Jn11:54*

---

1 Bullinger (Companion Bible, appendix 148) points out that the Jews required at least three days burial to certify a death. This was one reason that Christ waited four days to resurrect Lazarus to negate any doubts as to the certainty of his death.

CHAPTER 30
The imprisonment of John

A Herod the tetrarch was rebuked by John for making Herodias his wife, because she was his brother Philip's wife and also for all the other evils which he had done.	*Mt14:4; Mk6:18 Lk3:19*
B Herod added to his wickedness by imprisoning John.	*Mt14:3; Mk6:17 Lk3:20*

CHAPTER 31
Christ begins his closing Ministry

A When Jesus heard that John was imprisoned, he left for Galilee,	*Mt4:12; Mk1:14*
B and stayed, not in Nazareth, but in Capernaum, which is on the shore of the Sea of Galilee, at the borders of Zabulon and Nephthalim.	*Mt4:13*
C This fulfilled the prophecy of Esaias, which said	*Mt4:14*
D 'To the land of Zabulon and Nephthalim, which borders the sea beyond Jordan, in the region of Galilee, where there are many gentiles;	*Mt4:15*
E 'The people which sat in darkness saw a great light. Light has indeed shone on they which sat in a land covered with the shadow of death[1]'.	*Mt4:16*
F From that time, Jesus began to preach saying 'Repent and believe the good news that God is about to inaugurate a divine government over the earth'.	*Mt4:17; Mk1:14,15*

---

1 Is 9:1~2

The Harmonized Gospels — Apocalyptic Version

CHAPTER 32

The calling of Simon Peter, Andrew, James and John to full time service[1]

A Jesus went to the sea of Galilee, to the place where the two brothers, Simon called Peter, and Andrew, who were fishermen, were casting a net into the sea.	Mt4:18; Mk1:16
B He said to them 'Come with me and I will make you fishers of men'.	Mt4:19; Mk1:17
C They straight away left their nets, and followed him.	Mt4:20; Mk1:18
D Going on a little distance, he saw two other brothers, James the son of Zebedee, and John his brother. They were in a fishing boat with Zebedee their father, mending their nets. He also called them,	Mt4:21; Mk1:19
E and they immediately left their father in his boat, and followed him.	Mt4:22; Mk1:20

CHAPTER 33

Jesus casts out a demon in Capernaum

A Together they went into Capernaum, a city of Galilee, and on the Sabbath day Jesus entered the synagogue and taught.	Mk1:21; Lk4:31
B There the people were impressed with his teaching, for he spoke authoritatively, and quite unlike the scribes.	Mk1:22; Lk4:32
C There was also in their synagogue at that time, a man possessed with a demon and he accosted Jesus	Mk1:23; Lk4:33
D saying 'Leave us alone. We have no business with you, Jesus of Nazareth. Have you come to destroy us? I know that you are the Holy One of God'.	Mk1:24; Lk4:34
E Jesus rebuked the demon saying 'Be quiet and come out of him'.	Mk1:25; Lk4:35
F At this the demon shook up the man and came out of him with loud shrieks.	Mk1:26; Lk4:35
G All who were there were amazed, making statements among themselves such as 'What is happening here? What new doctrine is this? Look, he commands the demons with authority and they obey him'.	Mk1:27; Lk4:36
H (After that incident, word of his fame was spread throughout the region around Galilee.)	Mk1:28; Lk4:37

---

1 Before this incident, Simon Peter, Andrew, James and John met Jesus a few times (John 1:40 ~ 42; Luke 5:2 ~10) and likely listened to his sermons. This was the point of their call to service, when they gave up their trade and became full time disciples.

CHAPTER 34
Jesus heals Simon's mother-in-law

A When they left the synagogue they came to the house of Simon and Andrew, with James and John.	Mk1:29; Lk4:38
B There they found Simon's mother-in-law sick in bed with a fever.	Mt8:14; Mk1:30; Lk4:38
C Jesus went to her and taking her by the hand, he rebuked the fever. The fever immediately left her and she got up and proceeded to serve them.	Mt8:15; Mk1:31; Lk4:39

CHAPTER 35
Jesus heals following the Sabbath

A That evening, after the sun had set[1], people brought to him those that were diseased or possessed with demons.	Mt8:16; Mk1:32; Lk4:40
B Eventually all in the city came and congregated outside the door.	Mk1:33
C There Jesus healed a multitude that were sick of various diseases, and he cast out demons from many, but he forbade the demons from speaking, because they knew who he was.	Mk1:34; Lk4:41
D This fulfilled the prophecy of Esaias the prophet, that says 'He took away our infirmities, and removed our sicknesses'[2].	Mt8:17
E When Jesus saw the large crowd about him, he gave instructions to move to the another location.	Mt8:18

CHAPTER 36
Jesus prays in a solitary place

A In the morning, Jesus got up long before daybreak and went to a solitary place and prayed.	Mk1:35; Lk4:42
B Simon and his companions got up later and went looking for him.	Mk1:36
C When they had found him, they said 'Everyone is looking for you'. The people also pressed on him to stay with them.	Mk1:37; Lk4:42
D He then said to them 'We must go into the other towns so that I may witness to them also. This is why I have been sent'.	Mk1:38; Lk4:43

---

1 The people waited till the Sabbath was ended to bring their sick.
2 Is 53:4

The Harmonized Gospels — Apocalyptic Version

CHAPTER 37
Christ ministers in Galilee

A Jesus went through Galilee, teaching in their synagogues, and preaching the good news of a divine government over the earth. He also healed the people of all kinds of sicknesses and diseases.	Mt4:23; Mk1:39 Lk4:44
B His fame spread throughout Syria and they brought to him many sick people that had various diseases and pains. They also brought lunatics, those possessed with devils and the otherwise incapacitated. He healed them all	Mt4:24; Mk1:39
C and great multitudes followed him from Galilee, Decapolis, Jerusalem, Judaea and from beyond the Jordan.	Mt4:25

CHAPTER 38
The Sermon on the mount[1] - Part I:
The Beatitudes[2]

A Leaving the multitudes, he went up into a mountain and sat down with his disciples,	Mt5:1; Lk6:20
B to teach them. This is what he said:	Mt5:2
C 'Blessed are you with a contrite spirit[3]. God's divine government is for you[4].	Mt5:3; Lk6:20
D 'Blessed are you hungry, for you shall have your fill.	Lk6:21
E 'Blessed are you that weep now, for you shall laugh.	Lk6:21
F 'Blessed are those who are in distress, for they shall be comforted.	Mt5:4
G 'Blessed are those who are gentle and teachable and who respect others, for they shall rule over the earth.	Mt5:5

---

1 The Sermon on the Mount refers to the discourse recorded in Matt 5, 6 and 7 where Christ defines the standards to which His followers must adhere. Starting from the basis of the Ten Commandments, Christ expands their requirements to encompass their spiritual intent. (Luke 6:20~49; Ezek 36:26; Heb 10:16). Though Matt 5:1 and Luke 6:20 indicate that the Sermon on the Mount was directed at His disciples, it is likely that the Christ repeated elements of it at various times, and to various gatherings, during his ministry (Luke 7:1).
2 The 'beatitudes' from the Latin 'beatitudo' meaning 'blessedness', refers to those verses of the Sermon on the Mount that begin with 'Blessed are', in the King James Version. Matthew has nine verses with this opening (Matt 5:2 ~ 11) and Luke 6:20 ~ 22 contains four more. These have been combined here in eleven beatitudes.
3 Ps 34:18; Ps 51:17; Is 57:15; Is 66:2
4 Christ's message of hope is for a future time when He will return and take over all the Governments of the earth. At that time, the faithful will be resurrected or changed to a non-physical constitution and be given positions of authority in the new world government. (Rev 11:15; Rev 1:6; John 3:3,8; ICor 15:53~54).

The Harmonized Gospels — Apocalyptic Version

H 'Blessed are those who hunger and thirst for righteousness, for they shall be satisfied.	*Mt5:6*
I 'Blessed are those who show mercy, for they shall obtain mercy.	*Mt5:7*
J 'Blessed are the pure in heart, for they shall see God.	*Mt5:8*
K 'Blessed are those who seek peace, for they shall be called the children of God.	*Mt5:9*
L 'Blessed are those who would suffer persecution for doing right, for they shall rule in God's divine government.	*Mt5:10*
M 'Blessed are you, when men shall hate you, revile you, ostracize you and call you evil for my sake.	*Mt5:11; Lk6:22*
N 'Be happy and filled with joy, for exceedingly great is your reward. Did they not do the same to the prophets they persecuted before you?	*Mt5:12; Lk6:23*
O 'But too bad for you that are rich! You have received your consolation.	*Lk6:24*
P 'Too bad for you that are full! You shall hunger.	*Lk6:25*
Q 'Too bad for you that laugh now! You shall mourn and weep.	*Lk6:25*
R 'Too bad for you, when all men shall speak well of you! Did not their fathers do the same of the false prophets'.	*Lk6:26*

CHAPTER 39
The Sermon on the mount - Part II:
Charge to his disciples

A 'You are the salt of the earth. If the salt loses its saltiness, of what use is it? It has become good for nothing, and must be cast out, to be trodden underfoot.	*Mt5:13*
B 'You are the light of the world. A city that is set on an hill is not put there to be hidden,	*Mt5:14*
C 'nor do men light a candle and then cover it under a pot, but they put it on a candlestick so it can give light to the whole house.	*Mt5:15; Mk4:21 Lk8:16; Lk11:33*
D 'So likewise, let your light shine before men, that they may see your good works, and give glory to your Father which is in the heavens.	*Mt5:16*
E 'If any man have ears to hear, let him hear'.	*Mk4:23*

The Harmonized Gospels — Apocalyptic Version

CHAPTER 40

The Sermon on the mount - Part III:
The spiritual intent of the law

A 'Do not think that I have come to destroy what was written in the books of Moses or the prophets? I am come, not to destroy but to fulfil.	*Mt5:17*
B 'I tell you with certainty, that the universe will cease to exist, before the smallest matter written of in these books, fail to come to pass[1].	*Mt5:18; Lk16:17*
C 'If anyone shall reject what was written in these books, or tell others so, they shall be rejected in God's new world order. However, anyone who lives by it and teaches it to others, shall be greatly honored when the world is under divine rule.	*Mt5:19*
D 'I tell you now, except your righteousness exceeds that of the scribes and Pharisees, you cannot be part of God's new world order.	*Mt5:20*
E 'You have heard before that "You shall not murder" and you know that he who kills someone shall be held accountable.	*Mt5:21*
F 'But I tell you now that he who is even angry with another shall be held accountable, especially if unprovoked. He who tells someone that they are worthless, risks being punished and he who calls another "a fool", risks suffering the final destruction[2].	*Mt5:22*
G 'Therefore, if you would bring your offering to God and then remember that someone is unhappy with your conduct,	*Mt5:23*
H 'turn back and go find that person. First settle your differences and then present your offering.	*Mt5:24*
I 'For even in human courts, if you do not come to terms with your opponent while you have the chance, the judge will send you to prison under guard,	*Mt5:25; Lk12:58*
J 'where you shall not be allowed your freedom until you have paid the last penny.	*Mt5:26; Lk12:59*
K 'You have heard from before that "You shall not commit	*Mt5:27*

---

1 Christ here confirms the authenticity of the Old Testament and God's commitment to uphold its promises. In the rest of the 'Sermon on the Mount,' Christ addresses a number of the commands given in the books of the Law and expands on the spiritual requirements, thus fulfilling a prophecy given in Is 42:21.

2 Prior to Christ, the sixth commandment, which is the injunction against murder, carried a penalty, only when an actual murderous act occurred. Here Christ indicates that even feelings of ill-will, put one in jeopardy of transgressing the spiritual intent of the sixth commandment. In the new dispensation, the minutest verbal expression of hatred and scorn, was sufficient to condemn one to a final termination that occurs in the last destruction at the end of the millennium. (Ex 20:13; Mt19:18; Num 35:11~34; IJohn 2:11; Luke 12:5; Rev 20:13; Matt 25:31 ~ 46.)

The Harmonized Gospels — Apocalyptic Version

adultery,"	
L 'but I tell you, that he who looks on a woman with lust, is committing adultery with her in his heart[1].	Mt5:28
M 'If your right eye is causing you to sin, pluck it out and throw it away. Is it not better that one part of your body be destroyed, than if your whole body is destroyed in the final destruction?	Mt5:29; Mt18:9; Mk9:47
N 'If your right hand is causing you to sin, cut it off and throw it away. Is it not better that one part of your body be destroyed, than if your whole body is destroyed in the final destruction[2]?	Mt5:30; Mt18:8; Mk9:43, 45
O 'You have heard that "Whosoever wishes to end his relationship with his wife, can divorce her",	Mt5:31
P 'but I tell you, that you shall not divorce your wife, except for the cause of adultery. Both the woman, who is divorced in such circumstances, and he who marries her, are committing adultery.	Mt5:32; Lk16:18
Q 'You have also heard since ancient times that "You shall not make empty promises to God, but shall perform your oaths to Him"[3],	Mt5:33
R 'but I tell you, do not swear at all, whether by heaven, for it is God's throne,	Mt5:34
S 'or the earth, for it is his footstool, or by Jerusalem, for it is the city of the great King.	Mt5:35
T 'Do not even swear by your own head, because you cannot make one hair white or black.	Mt5:36
U 'Rather, let your commitment be either "Yes" or "No". Anything more than this springs from evil.	Mt5:37
V 'You have heard from before "An eye for an eye, and a tooth for a tooth[4],"	Mt5:38
W 'But I say to all you who will hear, Love your enemies. Do	Lk6:27; Mt5:44

---

1 Christ explains that a person will be judged to have committed adultery if they even harbor unlawful desire in the mind. The penalty for adultery is death. (Ex 20:14; Lev 20:10)

2 Christ is not suggesting that we actually cut off our body parts involved in sinful actions, because we know that sin occurs after it is conceived in the mind, and that removing the offending part will not purge the mind of the evil it conceived (Matt 15:18). Lev 21:5 expressly forbids mutilation of any sort. Christ is trying to convey the seriousness with which we should view sin, since it has the potential to deny us eternal life on resurrection and a part in God's new world order. We should, therefore, be extremely unrelenting on our war on sin, to the point that we would rather lose a body part than sin. Christ, later on, explained that His followers must be willing to even give up their physical lives for righteousness, (Mt15:18~19; Jas 1:14~15; Rev 21:7~8; Mt10:28, 39).

3 Num 30:2.

4 This principle of fair judgment, first described in Ex 21:24, is clearly a metaphor, as evidenced by the instructions in the rest of the chapter. For example, Ex 21:26 specifically deals with the instance of the loss of an eye and specifies a compensatory penalty. Only in the case of murder was the penalty to be exactly as the crime, and even for this God allowed some reprieve. (Lev 24:21; Num 35:15~28).

The Harmonized Gospels — Apocalyptic Version

good to those who hate you.

X 'Bless them who curse you and pray for those which callously use you. — *Lk6:28; Mt 5:44*

Y 'Only then can you be children of your heavenly Father, for he makes his sun to rise on both the wicked and the good, and he sends rain on both the just and the unjust. — *Mt5:45*

Z 'I tell you now, that you must not retaliate to evil. If someone should smite you on your right cheek, allow him to strike the other also[1]. — *Mt5:39; Lk6:29*

AA 'If someone sues you for your coat, give him your cloak also. — *Mt5:40; Lk6:29*

AB 'If someone forces you to bear a load for a mile, willingly carry it for two. — *Mt5:41*

AC 'Accommodate anyone that makes a request of you, and do not turn away anyone who seeks to borrow from you. If anyone borrows from you, do not ask back for what you loaned them. — *Mt5:42; Lk6:30*

AD 'You have heard it said "Love you friend, but hate you enemy". — *Mt5:43*

AE 'But if you only love those who love you, what is exceptional about that? Do not sinners also love those that love them? — *Lk6:32*

AF 'If you are only good to those who are good to you, how exceptional are you? Don't the wicked tax collectors even do this? — *Mt5:46; Lk6:33*

AG 'If you are only kind to your friends, how different are you from others? Don't the wicked tax collectors even do this? — *Mt5:47*

AH 'If you only lend to those who you expect to repay, how noble are you? Do not the sinners also lend to other sinners, with the expectation to be repaid. — *Lk6:34*

AI 'So love your enemies and do good. Lend expecting nothing in return and your reward shall be great, for you shall be the children of the Highest. Indeed, is He not kind to the unthankful and to the evil. — *Lk6:35*

AJ 'Give, and it shall be given unto you. A good measure, compacted, shaken together and overflowing shall men give into your arms. The same measure that you use will be used to reward you. — *Lk6:38*

AK 'Be merciful therefore , as your Father is merciful. — *Lk6:36*

AL 'Strive to be perfect, because your Father in heaven is perfect'. — *Mt5:48*

---

1 The principle of not avenging oneself, was understood from old testament times. (ISam 24:12; Rom 12:19). In this section of scripture, Christ here extended this principle to one's attitude, so that forgiveness replaces a desire to exact revenge on a perpetrator. Christ's primary concern is the state of one's own nature, that it be not tarnished with any remnant of evil. (Mark 7:20 ~ 23). The standard with which we are to assess ourselves is God Himself.

CHAPTER 41

The Sermon on the mount - Part IV:
Warning on seeking the praise of men[1]

A 'When doing good, beware that you do it just to impress others, for then you shall have no blessing from your heavenly Father.	Mt6:1
B 'When you give charity, do not announce it with trumpets, as the hypocrites do in the synagogues and in the streets, just so that they may impress men. I tell you with certainty that they have no more reward to receive.	Mt6:2
C 'When you give charity, do not let your left hand know what your right hand is doing.	Mt6:3
D 'Let your charity be in secret and your Father, who sees all secrets, will bless you.	Mt6:4
E 'When you pray, do not be as the hypocrites, for they love to stand up and pray in synagogues and in street-corners, to be seen in public. I tell you, they have no more reward to receive.	Mt6:5
F 'When you would pray, enter your room and close the door. Pray to your Father in secret and your Father which sees all secrets, shall hear you.	Mt6:6
G 'When you fast, don't do as the hypocrites, who make glum faces to show others that they are fasting. I tell you now, they have received their reward.	Mt6:16
H 'When you fast, anoint you head and wash your face.	Mt6:17
I 'Don't try to show off to others that you are fasting, but let your fast be to your Father only. Then your Father, which sees all secrets, shall openly bless you'.	Mt6:18

---

1 The desire to seek the praise and adulation of others puts the opinions of humans above that of God and is rooted in the ego. On both counts it is idolatry, which is the replacement of God and His values with falsehoods.

CHAPTER 42
The Sermon on the mount - Part V: On praying

A One of his disciples said 'Lord, teach us to pray, as John taught his disciples'.	Lk11:1
B Jesus replied 'When you pray, do not keep saying the same thing over and over again, like the heathens, for they think that the more they repeat themselves, the more likely are they to be heard.	Mt6:7
C 'Do not be like them, for your Father knows what you need before you ask him.	Mt6:8
D 'You should pray after this pattern: Our Father in heaven, Holy One.	Mt6:9; Lk11:2
E 'We look forward to your intervention on the earth, so that its inhabitants will obey you, even as is done in the heavens.	Mt6:10; Lk11:2
F 'Provide us with our daily sustenance,	Mt6:11; Lk11:3
G 'and forgive us all the wrong we do, as we forgive those who wrong us.	Mt6:12; Lk11:4
H 'Guide us so that we are not overcome by temptation, and deliver us from all evil, *for all authority and power and glory is yours forever. Amen*[1].	Mt6:13; Lk11:4
I 'Know this. If you forgive those who wrong you, your heavenly Father will also forgive you.	Mt6:14; Mk11:25
J 'If however, you do not forgive those who wrong you, neither will your Father forgive you the wrongs that you do.	Mt6:15; Mk11:26
K 'Consider the situation where you go to your neighbor at midnight and say "Lend me three loaves,	Lk11:5
L '"for a friend of mine on his journey has stopped at my home and I have nothing to set before him?"	Lk11:6
M 'If your neighbor replies "Don't bother me. My home is closed up and my children are asleep with me in bed. I cannot get up to give you anything".	Lk11:7
N 'I tell you that though he will not get up and help you because he is your friend, he will get up because of your constant pleading to give you what you need.	Lk11:8
O 'So I say to you, ask and it shall be given to you. Seek and you will find. Knock and it shall be opened for you.	Lk11:9; Mt7:7
P 'For every one that asks will receive, and he that seeks shall find. He that knocks will be attended to.	Lk11:10; Mt7:8
Q 'If any of you have a son who asks bread from you, his	Lk11:11; Mt7:9, 10

---

1 The words in italics are left out in the Arabic and Vulgate Latin versions.

The Harmonized Gospels — Apocalyptic Version

father, will you give him a stone? If he ask a fish, will you give him a serpent instead?	
R 'If he asks for an egg from you, will you give him a scorpion?	Lk11:12
S 'If you then, being evil, know how to give good gifts to your children, how much more shall your Father in heaven give the Holy Spirit to those that ask him?'	Lk11:13; Mt7:11
T Jesus also gave them a parable with the intent to encourage them to pray always and not lose heart.	Lk18:1
U He said 'In a certain city there was a judge who had no fear of God or any interest in what men think of him.	Lk18:2
V 'There was also a widow in that city and she came to him and said "Judge for me against he who has wronged me".	Lk18:3
W 'The judge ignored the woman's request for some time, but then he said himself "Though I have no fear of God or any interest in what men think of me,	Lk18:4
X '"because this widow keeps pestering me, I will attend to her case so that she will stop bothering me".'	Lk18:5
Y Jesus continued 'Do you see how the unjust judge acted?	Lk18:6
Z 'Don't you think that God would avenge his own elect, who cry day and night to him? Even though he is long suffering,	Lk18:7
AA 'I tell you that he will avenge them before long. Nevertheless, when I return to this earth, will I find any who trusts in God ?'	Lk18:8

CHAPTER 43
The Sermon on the mount - Part VI:
On material concerns

A When one of the company said to him 'Master, speak to my brother, that he divide the inheritance with me',	Lk12:13
B he replied 'Man, who made me a judge or a divider over you?'	Lk12:14
C To the assembly he said 'Be very careful of covetousness, for a man's life is not measured by the abundance of the things which he owns'.	Lk12:15
D Jesus then gave this parable. 'The fields of a certain rich man yielded bountifully,	Lk12:16
E 'and he thought to himself "What should I do, seeing that I have no more room to store my fruits?"	Lk12:17
F 'So he said "I know what I should do. I will demolish my barns, and build bigger ones to store all of my fruits and my goods.	Lk12:18
G '"Then I can say to myself 'I have goods to last me many years. I can now relax and eat, drink, and be merry' ".	Lk12:19
H 'But God said to him "Not so, for tonight your life will come	Lk12:20

The Harmonized Gospels — Apocalyptic Version

to an end". Tell me, what shall become of the things he has laid up?

I 'This is what happens to someone who is preoccupied with accumulating material things but who is not rich toward God. — *Lk12:21*

J 'Do not seek to accumulate wealth during your stay on earth, where the moth and the rust can ruin it, and where thieves can steal it. — *Mt6:19: Lk12:33*

K 'Rather, sell what you have and give it to charity and so provide for yourselves treasure which will never grow old. Increase your store of riches in heaven, where neither moth nor rust can destroy it, and where thieves cannot steal it, — *Mt6:20; Lk12:33*

L 'knowing that your treasure shows where your heart is. — *Mt6:21; Lk12:34*

M 'The soundness of your being is determined by your mind. If your mind is righteous, your whole being shall be full of light. — *Mt6:22; Lk11:34*

N 'But if your mind is evil, your whole being shall be full of darkness. If the best things you can do are evil, how great is that darkness! — *Mt6:23; Lk11:34*

O 'Be careful therefore that the core of your being is not darkness. — *Lk11:35*

P 'If you are full of light with no dark parts, you will truly be full of light, and shining as the bright flame of a candle. — *Lk11:36*

Q 'No man can serve two masters. He must either hate one and love the other, or obey one and ignore the other. So too, you cannot serve both God and greed. — *Mt6:24; Lk16:13*

R 'Therefore I tell you, do not be fearful for your life, or what you will have to eat or drink. Neither be concerned about what you have to wear, for there is more to life than food and clothes. — *Mt6:25; Lk12:22, 23*

S 'Look at the birds in the air. They do not sow or reap, neither do they gather into barns, but their food is provided by your heavenly Father. Are you not much more valuable than they? — *Mt6:26; Lk12:24*

T 'Can any of you add one measure to his stature by thinking about it? — *Mt6:27; Lk12:25*

U 'If you can't do such a little thing, why worry about the rest? — *Lk12:26*

V 'So why do you spend time worrying about having clothes to wear? Look at the lilies in the fields and how they grow. They do not have to labor or spin, — *Mt6:28; Lk12:27*

W 'but I tell you that not even Solomon in his finest attire could measure up to one of them. — *Mt6:29; Lk12:27*

X 'Just think for a moment, if God takes so much care in beautifying the grass of the field, which is here for a day and cast in the oven tomorrow, shall he not take much more care in providing for you? How little do you trust in God? — *Mt6:30; Lk12:28*

Y 'Therefore, do not spend your time worrying about how you will get food or drink or clothing, — *Mt6:31; Lk12:29*

Z 'as the unbelievers do, for your heavenly Father already knows what you need. | Mt6:32; Lk12:30

AA 'Rather, aspire to be in the God's new world order by pursuing His righteousness, and all these physical things shall be provided to you. | Mt6:33; Lk12:31

AB 'Do not be afraid, little flock, for it is your Father's desire to give you all that is his. | Lk12:32

AC 'Do not be concerned about tomorrow, for tomorrow will have enough time to address its own problems. The problems of today are more than enough for today'. | Mt6:34

CHAPTER 44

The Sermon on the mount - Part VII: On judging others

A 'Do not judge others, for then you shall not be judged. | Lk6:37

B 'Be careful of condemning others, lest you condemn yourself. | Mt7:1; Lk6:37

C 'Forgive and you shall be forgiven. | Lk6:37

D 'For just as you judge others, you will also be judged. Just as you do to others, will be done to you. | Mt7:2; Mk4:24

E 'The message of the books of the Law and the Prophets is this: In the manner that you would like others to behave to you, you should behave to them. | Mt7:12; Lk6:31

F 'Why do you obsess yourself about the speck in your brother's eye, when there is a beam in your own eye? | Mt7:3; Lk6:41

G 'How can you say to your brother, "Let me help you get out the speck from your eye", when there is a beam is in your own eye? | Mt7:4; Lk6:42

H 'Do not be the hypocrite. First remove the beam from your own eye, and then you can see clearly enough to take the speck from your brother's eye. | Mt7:5; Lk6:42

I 'In any case, you do not speak of holy things to dogs, neither do you give pearls to swine, for they will trample them underfoot, and then turn on you to tear you apart'. | Mt7:6

CHAPTER 45

The Sermon on the mount - Part VIII: How to be part of God's new world order

A Then one asked 'Lord, will only a few be saved?' Jesus replied,	Lk13:23
B 'if you would be part of God's new world order, know that the way is difficult. There are numerous easy ways that lead to destruction, and many choose them,	Mt7:13; Lk13:24
C 'but difficult is the way to eternal life, and few will find it.	Mt7:14; Lk13:24
D 'Beware of false leaders, who come to you in sheep's clothing, but with the hearts of ravenous wolves.	Mt7:15
E 'You shall know them by their fruits. Do you gather grapes from thorns, or figs from thistles?	Mt7:16
F 'Every good tree bears good fruit, and the sick tree bears defective fruit.	Mt7:17; Lk6:43
G 'A good tree does not bear bad fruit, neither can the sick tree bear good fruit.	Mt7:18
H 'For every tree is known by its fruit. Can figs be harvested from a thorn or grapes be gathered from a bramble bush?	Lk6:44
I 'The tree that does not bear good fruit is to be cut down and burnt.	Mt7:19
J 'You shall know them therefore, by their fruits.	Mt7:20
K 'I tell you that once the master of the house has shut the door, even though you stand outside and knock saying "Lord, Lord, open the door for us," he will say to you "I do not know who you are"	Lk13:25
L 'Why do you call me "Lord" and do not do the things which I say?	Lk6:46
M 'Not because you call me Lord, Lord, can you be in God's new world order, but only if you do the will of my Father in heaven.	Mt7:21
N 'At the time of the new dispensation, many will say "Have we not eaten and drunk with you" or "Lord, Lord, have we not taught in your name?" or "Have we not cast out devils in your name?' or "Have we not done many good works in your name?"	Mt7:22; Lk13:26
O 'But I will tell them "I never knew you. Depart from me, you workers of iniquity".	Mt7:23; Lk13:27
P 'I tell you now, that whosoever hears what I have said here and does them, I will liken to a wise man, who dug deep and laid the foundation of his house upon a rock.	Mt7:24; Lk6:47 Lk6:48
Q 'When the rain poured down and the floods came, and when the winds and the flood buffeted the house, it will not fall, for it is built on rock.	Mt7:25; Lk6:48

R 'They who hear what I said here and do not do them, shall be likened to a foolish man who built his house upon the sand.	Mt7:26; Lk6:49
S 'When the rain poured down and the floods came, and when the winds and the flood buffeted that house, it will collapse into a great pile of rubble'.	Mt7:27; Lk6:49
T When Jesus had concluded his discourse, all who heard were amazed by his teachings,	Mt7:28
U for he spoke with power and authority. No scribe had taught like this.	Mt7:29

CHAPTER 46
Healing of a leper

A When he came down from the mountain, a great multitude was waiting for him.	Mt8:1
B One of them, a man covered with leprosy, came and casting himself at *Jesus'* feet said 'Lord, if you will, you can heal me'.	Mt8:2; Mk1:40 Lk5:12
C At this, Jesus stretched out his hand and touched him, saying 'I will. Be cleansed,' and immediately the man's leprosy was cured.	Mt8:3; Mk1:41, 42 Lk5:13
D Jesus then said to him 'Tell no one about this, but go to the priest and offer the sacrifice that Moses commanded, that they may certify your cleansing[1]'.	Mt8:4; Mk1:43, 44 Lk5:14
E But the man went out and began to publicize the matter wherever he went. Jesus' fame spread abroad and great multitudes came to hear him and to be healed by him.	Mk1:45; Lk5:15
F Jesus could not enter into the city without being mobbed, so he kept to the less populated areas, especially so he could pray. Yet people from every region followed him there.	Lk5:16

---

1 Lev 14:1 ~ 34.

CHAPTER 47

Healing of the Centurion's servant

A After speaking to the people, Jesus went into Capernaum. *Mt8:5; Lk7:1*

B A certain centurion there had a servant who was very dear to him. The servant fell sick and was close to death. *Lk7:2*

C Hearing about Jesus, the centurion sent the elders of the Jews to him, to beseech him to come and heal his servant. *Lk7:3*

D The elders came to Jesus with the centurion's message 'Lord, my servant at home lies in bed, incapacitated and in terrible pain'. They then pleaded with him passionately saying 'He who asks this is a good man, *Mt8:6; Lk7:4*

E 'For he loves our nation and has built us a synagogue'. *Lk7:5*

F Jesus responded 'I will come and heal the sick'. *Mt8:7*

G So Jesus went with them and when they were not far from the house, the centurion sent some friends to him, with the message 'Lord, there is no need to put yourself out, for I am not worthy enough that you should come under my roof. *Mt8:8; Lk7:6*

H 'This is also why I did not come to you myself. You need but say the word and my servant shall be healed. *Lk7:7*

I 'For I too am a man under authority and having soldiers under me. When I say to one "Go", he goes. To another I say "Come" and he comes, and when I say to my servant "Do this" he does it'. *Mt8:9; Lk7:8*

J When Jesus heard this he was astounded and turning to the people behind him, he said 'I tell you that I have not found so great a faith, not even in all of Israel'. *Mt8:10; Lk7:9*

K 'I say to you, That many shall come from the east and west, and shall stand with Abraham, Isaac and Jacob, in the God's new world order, *Mt8:11; Lk13:29*

L 'but the children of the patriarchs shall be shut outside, weeping and gnashing their teeth'. *Mt8:12; Lk13:28*

M Jesus then said 'Go on home. As he believed, so has it been done'. At that instant, the servant was healed. *Mt8:13*

N When those that had been sent out returned to the house, they found the servant that had been sick, fully recovered. *Lk7:10*

CHAPTER 48
Resurrecting the Widow's dead son

A The next day Jesus left for the town of Nain and he was accompanied by many of his disciples and a multitude of people.	Lk7:11
B When they were almost at the gate of the town, they saw a dead man been carried out, who was the only son of his widowed mother. Many of the townsfolk were with her.	Lk7:12
C When the Lord saw her, he was moved with compassion and said to her 'Do not weep'.	Lk7:13
D Then he stopped the pallbearers and said 'Young man, arise'.	Lk7:14
E At this, the dead man sat up and began to speak. Jesus then took him to his mother.	Lk7:15
F The people were sobered and they glorified God, saying that a great prophet was raised up among them and that God had visited his people.	Lk7:16
G News of this incident travelled throughout all of Judaea, and the region round about.	Lk7:17

CHAPTER 49
Commitment required of Jesus' followers

A As he was leaving, a scribe came to him and said 'Master, I will follow you wherever you go'.	Mt8:19; Lk9:57
B Jesus replied, 'The foxes have dens and the birds have nests, but I have nowhere to lay my head'.	Mt8:20; Lk9:58
C He said to another 'Follow me'.	Lk9:59
D But the disciple said 'Lord, grant me leave to go and bury my father'.	Mt8:21; Lk9:59
E Jesus said to him 'Let the dead bury their dead. You go and preach the coming government of God'.	Mt8:22; Lk9:60
F Another disciple said 'Lord, I will follow you, but let me first go home and bid farewell to my kin'.	Lk9:61
G Jesus said to him 'No man who having put his hand to the plough and looks back, is fit for God's new world order'.	Lk9:62

The Harmonized Gospels — Apocalyptic Version

CHAPTER 50
Jesus calms the sea

A On one occasion, at evening, Jesus said to his disciples 'Let us cross the lake to the other side'. After sending away the multitude they went into a ship and cast off. Some smaller vessels also followed them.	Mt8:23; Lk8:22 Mk4:35, 36
B On the way, a fierce storm arose and the waves washed over the ship till it was swamped.	Mt8:24; Mk4:37 Lk8:23
C All this time, Jesus was inside the ship, sleeping on a cot. They woke him up and said 'Master, are you not afraid that we are about to perish?'	Mt8:24 ~ 25; Mk4:38; Lk8:24
D Jesus turned to them and said 'Why are you so fearful? How is it that you do not trust in God?	Mt8:26; Mk4:40 Lk8:25
E He arose and rebuked the wind and said to the sea 'Cease your turbulence and be still'. The wind ceased and a great calm settled over the sea.	Mt8:26; Mk4:39 Lk8:24
F At this, the men were amazed, wondering 'What manner of man is this, that even the winds and the sea obey him?'	Mt8:27; Mk4:41 Lk8:25

CHAPTER 51
Casting out the demons at Gergesenes

A When they disembarked on the other side at Gergesenes, two men who were possessed with devils came out from the graveyard and accosted them. They were violent and permitted no one to pass that way[1].	Mt8:28; Mk5:1, 2; Lk8:26 ~ 27
B One of the men was possessed by devils for a long time and wore no clothes. No one could bind him, even with chains,	Mk5:3; Lk8:27
C for many times he had been shackled, but he broke them into pieces as if they were nothing. No one could control him	Mk5:4; Lk8:29
D and he was night and day in the mountains or the tombs, making noises and cutting himself with stones.	Mk5:5; Lk8:29
E When he saw Jesus in the distance, he ran to him and made obeisance to him.	Mk5:6
F and loudly beseeched him saying 'What business do you have with me Jesus, Son of the Almighty God? I beg of you in the name of God, that you do not trouble me.	Mk5:7; Lk8:28
G (The man said this because Jesus had said to him 'Come out of the man, you demon'.)	Mk5:8; Lk8:29

---

1 Traditional translations of Matt 8:28 indicate that there were two men possessed by devils, while both Mark 5:2 and Luke 8:28 focus on one of the men.

The Harmonized Gospels — Apocalyptic Version

H Then Jesus asked him 'What is your name?' The man replied 'My name is "Legion" for we are many'.	*Mk5:9; Lk8:30*
I The devils also cried out saying 'Why have you come here, Jesus, Son of God? Have you come to trouble us before the time?'	*Mt8:29*
J and they entreated Jesus not to send them out of that country to another place.	*Mk5:10* *Lk8:31*
K There was a large herd of swine feeding nearby,	*Mt8:30; Mk5:11*
L and the devils pleaded 'Send us into the swine, that we may possess them'.	*Mt8:31; Mk5:12* *Lk8:32*
M Jesus granted them their request and the demons left the men and went into the swine. At this the herd of about two thousand, panicked and bolted down a steep incline into the sea, where they drowned[1].	*Mt8:32; Mk5:13* *Lk8:32 ~ 33*
N The keepers of the swine ran off and reported what happened to all they met in the town and countryside and they came to see what had happened.	*Mt8:33; Mk5:14* *Lk8:34*
O When they came to Jesus, they saw the one possessed with the legion of demons sitting, clothed and in his right mind. The people were afraid,	*Mk5:15; Lk8:35*
P and when those who witnessed the incident reported on what had happened to the *ones* possessed with demons and what became of the swine,	*Mk5:16; Lk8:36*
Q the people entreated Jesus to leave their territory.	*Mt8:34; Mk5:17* *Lk8:37*
R Jesus returned to the ship and the one possessed with the demons who had spoken to him, asked to go with him.	*Mk5:18; Lk8:38*
S Jesus declined his request and said to him 'Go home and tell your friends the wonderful things that the Lord has done for you and how he had compassion on you.	*Mk5:19; Lk8:39*
T The man went and publicized in the town of Decapolis the great work that Jesus had done for him, and all who heard were impressed.	*Mk5:20; Lk8:39*

---

1 The desire of the devils to possess the herd of swine for the fleeting moments before they drowned is evidence of their warped attitude.

CHAPTER 52
Healing of the bed-ridden man

A Jesus boarded a ship, and crossed the sea to Capernaum, where it soon became public knowledge that he was in a house. — Mt9:1; Mk2:1

B In a short time, a multitude gathered and there were so many that they could not fit inside the room, but spilled outside the door to hear him preach and to be healed by the power of the God. — Mk2:2; Lk5:17

C Someone sick with an infirmity was carried on a stretcher to the gathering by four bearers. — Mt9:2; Mk2:3; Lk5:18

D They couldn't get through the crowd to Jesus, so they climbed on the roof and made and opening, through which they let down the bed carrying the one who was sick. — Mk2:4; Lk5:19

E When Jesus saw their fervency, he said to the sick man 'Son, be of good cheer. Your sins are forgiven'. — Mt9:2; Mk2:5; Lk5:20

F In the crowd, there were some Pharisees, Scribes and experts in the law who had come from many towns. These spoke among themselves saying, — Mt9:3; Mk2:6; Lk5:17

G 'Why is this man blaspheming? Who can forgive sins but God?' — Mt9:3; Mk2:7; Lk5:21

H Jesus perceived what they were thinking, so he said to them 'Why do you let evil enter your hearts? What do you think? — Mt9:4; Mk2:8; Lk5:22

I 'Is it easier to say to the one sick with the infirmity "Your sins are forgiven", or to say "Stand up from your bed, and carry it out with you?" — Mt9:5; Mk2:9; Lk5;23

J 'But this I do, that you may know that I have been given power on earth to forgive sins'. Then, turning to the man who was sick with the infirmity, he said 'Stand up, take your bed with you and go to your house'. — Mt9:6; Mk2:10, 11; Lk5:24

K Straight away, the man got up from his bed, and lifting it up, he walked out in front the assembly, all the while glorifying God. — Mt9:7; Mk2:12; Lk5:25

L When the multitudes saw this, they were amazed, and praised God for giving such power to men, saying 'We have never seen anything like this before'. — Mt9.8; Mk2.12; Lk5:26

CHAPTER 53
The calling of Matthew

A Jesus went to the seaside where a multitude came to him, and he taught them. — *Mk2:13*

B While leaving the area, he saw Levi, also called Matthew, the son of Alphaeus, sitting down at the custom-house collecting taxes. Jesus said to him 'Follow me' and Matthew immediately stopped whatever he was doing, got up and followed him. — *Mt9:9; Mk2:14; Lk5:27~28*

C Sometime later, Jesus and his disciples went to Levi's house to eat, and many publicans and sinners sat with them, for a large crowd followed him. — *Mt9:10; Mk2:15; Lk5:29*

D When the Scribes and Pharisees saw Jesus eating with publicans and sinners, they sneered at his disciples saying 'How come he eats and drinks with publicans and sinners?' — *Mt9:11; Mk2:16; Lk5:30*

E When Jesus heard of it, he said 'They that are in good health do not need the physician, but they that are sick do. I have come, not to call the righteous, but sinners to repentance. — *Mt9:12, 13; Mk2:17*

F 'Go therefore and learn what this means "I will have mercy, and not sacrifice"'. — *Lk5:31~32; Mt9:13*

CHAPTER 54
The need for a new way of thinking

A Some disciples of John also came and asked 'Why do we and the Pharisees fast often, but your disciples do not fast'? — *Mt9:14; Mk2:18; Lk5:33*

B Jesus replied 'Will the companions of the bridegroom fast while he is with them? As long as the bridegroom is with them, they will not fast. — *Mt9:15; Mk2:19; Lk5:34*

C 'But the days are coming when the bridegroom will be taken away from them. In those days, they will fast. — *Mt9:15; Mk2:20; Lk5:35*

D 'No man patches an old garment with a piece of new cloth, for the patch puts more strain on the garment and makes a bigger tear. The new piece is incompatible with the old. — *Mt9:16; Mk2:21; Lk5:36*

E 'Neither do men put new wine into old wineskins, for they will burst and both the wine and the wineskin will be lost. If the new wine is put into new wineskins, both are preserved. — *Mt9:17; Mk2:22; Lk5:37~38*

F 'And no man who has drunk old wine will straightway like a new one, for he thinks "The old is better".' — *Lk5:39*

CHAPTER 55
The healing of the woman with the bleeding

A Jesus crossed the sea by ship and when he landed, many people were there waiting to see him. While he was still at the seaside,	*Mk5:21; Lk8:40*
B a leader in the synagogue, named Jairus, cast himself at Jesus' feet, for his daughter of about twelve years in age, was very sick.	*Mt9:18; Mk5:22 Lk8:41 ~ 42*
C pleading 'My young daughter is at the point of death. I beg you, please come and lay your hands on her and heal her that she may live'.	*Mt9:18; Mk5:23 Lk8:41*
D Jesus and his disciples started out followed by a huge crowd of people all around him.	*Mt9:19; Mk5:24*
E In the crowd was a woman, who was sick with a bleeding for twelve years.	*Mt9:20; Mk5:25 Lk8:43*
F She had spent all her income on various treatments from many physicians, but instead of getting better, her condition worsened.	*Mk5:26; Lk8:43*
G While Jesus was on the way to Jairus' daughter, the woman pushed through the crowd and touched his clothing,	*Mt9:20; Mk5:27 Lk8:44*
H for she thought to herself 'If I could but just touch his clothes, I will be healed'.	*Mt9:21; Mk5:28*
I Immediately she was healed, her bleeding stopped and she felt in her body that her sickness was gone.	*Mk5:29; Lk8:44*
J Jesus straightaway knew that the healing had come from him, so he stopped and said to the crowd 'Who touched my clothes?'	*Mk5:30; Lk8:45*
K Peter and the other disciples said somewhat puzzled 'There is a crowd pressing around you and yet you ask "Who touched me?"'	*Mk5:31; Lk8:45*
L But Jesus said 'Somebody has touched me, for I perceive that healing has proceeded from me' and he looked around to see who the person was.	*Mk5:32; Lk8:46*
M Then the woman knowing what had happened to her, and that she had been found out, came trembling before him. She fell at his feet and disclosed all that had happened.	*Mk5.33, Lk8.47*
N Jesus then said to her 'Daughter, because you believed, you have been healed. Go in peace and be healed of your sickness'.	*Mt9:22; Mk5:34 Lk8:48*

CHAPTER 56
Restoring Jairus' daughter to life

A While on the way, one came from the house of the leader in the synagogue and said 'Your daughter is dead. You do not need to trouble the Master any further'.	Mk5:35; Lk8:49
B But as soon as Jesus heard this he said to the ruler of the synagogue 'Do not be afraid, but believe and she will be restored'.	Mk5:36; Lk8:50
C The entourage with him stopped at the house and he entered with child's parents, Peter, James, and John, who was the brother of James.	Mk5:37; Lk8:51
D In the house, they saw many who were weeping and wailing,	Mt9:23; Mk5:38
E and Jesus said 'Why all this fussing and weeping? The girl is not dead, but asleep'.	Mt9:24; Mk5:39 Lk8:52
F They laughed in derision. Jesus put them all out and taking the father and the mother of the girl, and his aforementioned disciples with him, they entered the room where she was lying.	Mt9:25; Mk5:40 Lk8:53
G There he took the hand of the girl and said to her 'Talitha cumi', which means 'Young lady, arise'.	Mt9:25; Mk5:41 Lk8:54
H Immediately the girl got to her feet and started to walk. The people there were shocked and greatly amazed.	Mk5:42; Lk8:55
I Jesus cautioned them to tell no one and instructed that they should give the girl something to eat,	Mk5:43; Lk8:54 ~ 55
J But the fame of this incident was spread throughout that land.	Mt9:26

CHAPTER 57
Healing of two blind men

A As Jesus was leaving, two blind men who followed him entreated him saying 'Son of David, have mercy on us'.	Mt9:27
B When Jesus arrived at his destination and entered the house, the blind men came to him and Jesus asked 'Do you believe that I am able to do this? They replied 'Yes Lord'.	Mt9:28
C Jesus then touched their eyes and said 'Let it be as you believe',	Mt9:29
D and their eyes were immediately opened. Jesus then told them 'Tell no one of this'.	Mt9:30
E However, when they were left, they spread abroad his fame in all that territory.	Mt9:31

CHAPTER 58
Jesus teaches throughout the region

A Jesus went through many of the cities and villages, teaching in the synagogues, as he made his way to Jerusalem. He announced the good news of God's coming worldwide government and healed all the sick and diseased that was brought to him.   *Mt9:35; Lk13:22*

B When he saw the multitudes, he was moved with compassion, because they were weighed down with worry, as sheep without a shepherd.   *Mt9:36*

C At one time a huge crowd gathered, so that they could not even sit for a meal.   *Mk3:20*

D When his disciples saw what was happening, they sought to get Jesus to take a break, for they saw that he was fixated on his work.   *Mk3:21*

E To his disciples he said 'The harvest is huge, but the laborers are few,   *Mt9:37; Lk10:2*

F 'pray therefore to the Lord of the harvest, that he send more laborers to attend to his harvest'.   *Mt9:38; Lk10:2*

CHAPTER 59
Jesus selects twelve apostles

A One day Jesus went out into a mountain to pray and he was up all night praying to God. — *Mk3:13; Lk6:12*

B At daybreak, he called his disciples and named twelve to be sent out as apostles, bestowing on them the authority to cast out demons and to heal all kinds of sicknesses and diseases. — *Mt10:1; Mk3:14, 15; Lk6:13; Lk9:1*

C These are the names of the twelve apostles. First named was Simon, also called Peter, and his brother Andrew. The others were James, the son of Zebedee, together with John his brother. These two he titled Boanerges, which means 'Sons of thunder'. — *Mt10:2; Mk3:16 ~ 18; Lk6:14*

D Philip, Bartholomew, Thomas, Matthew the tax collector, James (of Alphaeus) and his relative Judas called Lebbaeus (surnamed Thaddaeus), — *Mt10:3; Mk3:18; Lk6:14 ~ 16*

E Simon the Canaanite, called Zealotes, and Judas Iscariot, who also betrayed him. — *Mt10:4; Mk3:19*

F Jesus sent out these twelve in pairs. — *Mt10:5; Mk6:7*

G Afterwards, the Lord appointed another seventy of his disciples and likewise sent them in pairs, to go before him to all the places that he planned to visit. — *Lk10:1*

H He instructed his disciples 'Do not go to the Gentiles or enter the cities of the Samaritans, — *Mt10:5; Mk6:7*

I 'but go to the lost sheep of the house of Israel. — *Mt10:6*

J 'Wherever you go, preach to them, saying "A new government of God is coming soon ". — *Mt10:7; Lk9:2; Lk10:9*

K 'Heal the sick, cleanse the lepers, raise the dead, cast out devils. You receive these things without charge, therefore give of it without charge. — *Mt10:8; Lk9:2; Lk10:9*

L 'Take no gold, or silver, or brass in your purses. — *Mt10:9; Mk6:8; Lk10:4*

M 'Take no provisions for your journey, nor any extra coats, or shoes, or staves, for the workman is deserving of his hire. — *Mt10:10; Mk6:9; Lk9:3; Lk10:4, 7*

N 'While on your way, do not turn aside to visit anyone. — *Lk10:4*

O 'When you enter a city or town, ask for who is respectable and stay with them for the duration. — *Mt10:11; Mk6:10; Lk9:4*

P 'When you come to the house, greet them with peace and happiness. — *Mt10:12; Lk10:5*

Q 'If the house is worthy, peace will come upon it, but if it is not worthy, your peace will return to you. — *Mt10:13; Lk10:6*

R 'Stay in one house and eat what they provide. Do not go from house to house. — *Lk10:7*

S 'When you come to a town and they receive you, accept whatever they provide. — *Lk10:8*

The Harmonized Gospels — Apocalyptic Version

T 'If a house or a city refuses to receive you or hear your words, shake the dust off your feet when you leave them and say,	Mt10:14; Mk6:11 Lk9:5; Lk10:10
U 'Even the dust of your city, which lies on our feet, we wipe off, for a testimony against you. Nevertheless, know that the government of God is coming.	Mt10:14; Mk6:11 Lk9:5; Lk10:11
V 'I assure you that their actions will be considered worse than the inhabitants of Sodom and Gomorrha, when they are both raised at the period of the Judgment[1].	Mt10:15; Mk6:11 Lk10:12
W 'I now send you out as sheep in the midst of wolves. Therefore, be wise as serpents, and harmless as doves.	Mt10:16; Lk10:3
X 'Be careful of men, for they will take you before the courts, and they will scourge you in their synagogues.	Mt10:17
Y 'You shall be brought before governors and kings for my sake, so you could preach to them and the Gentiles.	Mt10:18
Z 'When they bring you up before the synagogues and magistrates, do not be concerned about what to say. You will know at that time what to say,	Mt10:19; Lk12:11
AA 'for you will not speak on your own, but your Father will show you what to say.	Mt10:20; Lk12:12
AB 'Brother will condemn brother to death, and the father will condemn the child. Children shall accuse their parents, and cause them to be put to death.	Mt10:21
AC 'Know that you will be hated by all mankind for my sake, but he that is faithful to the end shall be saved.	Mt10:22
AD 'When they persecute you in one city, escape to another. I tell you, You will not have gone to all the cities of Israel, before I return.	Mt10:23
AE 'A disciple is not greater than his master, nor is the servant regarded more than his lord.	Mt10:24; Lk6:40
AF 'The best that can be expected is for the disciple to be as his master, and the servant to be as his lord. If they have called the master of the house Beelzebub, how much worse will they call those in his household?	Mt10:25; Lk6:40
AG 'However, do not be afraid of them, for in time, there is nothing that is hidden that will not be revealed and nothing that is secret that will not be exposed.	Mt10:26; Mk4:22 Lk8:17; Lk12:2
AH 'Whatsoever you have spoken in the darkness shall be heard in the light and that which you whispered secretly behind closed doors shall be proclaimed upon the house	Lk12:3

---

1 All who died being truly converted and having Christ in-dwelling, will be resurrected to immortality at Christ's return. The rest of humanity will be raised to physical life a thousand years afterwards during a period of judgment when Satan is restrained and God extends His Spirit to them. Those who chose to accept God then, will also be made immortal sons of God, but those who do not will be destroyed. (IThess 4:16 ~ 17; Rev 20:5,10 ~ 15; Ezek 11:19).

The Harmonized Gospels — Apocalyptic Version

tops.

AI 'So too, whatever I tell to you in private, you must tell it to the world, and whatever I whisper in your ear, you must shout over the rooftops. — *Mt10:27*

AJ 'Do not be afraid of those who can kill you in the flesh, for they are not able to prevent your resurrection. Rather, fear the one who will determine whether you are to be saved from the final destruction. — *Mt10:28; Lk12:4, 5*

AK 'Consider that two sparrows are sold for a coin and five sparrows are sold for a two coins. Yet not one of them falls to the ground without the knowledge of your Father. — *Mt10:29; Lk12:6*

AL 'In your case, he even knows how many hairs you have on your head. — *Mt10:30; Lk12:7*

AM 'Therefore, do not be afraid, for you are more value than many sparrows. — *Mt10:31; Lk12:7*

AN 'If anyone is not afraid to admit their association with me to men, I will present him to my Father in heaven before the angels. — *Mt10:32; Lk12:8*

AO 'If anyone should disavow me before men, I will also disavow them before my Father in heaven and the angels with him — *Mt10:33; Lk12:9*

AP 'I have come to set a fire on the earth and it is already kindled? — *Lk12:49*

AQ 'But I have a baptism to be baptized with, and I am consumed with it till it be accomplished. — *Lk12:50*

AR 'Do not think that the world will be at peace because I am here. My coming at this time, will not bring peace, but strife. — *Mt10:34; Lk12:51*

AS 'Because of me, a man will get into conflict with his father and the daughter will be in disagreement with her mother. The daughter-in-law also, will be in opposition to her mother-in-law. — *Mt10:35; Lk12:53*

AT 'People will find themselves at odds with members of their own household. There shall be five in one house divided, three against two, and two against three. — *Mt10:36; Lk12:52*

AU 'Anyone that strives to please their father or mother by disobeying me, is not worthy of me, and anyone that pleases their son or daughter by going contrary to me is not worthy of me and cannot be my disciple. — *Mt10:37; Lk14:26*

AV 'Those that are not willing to suffer affliction for following me, are not worthy of me. — *Mt10:38*

AW 'Anyone who compromises to save his life shall lose life, but anyone who gives up their life for my sake shall be given eternal life. — *Mt10:39*

AX 'They that accept you, accept me, and any that accepts me, accepts the one that sent me. — *Mt10:40*

AY 'He that listens to you listens to me, and he that spurns you, spurns me. He that spurns me spurns him that sent me.	Lk10:16
AZ 'Those that provide for a prophet for his work's sake, shall share in his reward, just as any who assists a righteous man in doing good, shall share in his blessing.	Mt10:41
BA 'Anyone who provides even a cup of cold water to these little ones because they are my disciples, shall likewise, not go unrewarded'.	Mt10:42
BB After Jesus had given his disciples their instructions, he also left for other cities, to announce his message and to teach them.	Mt11:1
BC The disciples went out and preached the good news of the coming Government of God and that men should repent.	Mk6:12; Lk9:6
BD They cast out many demons, and when they anointed the sick with oil, they were healed.	Mk6:13; Lk9:6
BE When the disciples returned they were all excited and said to Jesus "Lord, even the devils are subject to us through your name".	Mk6:30; Lk9:10 Lk10:17
BF He replied "I see Satan as the lightning falling from the sky.	Lk10:18
BG 'See, I give you power over Satan and his sting, and over all the machinations of the enemy. They have no power at all to harm you.	Lk10:19
BH 'Nevertheless, do not rejoice because the spirits are subject to you, but rather that your name is written in heaven'.	Lk10:20
BI Jesus' heart was filled with joy and he said 'I thank you Father, Lord of the heavens and the earth, that you have hidden these things from the wise and prudent, and has revealed them to babes. Let it be so, Father, for it is good in your sight'.	Mt11:25, 26 Lk10:21

CHAPTER 60
Jesus speaks of John the Baptist

A The disciples of John the Baptist, who was in the prison, told him about the works that Christ did. John then sent two of his disciples	Mt11:2; Lk7:18
B to Jesus to ask him the question 'Are you the one that was sent, or are we to wait for another'?	Mt11:3; Lk7:19
C John's disciples did as he requested and	Lk7:20
D while they were with Jesus he cured many who suffered from various infirmities and sicknesses. He also freed some from evil spirits and gave sight to many that were blind.	Lk7:21
E Jesus said to them 'Go and tell John of the things which you hear and see.	Mt11:4; Lk7:22
F 'The blind can see, the lame walk, the lepers are healed, the deaf can hear, the dead are raised up, and the poor have the	Mt11:5; Lk7:22

The Harmonized Gospels — Apocalyptic Version

good news of the God's new world order preached to them.

G 'Blessed are they who do not stumble, because they doubt me'. — *Mt11:6; Lk7:23*

H As the disciples of John left, Jesus spoke to the multitudes about John, saying 'What do you expect to see in the wild besides the reeds shaken with the wind? — *Mt11:7; Lk7:24*

I 'Surely it was not a man dressed in fine clothes, for you will only find them in houses of the wealthy or in the kings' courts. — *Mt11:8; Lk7:25*

J 'If though you went to see a prophet, I tell you that you indeed saw more than a prophet. — *Mt11:9; Lk7:26*

K 'For it is written of him "Behold, I will send my messenger before you, to prepare the way for you". — *Mt11:10; Lk7:27*

L 'I tell you that of all mankind, there has been none greater than John the Baptist. Yet, in God's new world order, the lowest in rank will have far greater ability than John showed as a human. — *Mt11:11; Lk7:28*

M 'Since the work of John the Baptist, the government of God draws closer, and only with determination and commitment can one be part of it. — *Mt11:12; Lk16:16*

N 'For the books of the law and prophets spoke of John. — *Mt11:13; Lk16:16*

O 'If you will believe, he is Elias, which was promised to come[1]. — *Mt11:14*

P 'Those that are given to understand will understand'. — *Mt11:15*

Q When they heard this, many of the common folk and the publicans accepted this as fulfillment of what God had prophesied, because they were baptized of John. — *Lk7:29*

R The Pharisees and lawyers, however, rejected that this was according to the word of God and thus condemning themselves, because they were not baptized of John. — *Lk7:30*

S Jesus continued 'How can I describe this generation? — *Mt11:16; Lk7:31*

T 'It is like children sitting down in the marketplace and saying to one another, — *Mt11:16; Lk7:32*

U 'We have played happy music for you, but you have not danced. We have played sad music for you and you did not weep. — *Mt11:17; Lk7:32*

V 'For John did not eat nor drink common food and they say "He is possessed by devil". — *Mt11:18; Lk7:33*

W 'I come eating and drinking, and they say "He is a gluttonous alcoholic, and associates with publicans and sinners". — *Mt11:19; Lk7:34*

X Thankfully, wisdom knows her children'. — *Mt11:19; Lk7:35*

---

1 John the Baptist was like Elijah, a notable prophet of God who turned Israel to God. Christ prophesied of another one like Elijah to come again before His return. IKings 18:21 ~ 40; Mt17:1 ~ 4; IIKings 2:9, 15; Is 40:3; Mal 3:1; Mal 4:5; Luke 1:17; Mt17:11 ~ 12; Rev 11:3,6

CHAPTER 61
Jesus rebukes the cities of Judah

A Jesus then began to rebuke the cities which did not believe him, even after his many miracles, saying — *Mt11:20*

B 'Shame on you, Chorazin! Shame on you, Bethsaida! If the miracles done in you, had been done in Tyre and Sidon, they would have repented long ago in sackcloth and ashes. — *Mt11:21; Lk10:13*

C 'I tell you that Tyre and Sidon will be judged more honorable than you, when you are both raised up at the period of Judgment. — *Mt11:22; Lk10:14*

D 'You too Capernaum, which sits on a mountain, shall be brought low, for if the miracles done in you, had been done in Sodom, it would have remained until this day. — *Mt11:23; Lk10:15*

E 'I tell you that Sodom shall be judged more honorable than you, when you are both raised up at the period of Judgment'. — *Mt11:24*

CHAPTER 62
Jesus' invitation

A 'All things have been revealed to me by my Father. No one truly knows the Son except the Father and no one has seen the Father except the Son, who is in the bosom of the Father. It is the Son that reveals the Father to whom he wills. — *Mt11:27; Lk10:22; Jn1:18*

B 'All of you that are struggling under heavy burdens, come to me and I will give you rest. — *Mt11:28*

C 'Put on my yoke and learn of me, for I am humble and meek, and you shall find peace. — *Mt11:29*

D 'For my yoke is gentle, and my burden is light'. — *Mt11:30*

The Harmonized Gospels — Apocalyptic Version

CHAPTER 63
Jesus on keeping the Sabbath[1]

A On one Sabbath day, Jesus and his disciples were walking through a grain field. His disciples, being hungry, picked some of the grain and ate of it.	*Mt12:1; Mk2:23*
B On the next Sabbath, they again picked some grain and rubbed them with their hands to break out the kernels, which they ate.	*Lk6:1*
C When the Pharisees found out, they said 'Look, your disciples do things which are not lawful to do on the Sabbath day'.	*Mt12:2; Mk 2:24 Lk6:2*
D Jesus replied 'Have you not read of what David did, when he was in a difficult situation with his companions? How they were hungry,	*Mt12:3; Mk2:25 Lk6:3*
E and went into the house of God in the days of Abiathar the high priest, and ate of the showbread, which is only lawful to be eaten by the priests?	*Mt12:4; Mk2:26 Lk6:4*
F 'Have you not also read in the book of the law, how on the Sabbath days, the priests in the temple are allowed to work on the Sabbath, and are blameless?	*Mt12:5*
G 'I tell you, that standing here right now, is one who is greater than the temple.	*Mt12:6*
H 'If you had understood the scripture "I will have mercy, and not sacrifice", you would not have condemned the guiltless.	*Mt12:7*
I 'The Sabbath was made for man, and not man for the Sabbath.	*Mk2:27*
J 'Know that I am Lord, even of the Sabbath day'.	*Mt12:8; Mk2:28 Lk6:5*
K On another Sabbath, Jesus went into the synagogue, where there was a man, whose right hand was deformed.	*Mt12:9, 10; Mk3:1 Lk6:6*
L The Scribes and Pharisees were watching him seeking to find some fault with him and asked 'Is it lawful to heal on the Sabbath days'?	*Mt12:10; Mk3:2 Lk6:7*
M Jesus said to the man with the withered hand 'Come stand here'.	*Mk3:3; Lk6:8*
N He then addressed the gathering saying 'Is it lawful to do good on the Sabbath or to do evil, to save life or to kill?' But no one said anything.	*Mk3:4; Lk6:9*
O Jesus answered and said 'If you have a sheep and it falls	*Mt12:11*

---

1 This chapter brings together Jesus' comments on the keeping of the Sabbath that were made at different times.

The Harmonized Gospels — Apocalyptic Version

into a pit on the Sabbath day, is there any among you who would not take it out from the pit?

P 'How much more precious is a man than a sheep? Therefore, it is lawful to save on the Sabbath days. | Mt12:12

Q He looked at them in disbelief, struck by their lack of compassion and turning to the man he said 'Stretch out your hand'. The man extended his hand and it was completely restored like his other hand. | Mt12:13; Mk3:5 Lk6:10

R Seeing this the Pharisees were filled with rage so they went to the Herodians to plot on how they could destroy him. | Mt12:14; Mk 3:6 Lk6:11

S When Jesus became aware of their plans, he left that area and was followed by a great multitude. | Mt12:15

T Jesus was teaching at a synagogue on another Sabbath, | Lk13:10

U and present there was a woman who was sick for eighteen years. She was bent over and could not straighten up herself. | Lk13:11

V When Jesus saw her, he called her to him, and said 'Woman, you are freed of your infirmity'. | Lk13:12

W He then laid his hands on her and she was made straight and glorified God. | Lk13:13

X At this, the chief of the synagogue was indignant because Jesus had healed on the Sabbath and said to the people 'There are six days allotted for men to work on. Come on these days to be healed and not on the Sabbath. | Lk13:14

Y The Lord then said to him 'You hypocrite. On the Sabbath, do not each of you loose his ox or his ass from the stall and take them to water? | Lk13:15

Z 'Should not therefore this woman, a daughter of Abraham, who was bound by Satan for these eighteen years, be loosed from this bond on the Sabbath?' | Lk13:16

AA When he said these things, his adversaries were ashamed and the people rejoiced for all the glorious things that were done by him. | Lk13:17

AB On another Sabbath day, Jesus was invited by one of the chief Pharisees to dine at his house, and all those there were observing him, | Lk14:1

AC as a man who had the dropsy came to him. | Lk14:2

AD Jesus said to the lawyers and Pharisees 'Is it lawful to heal on the Sabbath day?' | Lk14:3

AE No one said anything. Then Jesus called the sick man, healed him and sent him away. | Lk14:4

AF He said to the assembly 'Which of you having an ass or an ox fall into a pit on the Sabbath day and will not immediately pull him out?' | Lk14:5

AG No one had an answer to give him. | Lk14:6

CHAPTER 64
Parable on seeking the place of honor

A Jesus spoke a parable to the assembly when he observed how they sought out the best seats. He said — Lk14:7

B 'When you are invited to a wedding by someone, do not sit in the seat of honor, lest a higher official than you, who was also invited, turns up. — Lk14:8

C 'Then the host must come and ask you to give up your place to the other and you would shamefacedly have to take a seat of lower rank. — Lk14:9

D 'When you have been invited, go and sit down in a common seat, so that when the host sees you he will say "Friend, come up to a seat of higher rank" and you shall have the respect of the others sitting at the table. — Lk14:10

E 'For whosoever exalts himself shall be abased and he that humbles himself shall be exalted'. — Lk14:11

CHAPTER 65
Jesus ministers at the seaside

A Jesus went with his disciples to the seaside, where multitudes came to see him. They came from Galilee, Judaea, — Mk3:7

B Jerusalem and from Idumaea. When others from beyond Jordan in the region about Tyre and Sidon heard of him, they came in large numbers to see the great works that he did. — Mk3:8; Lk6:17

C There were so many crowding him that he told his disciples to get a boat for him to speak from. — Mk3:9

D There he healed many, and those that were diseased strove just to touch him. — Mk3:10; Lk6:19; Mt12:15

E When those possessed by demons were brought before him, they fell down before him and the demons proclaimed 'You are the Son of God,' — Mk3:11; Lk6:18

F but he ordered them not to disclose his identity. — Mk3:12; Mt12:16

G This fulfilled the prophecy of Esaias the prophet that says — Mt12:17

H 'Here is my servant, whom I have chosen and dearly loved, and who greatly pleases me. I will put my Spirit in him, and he shall teach judgment to the Gentiles. — Mt12:18

I 'He shall not be argumentative, nor will anyone hear him shouting in the streets. — Mt12:19

J 'He will not hurt the broken spirited, nor contend with the proud, but shall achieve the victory with righteousness. — Mt12:20

K 'In him will the Gentiles put their trust[1]'. | Mt12:21

CHAPTER 66
The Pharisees accuse Jesus of working miracles by the power of Beelzebub

A Someone who was possessed by a devil and made blind and dumb was brought to him. Jesus healed him and he immediately was able to speak and see. | Mt 9:32; Mt12:22

B The people were amazed and said 'Never was such a thing seen in Israel. Is this not truly the son of David?' | Mt 9:33; Mt12:23; Lk11:14

C When some Scribes and Pharisees, who came from Jerusalem heard it, they said 'He cast out devils by the power of Beelzebub, the prince of the devils'. | Mt 9:33 ~ 34; Mt12:24; Mk3:22; Lk11:15

D Jesus, who knew what they were thinking said 'How can Satan cast out Satan? | Mt12:26; Mk3:23

E 'If a kingdom is in internal conflict, that kingdom cannot stand. | Mt12:25; Mk3:24; Lk11:17

F 'If a house is in conflict, that house cannot stand. | Mt12:25; Mk3:25; Lk11:17

G 'If Satan casts out Satan, he is divided against himself. How then shall his kingdom stand? | Mt12:26; Mk3:26; Lk11:18

H 'If I cast out devils by Beelzebub, by whom do your children cast them out? Should this not be your yardstick for judging? | Mt12:27; Lk11:19

I 'However, if I cast out devils by the power of God, then the government of God is unveiled before you. | Mt12:28; Lk11:20

J 'When a strong man who is armed protects his house, his goods are safe. | Lk11:21

K 'Only when someone stronger overpowers him and takes away his armor, can he take away his goods. | Mt12:29; Mk3:27; Lk11:22

L 'I tell you with certainty, that all sins will be forgiven mankind, and all the blasphemies they speak. | Mt12:31; Mk3:28

M 'If anyone says anything against me, it shall be forgiven him. But if anyone blasphemes the spirit of God, by saying it is an unclean spirit, he will receive no forgiveness, not today, nor in the judgment to come. | Mt12:32; Mk3:29; Mk3:30; Lk12:10

N 'He that is not with me is against me and he that does not help me gather will cause scattering. | Mt12:30; Lk11:23

O 'The tree is good if its fruit is good, or else the tree is bad if its fruit is bad, for the tree is known by its fruit. | Mt12:33

---

1 Is 42:1 ~ 6; Is 49:6

P 'You generation of vipers, how can you, being evil, speak good things? For the mouth will speak of what is in the heart.	Mt12:34; Lk6:45
Q 'A good man out of the goodness in his heart will produce good things, but an evil man out of the evil in him will produce evil fruit.	Mt12:35; Lk6:45
R 'I tell you, that at the time of their resurrection in the period of Judgment, men will have to account for every idle word that they use.	Mt12:36
S 'For your words will either prove you righteous or they will prove your guilt.	Mt12:37

CHAPTER 67

Jesus tells of the sign of his authenticity

A A spokesman of the scribes and of the Pharisees came to Jesus and said 'Teacher, will you give us a sign?'	Mt12:38; Lk11:16
B Jesus answered 'An evil and adulterous generation looks for a sign, but no sign be given to it, except the sign of the prophet Jonas.	Mt12:39; Lk11:29
C 'Jonas was a sign to the Ninevites as I am a sign to this generation.	Lk11:30
D 'For just as Jonas was three days and three nights in the belly of a fish, so too, shall the Son of man be three days and three nights inside the earth.	Mt12:40
E 'When the inhabitants of Nineveh are raised together with this generation in the period of Judgment, they would be deemed more worthy, because they repented at the preaching of Jonas, and here before you is one greater than Jonas.	Mt12:41; Lk11:32
F 'The queen of the south too, shall put this generation to shame, when they are both raised up in the period of Judgment, because she came from the far corners of the earth to hear the wisdom of Solomon, and here before you is one greater than Solomon.	Mt12:42; Lk11:31
G 'When an unclean spirit leaves a man, it goes about seeking another place to stay. When it finds none,	Mt12:43; Lk11:24
H 'it will say to itself "I will return to my old place of abode". When it returns and finds it empty and attractive,	Mt12:44; Lk11:24, 25
I 'it will go and get seven other spirits, even more wicked than itself, to stay with it. So that man is going to end up far worse than he was previously. This is what will happen to this wicked generation'.	Mt12:45; Lk11:26

The Harmonized Gospels — Apocalyptic Version

CHAPTER 68
Salvation is by obedience, not association

A While he was speaking to the people, his mother and his siblings came but could not get to him because of the crowd.	Mt12:46; Mk3:31 Lk8:19
B Someone said to him 'Your mother and your family are outside and ask to speak with you'.	Mt12:47; Mk3:32 Lk8:20
C A woman among the crowd said 'Blessed is the womb that carried you and the breast at which you suckled'.	Lk11:27
D Jesus replied 'Rather, blessed are they that hear the word of God, and keep it.	Lk11:28
E 'Who is my mother and who are my brothers and sisters?'	Mt12:48; Mk3:33
F Turning to his disciples, he raised his hands and said 'My mother and my family are those who hear the word of God and do it.	Mt12:49; Mk3:34 Lk8:21
G 'If any chooses to do the will of my Father in heaven, the same shall be my brother, and sister, and mother'.	Mt12:50; Mk3:35

CHAPTER 69
The parable of the sower and the seed

A Jesus went throughout the cities and villages, teaching and announcing the good news that a new government will be set up by God. The twelve apostles accompanied him,	Lk8:1
B as well as certain women, who had been healed of evil spirits and infirmities. These included Mary called Magdalene, from whom seven devils were cast out,	Lk8:2
C Joanna the wife of Chuza, Herod's steward, and Susanna. Many others helped and contributed to support Jesus and the others.	Lk8:3
D Later that day, Jesus left and went to the seaside.	Mt13:1; Mk4:1
E A large multitude gathered around him, so he went and sat in an anchored ship, while the people gathered on the shore.	Mt13:2; Mk4:1
F Speaking to them in parables, he said 'A farmer went out to plant,	Mt13:3; Mk4:2,3 Lk8:4
G 'and as he scattered his seed, some fell on the pathway to the fields and the birds came and devoured them.	Mt13:4; Mk4:4 Lk8:5
H 'Some fell on stony ground, where there was little soil and sprang up quickly because the soil was shallow.	Mt13:5; Mk4:5 Lk8:6
I 'However, when the sun beat on them, they were scorched for lack of moisture, and because they had no root, they dried up.	Mt13:6; Mk4:6 Lk8:6

The Harmonized Gospels — Apocalyptic Version

J 'Some seeds fell among thorns, and the thorns grew with them and eventually choked them, so no fruit was obtained from them.	Mt13:7; Mk4:7 Lk8:7
K 'But other seed fell on good ground and brought forth fruit. Some produced a hundredfold, some sixty-fold and some thirty-fold.	Mt13:8; Mk4:8 Lk8:8
L 'To those given understanding, let them hear'.	Mt13:9; Mk4:9 Lk8:8
M Afterwards, his disciples came to him to explain the parables and asked 'Why do you speak to them in parables?'	Mt13:10; Mk4:10 Lk8:9
N Jesus answered 'You have been appointed to know the mysteries of the coming government of God, but not them.	Mt13:11; Mk4:11 Lk8:10
O 'For whoever has, shall be given more, so that he grows in abundance, but whoever lacks, shall lose even the little that he has.	Mt13:12; Mk4:25 Lk8:18
P 'For this reason, I speak to them in parables, so that even though they see and hear, they will not understand.	Mt13:13; Mk4:12 Lk8:10
Q 'These fulfill the prophecy of Esaias, that says "You shall hear, but not understand, and see but not perceive.	Mt13:14
R '"For this people is hard-hearted. They have blocked their ears and closed their eyes, because they do not want to see with their eyes, or hear with their ears, or understand with their heart, and be converted, so that I may heal them[1]".	Mt13:15; Mk4:12
S 'But blessed are your eyes, for they see, and your ears, for they hear.	Mt13:16; Lk10:23
T 'I tell you now, that many prophets and righteous men and kings have longed to see and hear what you are witnessing, and they did not'.	Mt13:17; Lk10:24
U He continued 'Don't you understand this parable? If not, how will you understand any parable?	Mk4:13
V 'Listen therefore, to the parable of the farmer.	Mt13:18
W 'The seed sown by the sower is the word of God.	Mk4:14; Lk8:11
X 'The seed that falls on the pathway to the field are those who hear the word, but as soon as they hear it, Satan immediately takes away the word that was sown in their hearts, lest they should believe and be saved.	Mt13:19; Mk4:15 Lk8:12
Y 'The seed that falls on stony ground, are those that hear the word, and immediately receive it with joy	Mt13:20; Mk4:16 Lk8:13
Z 'but having no strength of character, they only persevere for a time. As soon as difficulties or persecution come about from keeping the word, they quickly give it up.	Mt13:21; Mk4:17 Lk8:13
AA 'As for the seed sown among thorns, these are those	Mt13:22; Mk4:18

---

1 Is 6:9 ~ 10

who hear the word,   *Lk8:14*
AB 'but the cares of this world, the temptation of riches and various other lusts dominate their mind and so choke the word, that it bears no fruit to perfection.   *Mt13:22; Mk4:19; Lk8:14*
AC 'The seed sown on good ground are those who hear the word with an honest and good heart and act on it. These bring forth fruit, some thirty-fold, some sixty-fold, and some a hundred-fold'.   *Mt13:23: Mk4:20; Lk8:15*

CHAPTER 70
The parable of the wheat and the tares

A Jesus gave another parable saying 'The coming of God's new world order is illustrated by a man who sowed good seed in his field.   *Mt13:24*

B 'While he and his servants slept, the enemy came and sowed tares among the wheat, and secretly left.   *Mt13:25*

C 'When the wheat started to sprout its leaves, the tares were seen growing among them.   *Mt13:26*

D 'Seeing this, the servants came to him and said "Master, did we not sow good seed in your field? Where therefore, have the tares come from?"   *Mt13:27*

E 'The man replied "This is the work of the enemy". The servants then asked him "Should we go and pull out the tares"?   *Mt13:28*

F 'But the man said "No, for while you root out the tares, you may also root up the wheat with them.   *Mt13:29*

G '"Rather, let both grow together until the harvest. Then will I tell the reapers 'First gather the tares and bind them in bundles for burning, and then gather the wheat to put in my barn''.   *Mt13:30*

H After Jesus had dismissed the multitudes and went into the house, his disciples came to him and said 'Tell us the meaning of the parable of the tares of the field'.   *Mt13:36*

I Jesus then explained 'I am the one sowing the good seed.   *Mt13:37*

J 'The field is the world, and the good seed are the children of God's new world order. The tares are the children of the wicked one.   *Mt13:38*

K 'The enemy that sowed them is the devil and the harvest is at the end of this dispensation. The reapers are the angels.   *Mt13:39*

L 'As the tares are gathered and burned in the fire, so too will it be at the very end of this world era.   *Mt13:40*

M 'For I will send my angels, and they will remove all that transgress, and all who do wickedly,   *Mt13:41*

N 'and shall cast them into the fire. They shall weep when   *Mt13:42*

they see their destruction coming.
O 'Then, in God's new world order, the righteous shall be with their Father and shine as the sun. Let those given to understand hear me'. *Mt13:43*

CHAPTER 71
The parable of the sprouting seed

A He said too 'The coming government of God is likened to a man who throws some seed on the ground. *Mk4:26*

B 'Day after day he goes to sleep and awakes. During all this time the seed sprouts and grows but he does not know how, *Mk4:27*

C 'for the earth produces fruit by itself. First a blade appears, then an ear shows and afterwards the ear of corn becomes full. *Mk4:28*

D 'When the fruit is ready, he hastens to reap it with his sickle, because the time has come to harvest it'. *Mk4:29*

CHAPTER 72
The parable of the mustard seed

A Jesus gave another parable saying 'To what shall we liken God's new world order, and what shall we compare it to? *Mt13:31; Mk4:30 Lk13:18*

B 'It is like a grain of mustard seed. When it is planted, it is the smallest of the seeds, *Mt13:31,32; Mk4:31; Lk13:19*

C 'but after it is sown, it grows up and becomes the largest of the herbs. It's branches are such that the birds even build their nest under it'. *Mt13:32; Mk4:32 Lk13:19*

CHAPTER 73
The parable of the leaven

A Jesus continued 'What shall we liken God's new world order to? *Lk13:20*

B 'The coming of God's new world order is like a little leaven, which a woman took and secreted in three measures of meal, yet in time, all of the meal became leavened' *Mt13:33; Lk13:21*

C Jesus related many such parables to the gathering, throughout the time they were there, *Mt13:34; Mk4:33*

D and on that occasion he spoke only in parables to them. However, when he was alone with his disciples, he ex- *Mk4:34*

plained the parables to them.
E to fulfill the word of the prophet, which says 'I will speak in parables, and reveal mysteries, which have been kept secret from the foundation of the world[1]'.

Mt13:35

CHAPTER 74
The parables of the treasure and the pearls

A Jesus said 'God's new world order is like a treasure hidden in a field. When a man found it, he told no one, but was so delighted by it, he went and sold all that he had, and bought the field.

Mt13:44

B 'God's new world order is also like a merchant seeking fine pearls.

Mt13:45

C 'When he found the most exquisite pearl, he went and sold all that he had, and bought it'.

Mt13:46

CHAPTER 75
The parable on casting the net

A 'The coming of God's new world order is like a net that is cast into the sea, that catches every kind.

Mt13:47

B 'When it is full, they pull it to the shore and set about to sort it. The good is gathered into containers, but the bad is thrown away.

Mt13:48

C 'So shall it be at the very end of this world era, for the angels will go out and gather the wicked from among the just,

Mt13:49

D 'and shall cast them into fire. There they shall weep when they see their destruction coming'.

Mt13:50

E Jesus asked them 'Have you understood all these things?' They replied 'Yes Lord'.

Mt13:51

F Then he said to them 'To the master of the house, every disciple who is taught about the coming worldwide government, is like a new treasure added to what he has'.

Mt13:52

---

1 Ps 78:2.

CHAPTER 76
Jesus finds skepticism in his hometown

A When Jesus had finished speaking these parables, he left that territory,	Mt13:53
B and went to Capernaum with his mother, his siblings and his disciples, where they stayed for a short time.	Jn2:12
C From there Jesus, inspired by God, visited regions of Galilee and news of him spread throughout the environs,	Lk4:14
D for he taught in their synagogues, and was praised by all.	Lk4:15
E He also visited Nazareth, where he had been brought up, and as was his custom, he went into the synagogue on the Sabbath day and stepped forward at the time of reading.	Lk4:16; Mt13:54 Mk6:1,2
F The book of the prophet Esaias was handed to him and when he opened the book, he turned to a section and read from what was written,	Lk4:17
G 'The power of the Lord is upon me, because he has anointed me to preach the good news to the poor. He has sent me to heal the brokenhearted and to preach deliverance to those in bondage; to give sight to the eyes of the blind and to set at liberty the oppressed;	Lk4:18
H to preach the acceptable year of the Lord[1]'.	Lk4:19
I Then he closed the book, returned it the priest, and sat down. All those in the synagogue were looking him,	Lk4:20
J and he said to them 'Today this scripture that you just heard is fulfilled before your very eyes'.	Lk4:21
K All of them heard what he said and wondered at his profound words. They spoke among themselves saying 'Is not this Joseph's son'?	Lk4:22; Mt13:54 Mk6:1,2
L 'Is not this the carpenter's son, whose mother is called Mary and whose brothers are James, Joses, Simon and Judas?	Mt13:55; Mk6:3
M 'Aren't those his sisters with us? From where did he get all these things'?	Mt13:56; Mk6:3
N Thus they doubted him. Jesus said 'A prophet is not without honor, save in his own country, and in his own house.	Mt13:57; Mk6:3,4 Lk4:24; Jn4:44
O 'You will surely quote me the proverb "Physician, heal yourself", expecting that the things I did in Capernaum, should also have been done in your district.	Lk4:23
P 'Listen to these facts. There were many widows in Israel at the time of Elias, when there was drought for three years and six months, and a great famine extended throughout the	Lk4:25

---

1 Is 61:1; 49:9; 58:6; 42:7.

The Harmonized Gospels — Apocalyptic Version

land.
Q 'Yet Elias was not sent to any of these. Rather he was sent to Sarepta, a city of Sidon and to a widow there[1]. | *Lk4:26*

R 'There were many lepers in Israel at the time of Eliseus the prophet, but none of them were cleansed except for Naaman the Syrian[2]'. | *Lk4:27*

S When the people in the synagogue heard what he had said, they were filled with rage. | *Lk4:28*

T They seized him and took him out of the city to the brow of the hill on which their city was built, so that they could throw him off, | *Lk4:29*

U but he escaped through the crowd and went his way. | *Lk4:30*

V He did not do many works there except to lay his hands upon a few that were sick and heal them, | *Mt13:58; Mk6:5*

W and he marveled at their reluctance to believe. | *Mk6:6*

CHAPTER 77
The beheading of John the Baptist

A Herod had arrested John and put him in prison, because of Herodias, the wife of his brother Philip, whom he had subsequently married. | *Mt14:3; Mk6:17*

B This was because John had said to him 'It is not lawful for you to marry the woman who was your brother's wife'. | *Mt14:4; Mk6:18*

C Herodias held a grudge against John, and tried to have him killed but she was not successful, | *Mk6:19*

D because Herod had regard for John and knew that he was a righteous and holy man. He respected John and after listening to him he did many things John had said and was always willing to hear John's views. Herod was also wary of the people, because they considered John a prophet. | *Mt14:5; Mk6:20*

E The time came for Herod to celebrate his birthday, so he prepared a banquet for his chief administrators and generals, and the leading citizens of Galilee. | *Mk6:21*

F At the celebration for Herod, the daughter of Herodias danced before them, and pleased Herod. | *Mt14:6; Mk6:22*

G Herod the king then said unto the young lady 'Ask me for anything you would like and I will give it to you'. | *Mt14:7; Mk6:22*

H He even swore to her 'Whatsoever you shall ask of me, I will give you, up to half of my kingdom'. | *Mk6:23*

I The young lady went to her mother and said 'What shall I | *Mk6:24*

---

1 I Kings 17:10 ~16.
2 II Kings 5:1 ~ 14.

ask?' Her mother replied 'The head of John the Baptist'.
J The young lady hurried back to the king and said 'I would like if you could give me the head of John the Baptist on a tray'. — *Mt14:8; Mk6:25*
K The king was grieved in his heart, but because he had sworn in front of the whole assembly, he would not refuse her. — *Mt14:9; Mk6:26*
L The king immediately sent for an executioner, and commanded him to bring John's head. So the executioner went and beheaded John in the prison. — *Mt14:10; Mk6:27*
M He brought John's head on a tray and gave it to the young lady, who gave it to her mother. — *Mt14:11; Mk6:28*
N Johns' disciples came for his body, and after they buried it in a tomb, they went and told Jesus. — *Mt14:12; Mk6:29*
O When Jesus heard the news, he left by ship for an isolated area. — *Mt14:13*

CHAPTER 78
Feeding of the five thousand

A Jesus said to them 'Come let us go to an quiet area for a rest'. This was because they constantly had people coming to them so that they did not even have time to eat. — *Mk6:31; Lk9:10*
B They unobtrusively boarded a ship and sailed over the sea of Galilee, also called the sea of Tiberius. They landed at an isolated area under the jurisdiction of Bethsaida. — *Mt14:13; Mk6:32 Lk9:10; Jn6:1*
C However, the great multitude who came to see the miraculous healings observed them leaving. They hastening out of the city by foot, arriving ahead of Jesus and were waiting for him. — *Mt14:13; Mk6:33 Lk9:11; Jn6:2*
D When Jesus landed, he saw the mass of people, and he was moved with compassion for them because they were as sheep having no shepherd. So Jesus and his disciples went up on high ground and Jesus taught the multitude many things concerning the coming government of God and healed their sick. — *Mt14:14; Mk6:34 Lk9:11; Jn6:3*
E As daylight was coming to an end, Phillip said to him 'This is an isolated area and it is getting late. — *Mt14:15; Mk6:35 Lk9:12*
F 'Send the people away, that they may go to the nearby villages and buy food, for they have had nothing here to eat'. — *Mt14:15; Mk6:36 Lk9:12*
G Jesus said to Phillip 'Where can we buy bread to give them to eat?' — *Mt14:16; Mk6:37 Lk9:13; Jn6:5*
H Jesus said this to test him, for he knew what he was about to do. — *Jn6:6*

The Harmonized Gospels — Apocalyptic Version

I Philip answered 'Two hundred pennyworth of bread is not sufficient for them, even if they all get a small portion'.	*Jn6:7*
J Jesus asked 'How many loaves do you have? Go and see'.	*Mt14:17; Mk6:38 Lk9:13*
K When they had checked Andrew, Simon Peter's brother came and said,	*Jn6:8*
L 'There is a lad here with five barley loaves and two small fishes, but how can it suffice for so many'?	*Jn6:9*
M Jesus said to them 'Bring them to me'.	*Mt14:18*
N Jesus then instructed them to sit the people in companies on the grass.	*Mt14:19; Mk6:39 Lk9:14; Jn6:10*
O So the people were organized in groups of hundreds and fifties.	*Mk6:40; Lk9:15*
P Jesus then took the five loaves and the two fishes, and looking up he blessed it. Then he broke pieces of the loaves and gave them to his disciples to give to the people. He likewise divided the two fishes for everyone.	*Mt14:19; Mk6:41 Lk9:16; Jn6:11*
Q When all were finished eating, Jesus said to his disciples 'Gather up all the scraps that are left over, leaving nothing behind'.	*Mt14:20; Mk6:42 Jn6:12*
R They gathered together twelve baskets filled with the scraps of the five barley loaves and the fishes, which remained over after they had eaten.	*Mt14:20; Mk6:43 Lk9:17; Jn6:13*
S That day, the number who had eaten were about five thousand men, beside women and children.	*Mt14:21; Mk6:44 Lk9:14; Jn6:10*
T When the people saw this miracle that Jesus did they said 'This is truly the prophet that was expected to come into the world'.	*Jn6:14*
U When Jesus saw that they wanted to take him by force and make him king, he sent the people away and instructed his disciples to go by ship to the other side from Bethsaida.	*Mt14:22; Mk6:45*

CHAPTER 79
Jesus walks on the sea

A After he had sent the people away, Jesus went by himself up into a mountain to pray, and was there for a good part of the night. — Mt14:23; Mk6:46; Jn6:15

B His disciples were on a ship some distance from the shore and headed for Capernaum. It was late and they were rowing hard, as the ship was being tossed about by a contrary wind. — Mt14:24; Mk6:47, 48; Jn6:15 ~ 18

C At about 3 am that night, they were four miles from the shore when they saw Jesus walking on the sea at such a rate that he could have passed them. — Mt14:25; Mk6:48; Jn6:19

D When the disciples saw him walking on the sea, they were deeply troubled and cried out for fear, thinking it was an apparition. — Mt14:26; Mk6;49; Jn6:19

E Jesus however, spoke to them saying 'Do not be concerned. Fear not, it is I'. — Mt14:27; Mk6:50; Jn6:20

F On hearing his voice, Peter said 'Lord, if it is you, tell me to come to you on the water'. — Mt14:28

G Jesus replied 'Come'. So Peter stepped out of the ship on the water, and he started to walk to Jesus. — Mt14:29

H But when he saw the wind howling about him, he became afraid and beginning to sink, he cried out 'Lord, save me'. — Mt14:30

I Jesus immediately reached out and caught him, and said 'O you of little faith, why did doubt'? — Mt14:31

J They climbed aboard the ship and the wind died down. They were all greatly amazed, not fully understanding what was going on, — Mt14:32; Mk6:51; Jn6:21

K even after the incident with the loaves, because their understanding was not yet opened. — Mk6:52

L All those that were in the ship came and worshipped him, saying 'Indeed, you are the Son of God'. — Mt14:33

M The ship sailed on and landed in the district of Gennesaret. — Mt14:34; Mk6:53; Jn6:21

CHAPTER 80
On eating his flesh and drinking His blood

A The next day the people who were on the other side of the sea knew that there was no other boat there, except the one that his disciples had taken. They saw that Jesus did not go with his disciples into the boat, and that his disciples had left without him. — Jn6:22

B There were however, other boats from Tiberias some distance from the place where they ate the bread that had multiplied when the Lord had given thanks. — Jn6:23

C After some time the people realized that Jesus was not there, nor any of his disciples. They therefore went and took the nearby boats and came to Capernaum looking for Jesus. — Jn6:24

D They found him on the other side of the sea and asked 'Rabbi, when did you come over'? — Jn6:25

E Jesus replied 'I tell you with certainty that you seek me, not because you saw the miracles, but because you ate of the loaves and were filled. — Jn6:26

F 'Do not crave for the meat which is temporary, but for the meat which brings everlasting life. This the Son of man shall give you, for he has been granted this right by God the Father'. — Jn6:27

G They also asked him 'What should we do, that we might perform the works of God'? — Jn6:28

H Jesus replied 'The work of God is that you believe the one whom he has sent'. — Jn6:29

I They said 'What sign can you show us then, that we may see and believe you? What can you show us? — Jn6:30

J 'Our fathers did eat manna in the desert, for it is written "He gave them bread from heaven to eat"'. — Jn6:31

K Then Jesus said to them 'With certainty I tell you that Moses did not give you the bread from heaven, but my Father does give you the true bread from heaven. — Jn6:32

L 'For the bread of God is he who comes down from heaven, and gives life unto the world'. — Jn6:33

M Then they said 'Lord, give us this bread always'. — Jn6:34

N Jesus said 'I am the bread of life. Whosoever comes to me shall never hunger, and who believes in me shall never thirst. — Jn6:35

O 'But it is as I said to you. You have seen me and do not believe. — Jn6:36

P 'All that the Father give me shall come to me, and any that come to me, I will not cast out. — Jn6:37

Q 'For I came down from heaven, not to do my own will, but the will of him that sent me. — Jn6:38

R 'And what is the will of the Father who sent me? It is that of all those whom he has given me, I should lose nothing, but should resurrect them at the last day. — Jn6:39

The Harmonized Gospels — Apocalyptic Version

S 'This is the will of the one that sent me, that every one who sees the Son, and believes on him, may have everlasting life, and I will resurrect him at the last day'. — *Jn6:40*

T The Jews were also disturbed because he said 'I am the bread which came down from heaven'. — *Jn6:41*

U They said 'Is this not Jesus, the son of Joseph, whose father and mother we know? How is it then that he says 'I came down from heaven'? — *Jn6:42*

V Jesus told them 'You do not have to grumble among yourselves. — *Jn6:43*

W 'No man can come to me, except the Father who sent me, draws him, and I will resurrect him at the last day. — *Jn6:44*

X 'It is written in the book of the prophets "They shall be all taught of God". Every man therefore that has heard and has learned of the Father, comes to me. — *Jn6:45*

Y 'Not that anyone has seen the Father, except he who is from God. He indeed has seen the Father. — *Jn6:46*

Z 'I tell you with certainty that he that believes me shall have everlasting life. — *Jn6:47*

AA 'I am that bread of life. — *Jn6:48*

AB 'Your fathers did eat manna in the wilderness, and are dead. — *Jn6:49*

AC 'I speak of the bread which comes down from heaven that a man may eat of and not die. — *Jn6:50*

AD 'I am the living bread which came down from heaven. If any man eats of this bread, he shall live for ever. The bread which I will give is my flesh, which I will give for the life of the world'. — *Jn6:51*

AE The Jews questioned among themselves saying, 'How can this man give us his flesh to eat'? — *Jn6:52*

AF Jesus again said to them 'With certainty I tell you that except you eat my flesh and drink my blood, you have no life in you. — *Jn6:53*

AG 'Whosoever eats my flesh, and drinks my blood, has eternal life and I will resurrect him at the last day. — *Jn6:54*

AH 'For my flesh is meat indeed, and my blood is drink indeed. — *Jn6:55*

AI 'He that eats my flesh and drinks my blood lives in me, and I in him. — *Jn6:56*

AJ As the living Father has sent me and I live because of the Father, so he that eats of me shall likewise live because of me. — *Jn6:57*

AK 'This is that bread which came down from heaven. Your fathers did eat manna and are dead, but he that eats of this bread shall live for ever'. — *Jn6:58*

AL Jesus said these things in the synagogue, as he taught in Capernaum. — *Jn6:59*

AM When they had heard this, many of his disciples, said 'This is an hard thing he is saying. Who can understand it'? — *Jn6:60*

AN When Jesus sensed that his disciples were arguing about it, he said to them 'Does this offend you? — *Jn6:61*

AO 'What if you shall see the Son of man ascend up to the heavens from where he was before? — *Jn6:62*

The Harmonized Gospels — Apocalyptic Version

AP 'It is the spirit that gives life. The flesh profits nothing. The words that I speak unto you, they are spirit, and they are life.	Jn6:63
AQ 'But there are some of you who do not believe'.	Jn6:64
AR Jesus knew from the beginning all who did not believe and who would betray him.	Jn6:64
AS He continued 'That is why I said to you that no man can come unto me, except it were given unto him of my Father'.	Jn6:65
AT From that time many of his disciples departed and followed him no more.	Jn6:66
AU Jesus unto the twelve 'Will you also go away'?	Jn6:67
AV Simon Peter answered 'Lord, to whom shall we go? You have the words of eternal life.	Jn6:68
AW 'We believe and are sure that you are the Christ, the Son of the living God'.	Jn6:69
AX Jesus answered 'Have not I chosen you twelve, and one of you is a devil'?	Jn6:70
AY (He was speaking of Judas Iscariot, the son of Simon, who was one of the twelve and who would betray him.)	Jn6:71

CHAPTER 81

Jesus heals in the district of Gennesaret

A When the people of Gennesaret found out that Jesus had landed there, they sent out into the surrounding country, and brought all that were sick to him.	Mt14:34; Mk6:53
B Wherever he went, whether in the villages, or the cities, or in the countryside, they laid the sick in the streets, and pleaded with him to touch the sick with but the hem of his garment, and all who touched him were healed.	Mt14:35, 36; Mk6:54 ~ 56

CHAPTER 82

Jesus on the washings of the Pharisees

A Some Pharisees and Scribes from Jerusalem came to see him and a Pharisee invited Jesus to dine with them.	Mt15:1; Mk7:1 Lk11:37
B There they observed some of *Jesus'* disciples eating bread without washing their hands. They were disdainful of them because it was considered a defilement.	Mk7:2; Lk11:38
C The Pharisees, as well as all the Jews, do not eat unless they wash their hands, because it is an ancient tradition.	Mk7:3
D When the Jews come from the market, they do not eat unless they wash their hands. There are many other similar traditions which they keep, such as the washing of cups,	Mk7:4

The Harmonized Gospels — Apocalyptic Version

pots, brassware and tables.

E The Pharisees and Scribes asked Jesus 'Why do your disciples transgress the tradition of the elders, by not washing their hands before they eat'?	Mt15:2; Mk7:5
F Jesus replied 'Tell me, why do you transgress the commandment of God by your tradition?	Mt15:3
G 'For Moses said "Honor your father and your mother[1]" and also "Whosoever curses his father or mother, should be put to death[2]".	Mt15:4; Mk7:10
H 'But you say "If a man shall say to his father or mother 'The gift that you were expecting from me has been given as an offering in the temple' he shall be free of Moses' command".	Mt15:5; Mk7:11
I 'Thus you permit him to not honor his father or his mother,	Mt15:6; Mk7:12
J 'ignoring the word of God by your tradition, which you hold to. There are many similar instances when you do this'.	Mt15:6, 7; Mk7:13
K Jesus continued 'Esaias indeed described you well, you hypocrites, when he wrote "This people honor me with their lips, but their heart is far from me.	Mt15:7, 8; Mk7:6
L '"For they worship me in vain, teaching as doctrines the commandments of men[3]".	Mt15:9; Mk7:7
M 'For while you ignore the instructions of God, you hold on to the traditions of men, such as the washing of pots and cups, and many other similar things.	Mk7:8
N 'You knowingly reject the commandments of God so that you may keep your own tradition'.	Mk7:9
O Then he called the multitude near and said 'Understand this;	Mt15:10; Mk7:14
P 'it is not what goes into one's mouth that defiles them, but that which comes out of the mouth'.	Mt15:11; Mk7:15
Q 'Those given to understanding will understand'.	Mk7:16
R Afterwards, his disciples came and said 'Did you know that the Pharisees were offended after they heard what you just said?'	Mt15:12
S Jesus replied 'Every plant, which is not planted by my heavenly Father, shall be rooted up.	Mt15:13
T 'Leave them to their own devices. They are blind leaders of the blind, and if the blind leads the blind, they shall both fall into the ditch'.	Mt15:14; Lk6:39
U Peter then said 'Tell us what this parable means'.	Mt15:15; Mk7:17

---

1 Ex 20:12
2 Ex 21:17
3 Is 29:13

The Harmonized Gospels — Apocalyptic Version

V Jesus replied 'Are you still without understanding?	Mt15:16; Mk7:18
W 'Can you not see that something coming into a man cannot defile him,	Mt15:17; Mk7:18
X 'because it does not go into his heart but into his belly, and comes out into the waste, thus purging all that he eats?	Mt15:17; Mk7:19
Y 'But the things that come out of the mouth originated in the heart. These are the things that defile someone.	Mt15:18; Mk7:20
Z 'For from the inside, out of the heart, comes evil thoughts, adulteries, fornications, murders,	Mt15:19; Mk7:21
AA 'thefts, covetousness, wickedness, deceit, lusts, hatreds, blasphemy, pride and foolishness.	Mt15:19; Mk7:22
AB 'These are the things which defile someone, not eating without washing the hands'.	Mt15:20; Mk7:23

CHAPTER 83
The Canaanite woman in Tyre/Sidon

A Jesus then left that area and went to a house in the region of Tyre and Sidon, where they hoped they would not be recognized. But he could not be hidden for long,	Mt15:21; Mk7:24
B and a woman, whose young daughter was possessed with a demon, heard of him, and came and fell at his feet.	Mk7:25
C She was a Greek woman of Syrophenica, who dwelt in Canaan. She pleaded 'Have mercy on me, O Lord, Son of David, for my daughter is grievously troubled with a devil'.	Mt15:22; Mk7:26
D Jesus ignored her cries till his disciples came to him and said 'Tell her to go away, for she keeps crying out after us'.	Mt15:23
E Turning to her, Jesus said 'I have been sent only to the lost sheep of the house of Israel'.	Mt15:24
F The woman then threw herself at his feet and said 'Lord, help me'.	Mt15:25
G Jesus looked at her and said 'It is not fit to take the children's bread and throw it to the dogs'.	Mt15:26; Mk7:27
H To this the woman said 'That is true Lord, yet the dogs eat of the crumbs which fall from their masters' table'.	Mt15:27; Mk7:28
I Then Jesus said to her 'Woman, great is your faith. As you have asked, so be it. The devil is gone out of your daughter'.	Mt15:28; Mk7:29
J When the woman returned to her house, she found her daughter healed on her bed, and the demon gone.	Mk7:30

CHAPTER 84
Healing the deaf and dumb man

A Jesus departed the region of Tyre and Sidon and came to the sea of Galilee, passing by the coast of Decapolis. — *Mt15:29; Mk7:31*

B There they brought to him one that was deaf, and who had difficulty in speaking and they beseeched him to lay his hand upon him. — *Mk7:32*

C Jesus took him aside and put his fingers into the man's ears, and then he spat on his finger and touched the man's tongue. — *Mk7:33*

D Looking up he prayed and said to the man 'Ephphatha', which means 'Be opened'. — *Mk7:34*

E Immediately, the man's ears were opened, and the impediment in his speech was removed, so that he spoke plainly. — *Mk7:35*

F There great multitudes came to him, and lay before him their lame, blind, dumb, maimed, and otherwise suffering. Jesus healed them all, — *Mt15:30*

G and the multitudes were greatly amazed and glorified the God of Israel, when they saw the dumb speak, the maimed made whole, the lame walk, and the blind see. — *Mt15:31; Mk7:37*

H Jesus asked them to tell no one, but the more he asked them not to say anything, the more they proclaimed it. — *Mk7:36*

CHAPTER 85
Feeding the four thousand

A A huge multitude had gathered and they had nothing to eat. — *Mk8:1*

B Jesus called his disciples and said 'I am concerned for the multitude, because they have been here with me for three days, with nothing to eat. I will not send them away hungry, lest they faint on their way'. — *Mt15:32; Mk8:2, 3*

C His disciples asked 'Where in this wilderness can we get food for so great a multitude?' — *Mt15:33; Mk8:4*

D Jesus asked 'How many loaves do you have?' They replied 'Seven, and a few little fishes'. — *Mt15:34; Mk8:5*

E Jesus them instructed the multitude to sit down on the ground, — *Mt15:35; Mk8:6*

F and taking the seven loaves and the fishes, he gave thanks, and brake them, and gave to his disciples, who in turn passed it to the multitude. — *Mt15:36; Mk8:6, 7*

G All the people ate and were filled. When they collected — *Mt15:37; Mk8:8*

the scraps, they counted seven baskets full.
H At that time, four thousand men ate, beside women and children. *Mt15:38; Mk8:9*
I Jesus then dismissed the multitude, and left with his disciples by a ship for the coasts of Magdala in the region of Dalmanutha. *Mt15:39; Mk8:10*

CHAPTER 86
The Pharisees and Sadducees ask for a sign

A When they arrived in Magdala, the Pharisees and the Sadducees came to Jesus asking for proof of his authenticity, with a sign from heaven. *Mt16:1; Mk8:10, 11*
B Jesus sighed and said 'Why are you asking for a sign? *Mk8:12*
C 'When you see a cloud rise out of the west, straightway you say "A shower is coming" and so it happens. *Lk12:54*
D 'When you see the south wind blowing you say "It is going to be hot" and it comes to pass. *Lk12:55*
E 'When evening approaches and the sky is red, you say that the weather will be fair. *Mt16:2*
F 'However, if the sky is red in the morning, you say that the weather will become foul. *Mt16:3*
G 'You hypocrites, how is it you can read the signs in the sky, but you can't discern the signs of the times? *Mt16:3; Lk12:56*
H 'How then, can you not judge for yourselves what is right? *Lk12:57*
I 'A wicked and adulterous generation looks for a sign, but the only sign it shall be given, is the sign of the prophet Jonas'. *Mt16:4*
J Leaving them, he went into the ship and sailed to the other side. *Mk8:13*

CHAPTER 87
The leaven of the Pharisees and Sadducees

A When they got to the other side, the disciples realized that they had forgotten to bring anything to eat. — *Mt16:5; Mk8:14*

B Jesus said to them 'Hear me. Beware of the leaven of the Pharisees and of the Sadducees'. — *Mt16:6: Mk8:15 Lk12:1*

C Not fully understanding, they reasoned among themselves that he was talking about their situation with the lack of food. — *Mt16:7: Mk8:16*

D Jesus seeing their puzzlement, said 'Do you not yet see or understand? Is your hearts still hardened, so that having eyes, you do not see and having ears you do not hear? Why do you think that I am addressing our lack of victuals? — *Mt16:8; Mk8:17, 18*

E 'Do you not remember the five thousand we fed with five loaves, and the baskets of scraps that you gathered; — *Mt16:9; Mk8:19*

F 'or the seven loaves, with which we fed the four thousand, and the baskets of scrap you collected? — *Mt16:10; Mk8:20*

G 'How can you not see that I am not speaking to you about food, but that you should be careful of the leaven of the Pharisees and the Sadducees'? — *Mt16:11; Mk18:21*

H Then they understood that he was not speaking of the leaven in bread, but of the hypocritical doctrines of the Pharisees and Sadducees. — *Mt16:12; Lk12:1*

CHAPTER 88
On accidental destruction

A On one occasion, those who were with him told him about some Galilaeans, and how Pilate had butchered them on top of their sacrifices. — *Lk13:1*

B Jesus asked 'What do you think? Were these Galilaeans worse sinners than other Galilaeans, seeing that they suffered such things? — *Lk13:2*

C 'I assure you that this is not the case. But unless you repent, you shall all likewise perish. — *Lk13:3*

D 'Likewise, there were eighteen on whom the tower in Siloam fell, killing them. Do you think that they were worse sinners than the other people living in Jerusalem? — *Lk13:4*

E 'I assure you that this is not the case. But unless you repent, you shall all likewise perish'. — *Lk13:5*

CHAPTER 89
The parable of the unfruitful fig tree

A Jesus also spoke this parable: 'A certain man had a fig tree planted in his vineyard. One day he came looking for fruit on it but found none. — *Lk13:6*

B 'He then told the gardener in charge of his vineyard "For these three years I come seeking fruit on this fig tree and found none. Cut it down, for there is no reason to waste the space it takes up". — *Lk13:7*

C 'But the keeper of the vineyard said to him 'Lord, leave it for another year and I shall dig around it and put some manure. — *Lk13:8*

D 'If it bears fruit, that is good, but if not, then we can cut it down'. — *Lk13:9*

CHAPTER 90
Healing of the blind man at Bethsaida

A When they arrived at Bethsaida, a blind man was brought to him, and the people sought to have him touch the blind man. — *Mk8:22*

B Jesus took the blind man's hand, and led him out of the town. Then spitting on his hand, he applied it on the man's eyes and asked him if he saw anything. — *Mk8:23*

C The blind man looked up and said 'I see men walking, but they look like trees'. — *Mk8:24*

D Jesus again put his hands on the man's eyes, and when the man look up, his sight was restored and he saw clearly. — *Mk8:25*

E Jesus sent the man home and told him 'Do not go back into the town or tell anyone in town of what has happened'. — *Mk8:26*

CHAPTER 91
Jesus confirms that he is the Christ

A When they arrived in the coastal area of Caesarea Philippi, Jesus asked his disciples 'Who do people say that I am?'	Mt16:13; Mk8:27 Lk9:18
B His disciples replied 'Some say that you are John the Baptist, some say Elias, and others that you are Jeremias or one of the prophets who has been resurrected'.	Mt16:14; Mk8:28 Lk9:19
C Jesus said 'But who do you think I am?'	Mt16:15; Mk8:29
D Simon Peter answered 'You are the Christ, the Son of the living God'.	Mt16:16; Mk8:29 Lk9:20
E Jesus looked at him and said 'You are blessed, Simon son of Jona, for this knowledge did not come to you from someone of flesh and blood, but from my Father who is in the heavens.	Mt16:17
F 'I tell you now, that you are called Peter *(a rock)*, and starting with you rocks, I will build my church, which will triumph even against death itself,	Mt16:18
G 'and unto all of you[1] I will give authority from heaven, so that whatsoever you would bind on the earth will be bound in heaven, and whatsoever you would loose on earth shall be loosed in heaven'.	Mt16:19
H Then Jesus charged his disciples to tell no one that he was the Christ.	Mt16:20; Mk8:30 Lk9:21

CHAPTER 92
Jesus tells of his coming martyrdom

A Jesus then began to explain to his disciples, that he must go unto Jerusalem, to be persecuted and killed by the rulers, chief priests and scribes, but that he will be resurrected on the third day.	Mt16:21; Mk8:31 Lk9:22; Lk17:25
B At this Peter privately said to him 'This cannot be, Lord. This surely cannot happen to you'.	Mt16:22; Mk8:32
C But Jesus looked at Peter and said 'Get away from me, Satan. You are a stumbling block to me, for you do not delight in the things of God, but those of men'.	Mt16:23; Mk8:33

---

1 Jesus here declared his intent to commission the Church and demonstrate its heavenly authority with miracles and signs. Though Peter was uniquely used in this way to herald the formation of the church, (Acts 5: 1-11; 15), Matt 18:18 confirms that this authority extended to the other apostles, who were also vehicles of miracles (Acts 5:12). Paul was later used to demonstrate miracles, in impact second only to Peter, not just to confirm the church's heavenly commission, but also to confirm his later apostleship (Acts 15:12; 20:9 –10; 28:3-6; Gal 2:8). There is no historical evidence that the level of signs demonstrated through the apostles extended beyond their generation.

CHAPTER 93
Commitment required of disciples

A There was a large crowd following him, so he said to them 'If any man desires to be my disciple, he must deny himself, take up his cross, and follow me. Mt16:24; Mk8:34 Lk9:23; 14:25, 27

B 'Which of you who desires to build a tower, does not first sit down and work out if he has enough resources to finish it? Lk14:28

C 'You do not want to lay the foundation and then find out you cannot finish it, lest all that sees begin to mock, saying Lk14:29

D ' "This man began to build, and was not able to finish". Lk14:30

E 'Which king who is facing a battle with another king, does not first sit down and consider whether he is able with his army of ten thousand to defeat the other who has an army of twenty thousand? Lk14:31

F 'If not, even when the other is still far off, he will send a negotiator to ask for conditions of peace. Lk14:32

G 'So too, unless you are prepared to give up all you have, you cannot be my disciple. Lk14:33

H Whosoever seeks to save his life will lose it, but whosoever gives his life for my sake, shall have it. Mt16:25; Mk8:35 Lk9:24; Lk17:33

I 'Of what value is it, if a man shall gain the whole world, but lose his own life? Mt16:26; Mk8:36 Lk9:25

J 'What price can a man give in exchange for his life? Mk8:37

K 'For I shall return in glory from my Father, and with his angels. Then will I reward every man according to his works. Mt16:27

L 'If anyone in this adulterous and sinful generation is ashamed of me and my words, I will also be ashamed of him when I return in glory from my Father and with the holy angels'. Mk8:38; Lk9:26

CHAPTER 94
The transfiguration

A *Jesus said to his disciples* 'I tell you, that some standing here will not see their death, till they see how I shall be like, in the new world order'. Mt16:28; Mk9:1 Lk9:27

B Six days later, Jesus took with him Peter, and the brothers James and John, up into an high mountain, where they were alone. Mt17:1; Mk9:2 Lk9:28

C As Jesus prayed, he was changed before them, so that his face looked like the sun, and his clothes shone and became whiter than snow, with a whiteness exceeding anything that the best soap on earth can produce. Mt17:2; Mk9:3 Lk9:29

The Harmonized Gospels — Apocalyptic Version

D As they looked, two others appeared in similar glory, who seemed to be Moses and Elias, and they stood speaking with Jesus[1] of his coming death in Jerusalem.	Mt17:3: Mk9:4 Lk9:30~31
E They felt as though they were in a dream, and Peter said 'Lord, it is an honor for us to be here. If it pleases you, let us make three shelters; one for you, one for Moses, and one for Elias'.	Mt17:4; Mk9:5 Lk9:32~33
F He did not know what else to say, for they were exceedingly afraid.	Mk9:6
G Just as he finished speaking, a bright cloud appeared over them, and a voice out of the cloud said 'This is my beloved Son, in whom I am well pleased. Listen to him'.	Mt17:5: Mk9:7 Lk9:34~35
H When the disciples heard the voice, they fell on their faces, and were very afraid.	Mt17:6
I But Jesus came and touched them, saying 'Get up. Do not be afraid'.	Mt17:7
J When they got up, they saw no one else with them, but Jesus.	Mt17:8; Mk9:8 Lk9:36
K On their descent from the mountain, Jesus said 'Tell this vision to no one, until the Son of man is risen from the dead'.	Mt17:9; Mk9:9 Lk9:36
L They did honor his request, but spoke among themselves about what he meant by being risen from the dead.	Mk9:10

CHAPTER 95
The prophecy of Elias

A His disciples also asked 'Why do the scribes say that Elias must first come?'	Mt17:10; Mk9:11
B Jesus replied 'Elias must indeed come beforehand and remind people of all the things written of the Son of Man, about how he must suffer many things, and be ridiculed.	Mt17:11; Mk9:12
C 'I tell you, that Elias has indeed come, but they did not recognize him. They have also done to him all that they wished. In like manner, I must also suffer at their hands.	Mt17:12: Mk9:13
D Then the disciples understood that he was speaking of John the Baptist.	Mt17:13

---

1 This experience was entirely visionary (Mt17:9). Moses and Elijah are still dead and awaiting a resurrection (IThess 4;15 ~ 17). The purpose of the vision was to establish in the mind of the disciples, the authenticity of Christ, and was a preview of what Christ and other glorified individuals would look like in the New World Order (ICor 15:53).

The Harmonized Gospels — Apocalyptic Version

CHAPTER 96
The healing of the lunatic

A When they came back down to the multitude, he saw a large crowd about the disciples, and the scribes talking to them.	Mk9:14; Lk9:37
B The people were agitated and when they saw him they ran to him and welcomed him.	Mk9:15
C He said to the scribes 'Why are you questioning them'?	Mk9:16
D Then a man fell to his knees before Jesus and said,	Mt17:14; Mk9:17 Lk9:38
E 'Lord, have mercy on my son, who is my only child. He is a lunatic, and very troubled. The demon shakes him violently and causes him to foam at the mouth.	Mt17:15; Mk9:18 Lk9:38 ~ 39
F 'I brought him to your disciples, but they could not cure him'.	Mt17:16; Mk9:18 Lk9:40
G Then Jesus said 'A generation of doubters. This long I have been with you, and how much longer till you believe? Bring him to me'.	Mt17:17; Mk9:19 Lk9:41
H They brought the child to him and straightway the demon tore at the boy so that he fell on the ground, jerking violently.	Mk9:20; Lk9:42
I Jesus asked his father 'How long ago has this happened to him'? He replied 'Since he was a child.	Mk9:21
J 'Many times too, it has thrown him into the fire or tried to drown him in the water, seeking to destroy him. If you can do anything, please have compassion on us and help us'.	Mk9:22
K Jesus said 'If you would believe, all things are possible to one who believes'.	Mk9:23
L The father of the child cried out with tears 'Lord, I believe. Help me with my unbelief'.	Mk9:24
M With the people all around looking on, Jesus rebuked the evil demon saying 'You dumb and deaf demon, I command you to come out of the boy and to refrain from going back into him'.	Mt17:18; Mk9:25 Lk9:42
N At this the demon cried out and violently shook the boy before coming out of him, leaving him unconscious so that many said 'He is dead'.	Mk9:26 Lk9:42
O But Jesus took the boy by the hand and helped him to stand up.	Mk9:27
P All the people there were amazed at the mighty power of God.	Lk9:43
Q Afterwards, when Jesus had come into the house, his disciples asked him in private 'Why could not we cast him out?'	Mt17:19; Mk9:28

The Harmonized Gospels — Apocalyptic Version

R Jesus replied 'Because of your unbelief'.	*Mt17:20*
S The apostles said 'Lord, increase our faith'.	*Lk17:5*
T Jesus said 'I tell you, if your trust in God is as small as a grain of mustard seed, you can say to a mountain "Move from here to there" and it will obey. There is nothing that will be impossible for you.	*Mt17:20*
U 'Or if you say to this sycamine tree "Be uprooted and be re-planted in the sea" and it will do as you say.	*Lk17:6*
V 'However, this kind of devil will only go out with prayer and fasting'.	*Mt17:21; Mk9:29*

CHAPTER 97
Jesus again tells of his coming martyrdom

A They left that area and passed through Galilee unobtrusively, for Jesus did not want anyone to know.	*Mk9:30*
B While still in Galilee, Jesus told them 'I will be delivered into the hands of men,	*Mt17:22; Mk9:31 Lk9:44*
C 'and be killed, but on the third day I shall be raised up'. The disciples were deeply saddened when they heard this.	*Mt17:23; Mk9:31*
D They did not fully understand what he was saying, but were afraid to ask him to explain.	*Mk9:32; Lk9:45*

CHAPTER 98
God's view on greatness

A Jesus came to Capernaum and went with his disciples to a house. He asked them 'What was it that you were arguing about while we were on our journey?'	*Mk9:33*
B They did not answer, for on the way, they were arguing about who should be the greatest.	*Mt18:1; Mk9:34 Lk9:46*
C Jesus sat down, and calling the twelve to him, he said 'If any man desires to be greatest, he should be the least of all and the servant to all'.	*Mk9:35; Lk9:48*
D He then called a little child and held him in his arms,	*Mt18:2; Mk9:36 Lk9:47*
E and said "I tell you that, unless your nature is changed and you become as little children, you cannot be part of the new world order.	*Mt18:3*
F 'Whosoever humbles themselves as this little child, shall be greatest in the God's government.	*Mt18:4*
G 'If anyone receives a child like this who comes in my name, they receive me, and whosoever receives me, receives not just me, but the one that sent me'.	*Mt18:5; Mk9:37 Lk9:48*

The Harmonized Gospels — Apocalyptic Version

CHAPTER 99
Jesus pays tax

A While at Capernaum, the tax collectors came to Peter and asked him 'Does your master not pay tribute?' — *Mt17:24*

B Peter answered 'Yes' and came into the house. There Jesus detained him and asked 'Tell me Simon, from whom do the kings of the earth take customs or tribute? Is it of their own children, or of strangers'? — *Mt17:25*

C Peter answered 'Of strangers'. Jesus then said to him 'Then the children are not taxed. — *Mt17:26*

D 'Nevertheless, so as not to offend them, go down to the sea and cast a hook. When you catch the first fish, open its mouth and you will find a coin. Take it and pay the tribute for you and I'. — *Mt17:27*

CHAPTER 100
On forbidding others to preach Christ

A John told *Jesus* 'Master, we saw one casting out devils in your name, but he was not among those who were with us, so we told him to stop, because he was not one of us'. — *Mk9:38; Lk9:49*

B But Jesus said 'Do not stop him, for he that is not against us is for us. No man who does a miracle in my name is likely to speak evil of me. — *Mk9:39; Lk9:50*

C 'Someone who is not against us is on our side'. — *Mk9:40*

CHAPTER 101
Warning on offending Christ's disciples

A Jesus said to his disciples 'I assure you that whosoever gives you a cup of water to drink in my name, because you belong to Christ, will not lose his reward. — *Mk9:41*

B 'It is impossible for you not to suffer at the hands of others, but let him beware who offends you. — *Lk17:1*

C 'If anyone offends one of these little ones who believe in me, it is better for them, if a millstone be hung about their neck, and that they be drowned in the deepest part of the sea. — *Mt18:6; Mk9:42; Lk17:2*

D 'Let the world be warned for causing offence. For offences will indeed come, but let that person that causes the offence be warned. — *Mt18:7*

The Harmonized Gospels — Apocalyptic Version

E 'Therefore, if your hand or your foot cause you to transgress, cut them off and throw them away. For it is better to be on crutches or maimed, if it means you will attain eternal life, rather than having your two hands and two feet, but end up in the destroying fire. *Mt18:8; Mk9:43, 45*

F 'If your eye causes you to transgress, pluck it out and throw it away. It is better to be without an eye and to attain eternal life, than to end up in the destroying fire because you would keep your eye[1]. *Mt18:9; Mk9:47*

G 'There the worms are ever present, and the fire consumes all. *Mk9:44, 46, 48*
Mk9:48

H 'Be careful that you do not offend one of these little ones, for I tell you that their angels have constant access to my Father, who is in heaven. *Mt18:10*

I 'Even so, they must all be seasoned with fire, just as every sacrifice is seasoned with salt. *Mk9:49; Mt 5:13*

J 'Salt is good, but if the salt have lost his saltiness, what will you season with it? Maintain your saltiness, and have peace with one another'. *Mk9:50 Lk14:34,35*

CHAPTER 102
How to respond when offended

A 'Be careful to do this. If your brother offends you, go to him privately and discuss the offence. If he repents and accept his offence, forgive him and so you will still have your brother. *Mt18:15; Lk17:3*

B 'If he is unwilling to accept wrong, take two or three others with you, to witness the discussion. *Mt18:16*

C 'If he is still unwilling to accept wrong, bring the matter to the church. If he will not abide with the ruling of the church, let him be considered as an unbeliever and a publican. *Mt18:17*

D 'I tell you, that whatsoever you shall bind on earth shall be supported in heaven and whatsoever you shall loose on earth shall be supported in heaven. *Mt18:18*

E 'I tell you again, if two of you shall agree on anything and ask it of my Father in heaven, the same shall be done for you. *Mt18:19*

F 'Indeed, wherever two or three are gathered together in my name, I shall be among them'. *Mt18:20*

---

1 See note 2 on pg. 46 on Matt 5:29, 30.

CHAPTER 103
God's delight on the repentance of sinners

A Many publicans and those who ran afoul of the law came to hear him.	Lk15:1
B When the Pharisees and scribes saw this, they said to one another 'This man sits down with criminals and even eats with them'.	Lk15:2
C Jesus addressed them with a parable, saying,	Lk15:3
D 'Tell me, if someone has a hundred sheep and one of them goes astray, will they not leave the ninety-nine and search the mountains to find the lost one?	Mt18:12; Lk15:4
E 'When they do find it, I tell you that they rejoice over that one sheep, more than for the ninety-nine which did not go astray.	Mt18:13; Lk15:5
F 'They will carry it on their shoulders, rejoicing,	Lk15:5
G 'and when they come home, they will call their friends and neighbors, and say to them '"Rejoice with me, for I have found my lost sheep"	Lk15:6
H 'I tell you that likewise, there is more joy in heaven over one sinner that repents, than over the ninety-nine just persons who need no repentance. For your Father which is in heaven desires that not one of these little ones should perish.	Mt18:14; Lk15:7
I 'When a woman who has ten pieces of silver loses one piece, does she not light a candle, and diligently scour the house, till she find it?	Lk15:8
J 'When she finds it, does she not call her friends and neighbors and say "Rejoice with me, for I have found the piece which I had lost".	Lk15:9
K 'Likewise, I tell you, there is joy among the angels of God when one sinner repents'.	Lk15:10
L 'I have likewise come to save those that are lost'.	Mt18:11

CHAPTER 104
The parable of the unforgiving servant

A Peter then asked 'Lord, if my brother should sin against me, how often should I forgive him? Is it up to seven times?'	Mt18:21
B Jesus replied 'If he commits an offence against you seven times in a day, and these seven times he turns back to you and says "I repent", you shall forgive him.	Lk17:4
C 'But I tell you more. You shall not only do this for seven times, but seventy times seven.	Mt18:22

The Harmonized Gospels — Apocalyptic Version

D 'This is how the new world order will be like. A king calls his servants to give account of their stewardship.	Mt18:23
E 'Among them was found one who owed him ten thousand talents.	Mt18:24
F 'Since the servant could not pay, his lord commanded him to be sold, together with his wife, and children, to recover the debt.	Mt18:25
G 'However, the servant fell down before his Lord and begged "Give me some time and I will repay all".	Mt18:26
H 'The lord of that servant was moved with compassion, so he freed him and even forgave his debt.	Mt18:27
I 'Later, that same servant went out looking for of his fellow-servant, which owed him an hundred cents. When he found him, he grabbed him by the throat and demanded "Pay me what you owe".	Mt18:28
J 'The fellow-servant fell down at his feet, and begged "Give me some time and I will repay all".	Mt18:29
K 'But the servant would not relent and threw his fellow-servant into prison, till he should pay the debt.	Mt18:30
L 'When the other servants saw what had transpired, they were grieved, and reported what was done to their lord.	Mt18:31
M 'Then the lord called the servant and said "You wicked servant! I forgave you a huge debt, as you had requested,	Mt18:32
N '"Should you not have had compassion on your fellow-servant, just as I had compassion on you?"	Mt18:33
O 'So his lord was angry, and delivered the servant to the collectors, till he should pay all that he owed.	Mt18:34
P 'In like manner will my heavenly Father deal with you, if you do not truly forgive each other from your heart'.	Mt18:35

CHAPTER 105
Parable of the prodigal son

A Jesus said 'A certain man had two sons.	Lk15:11
B 'One day the younger one said to his father "Father, give me my share of the inheritance," and his Father did so.	Lk15:12
C 'Soon afterwards, the younger son took all that he had and went into a distant country, where he wasted his inheritance, partying and having a good time.	Lk15:13
D 'When he had nothing left, a terrible famine fell on the land. Being in want,	Lk15:14
E 'he went and hired out himself to a citizen of the country, who gave him a job to feed his swine.	Lk15:15
F 'Yet he was often hungry and even considered eating the husks that he fed the swine, but he was not even allowed that.	Lk15:16
G 'Then he came to his senses and thought "How many hired servants does my father have and every one of them have bread enough to spare, yet I perish here with hunger?	Lk15:17

The Harmonized Gospels — Apocalyptic Version

H '"I will leave this place and go to my father, and tell him 'Father, I have sinned against heaven and in your eyes.	Lk15:18
I "I no longer deserve to be called your son. Pray make me as one of your hired servants".	Lk15:19
J 'So he left and went to his father. When he was still some distance away, his father saw him and filled with joy, he ran to his son and gathered him in his arms and kissed him.	Lk15:20
K 'The son said to him "Father, I have sinned against heaven and in your eyes. I am no more worthy to be called your son".	Lk15:21
L 'But the father said to his servants "Bring out the best clothes for him and put a ring on his hand and shoes on his feet.	Lk15:22
M '"Go get the best calf and prepare it. Let us eat and be merry	Lk15:23
N "for this my son was dead and is alive again. He was lost but has been found". So they began to celebrate.	Lk15:24
O 'The elder son was in the field and as he came near the house, he heard music and dancing.	Lk15:25
P 'He called one of the servants, and asked what was going on.	Lk15:26
Q 'The servant replied "Your brother has come back and your father has killed the choice calf, because he has gotten him back safe and sound".	Lk15:27
R 'The elder brother was angry and would not join the festivities, so his father came out to find out what was wrong.	Lk15:28
S 'The elder son said to his father "For all these years I have served you and I have never refused to do anything you asked, yet you never gave me even a young goat to celebrate with my friends.	Lk15:29
T '"But as soon as this your son has come, who wasted your substance on harlots, you have killed for him the best calf".	Lk15:30
U 'The father replied "Son, you are always with me and all that I have is yours.	Lk15:31
V '"It is right that we should rejoice and be glad, for this your brother was dead, but is now alive again. He was lost, but is now found"'.	Lk15:32

CHAPTER 106
On divorce

A Jesus left Galilee for an area in Judaea away from the Jordan.	Mt19:1
B Great multitudes followed him and he taught them and healed many there.	Mt19:2; Mk10:1
C The Pharisees also came to him to find occasion to criticize and asked 'Is it lawful for a man to put away his wife for every cause'?	Mt19:3; Mk10:2
D Jesus replied 'Have you not read that he who made them at the beginning made them male and female,	Mt19:4; Mk10:6
E 'and proclaimed "For this cause shall a man leave his father and mother, and shall cleave to his wife, so the two shall become one flesh"?	Mt19:5; Mk10:7

F 'See that they are no more two, but one flesh. What therefore God has joined together, let not man tear apart'. — *Mt19:6; Mk10:8, 9*

G They asked 'Why then did Moses authorize a bill of divorce to put away one's wife'? — *Mt19:7; Mk10:4*

H Jesus said 'Because of the hardness of your hearts Moses suffered you to put away your wives, but from the beginning this was not so. — *Mt19:8; Mk10:3, 5*

I 'I tell you that whosoever puts away his wife, except for fornication, and marries another, commits adultery. Who also marries a woman that is put away in such a manner commits adultery'. — *Mt19:9; Mk10:11, 12; Lk16:18*

J Later in the house his disciples said to him 'If this is the case with a man and his wife, it is not good to marry'. — *Mt19:10 ; Mk10:10*

K Jesus said to them 'This is not for all men but to those so called. — *Mt19:11*

L 'For some are eunuchs from when they came from their mother's womb. Some are eunuchs, who were made so by the hands of men, and some are eunuchs, who have made themselves eunuchs for the sake of God's new world order. He that is called to receive it, let him receive it'. — *Mt19:12*

CHAPTER 107
Blessing of the children

A Some also brought their little children for Jesus so that he could lay his hands on them and pray for them, but the disciples tried to stop them. — *Mt19:13; Mk10:13 Lk18:15*

B When Jesus saw what they were doing, he was very displeased and told them 'Allow the little children to come to me. Do not stop them, for God's new world order is for those like them. — *Mt19:14; Mk10:14 Lk18:16*

C 'I tell you with certainty that someone who does not embrace the new world order as a little child does, cannot enter it'. — *Mk10:15; Lk18:17*

D He held the children in his arms, laid his hand on them and blessed them. — *Mt19:15; Mk10:16*

CHAPTER 108
The young man who couldn't

A As they were going on their way, an official ran to him and knelt down and asked 'Good Master, what good thing should I do so that I may have eternal life'? *Mt19:16; Mk10:17 Lk18:18*

B Jesus replied 'Why do you call me good? There is no one good but God. Nevertheless, if you will like to have eternal life, keep the commandments'. *Mt19:17; Mk10:18 Lk19:19*

C The man asked 'Which'? *Mt19:18*

D Jesus replied 'You shall not murder; You shall not commit adultery; You shall not steal or defraud; You shall not bear false witness; *Mt19:18; Mk10:19 Lk18:20*

E 'Honor your father and mother. In all things, you shall love your neighbor as yourself[1]'. *Mt19:19; Mk10:19 Lk18:20*

F The young man then said 'I have kept all these things since my youth. What do I lack'? *Mt19:20; Mk10:20 Lk18:21*

G Jesus, touched by his attitude said to him 'One thing is missing. If you would like to be perfect, go and sell all that you have and distribute it to the poor. Do this and you will have treasure in heaven, and then come, take up the cross, and follow me'. *Mt19:21; Mk10:21 Lk18:22*

H When the young man heard what Jesus said, he went away in sorrow, for he was very wealthy. *Mt19:22; Mk10:22 Lk18:23*

I Jesus saw the man's disappointment and said to his disciples 'I tell you, that a rich man shall find it very difficult to be in the new world order. *Mt19:23; Mk10:23 Lk18:24*

J The disciples were taken aback by what he said, but Jesus reiterated "It is indeed difficult for the rich to be in God's new world order. *Mk10:24*

K 'Truly, I say to you, that it is easier for a camel to go through the eye of a needle, than for a rich man to enter the new world order'. *Mt19:24; Mk10:25 Lk18:25*

L The disciples were astounded and asked 'Who then can be saved'? *Mt19:25; Mk10:26 Lk18:26*

M Jesus looked at them and said 'With men this is impossible, but with God, all things are possible'. *Mt19:26; Mk10:27 Lk18:27*

---

1 Lev 19:18

CHAPTER 109
The reward of his disciples

A Peter asked 'What of us. We have forsaken all and followed you. What shall become of us'?	Mt19:27; Mk10:28 Lk18:28
B Jesus replied 'I tell you with certainty, that in the coming worldwide government, when I shall sit in my throne of glory, you who have followed me, will also sit upon twelve thrones, judging the twelve tribes of Israel.	Mt19:28
C 'Every one that has forsaken their house, or brothers, or sisters, or father, or mother, or wife, or children, or possessions, for my sake, to preach the good news of the new world order, shall receive a hundred times more in this world, with persecutions, and shall also receive everlasting life in the new world order.	Mt19:29; Mk10:29, 30 Lk18:29 ~ 30
D 'But many who are first shall be as the last, and the last as the first.	Mt19:30; Mk10:31
E 'For the circumstances in the new world order is similar to a landowner, who went out early in the morning to hire laborers for his vineyard.	Mt20:1
F 'He agreed with the laborers to pay them a penny for the day and put them to work in his vineyard.	Mt20:2
G 'Later at about 9 am, he saw some others idle in the marketplace,	Mt20:3
H 'and told them "You too may go and work in my vineyard, and I will pay you whatever is fair". So these others took the offer.	Mt20:4
I 'He went out again about noon and at 3 pm and did likewise.	Mt20:5
J 'At about 5 pm, he again went out, and found others that were standing idle and asked them "Why are you standing idle here, all day long"?	Mt20:6
K 'They answered "No one has hired us". So he also told these, "You also, go and work in my vineyard and I will pay you whatever is fair".	Mt20:7
L 'When daylight was drawing to a close, the owner of the vineyard said to his steward "Call the laborers and give them their hire, beginning from the last group and finishing with the first".	Mt20:8
M 'When the group that was hired at 5 pm was paid, they were each given a penny.	Mt20:9
N 'When the first group came to be paid, they expected to receive more, but they also received a penny'.	Mt20:10
O 'On seeing what they received, they grumbled against the landowner,	Mt20:11

The Harmonized Gospels — Apocalyptic Version

P 'Saying "This last group only worked one hour, and yet you have paid them the same as us, although we did most of the work and labored in heat of the day".	*Mt20:12*
Q 'But he said to one of them "Friend, I have done you no wrong. Did you not agree to work for a penny?	*Mt20:13*
R '"Take what is yours and go your way. For I have chosen to give to those who came last, the same that I have given you.	*Mt20:14*
S '"Am I not entitled to do what I will, with what is mine? Why are you upset because I am generous?"	*Mt20:15*
T 'So shall the last be as the first, and the first be as the last, for many will be called, but few chosen'.	*Mt20:16; Lk13:30*
U 'When your servant who was plowing or feeding cattle come in from the field, which of you will say to him "Go and have your meal"?	*Lk17:7*
V 'You will more likely say to him "Prepare my meal and come and serve me. After I have eaten and drunk, you can then go and have your meal".	*Lk17:8*
W 'Does the master thank that servant because he did the things that was expected of him? I think not.	*Lk17:9*
X 'So likewise, when you have done all those things you were told to do, say "We are unprofitable servants. We have only done that which we are expected to do".	*Lk17:10*

CHAPTER 110
The healing of the ten lepers

A On the way to Jerusalem Jesus was passing through Samaria and Galilee.	*Lk17:11*
B As he entered a certain village, ten men who were lepers, stood some distance away,	*Lk17:12*
C and cried out to him 'Jesus, Master, have mercy on us'.	*Lk17:13*
D Jesus took notice of them and 'Go and show yourselves to the priests'. As they went to do this they were healed.	*Lk17:14*
E Then one of them, when he saw that he was healed, turned back, and with a loud voice glorified God,	*Lk17:15*
F and prostrated himself at Jesus' feet thanking him. This man was a Samaritan.	*Lk17:16*
G Jesus said 'Were there not ten cleansed? Where are the other nine?	*Lk17:17*
H 'None of them came back to give glory to God but this stranger'.	*Lk17:18*
I He then said to the man 'Stand up and go your way. Because you believed in me, you have been made whole'.	*Lk17:19*

CHAPTER 111
Jesus warns yet again of his coming sufferings

A They were on the way to Jerusalem, and the disciples were apprehensive[1]. Jesus spoke to the twelve disciples when they were alone, saying *Mt20:17; Mk10:32; Lk18:31*

B 'We are going to Jerusalem, where I will be delivered to the chief priests the scribes, who will condemn me to death, *Mt20:18; Mk10:33 Lk18:31*

C 'They will also deliver me to the Gentiles, who will ridicule me, scourge me, spit on me, and then crucify me. But on the third day I will be resurrected'. *Mt20:19; Mk10:34 Lk18:32 ~ 33*

D The disciples did not fully grasp what Jesus was saying for they could not visualize the things which he told them. *Lk18:34*

CHAPTER 112
The Zebedee brothers want to destroy Samaritans

A Close to the time when he was to be offered up, Jesus set about making his way to Jerusalem, *Lk9:51*

B He sent ahead some disciples into a village of the Samaritans, to prepare for the group, *Lk9:52*

C but the Samaritans did not welcome him, because they knew that he was just passing through on the way to Jerusalem. *Lk9:53*

D When his disciples James and John saw this, they said 'Lord, will you command fire to come down from the sky and consume them, just as Elias did[2]'? *Lk9:54*

E But he rebuked them saying 'You do not know the source of attitude you are showing. *Lk9:55*

F 'For I did not come to destroy men's lives, but to save them'. Then they went to another village. *Lk9:56*

---

1 John 11:8
2 IKings 18:1, 37 ~ 38

CHAPTER 113
The sons of Zebedee seek preeminence

A The mother of Zebedee's children came to Jesus with her sons, and bowing at his feet, she indicated that she had a request to ask of him. — *Mt20:20; Mk10:35*
B Jesus said to her 'What is your desire'? — *Mt20:21; Mk10:36*
C She replied 'When your new worldwide government is set up, grant me that my two sons will sit with you, one on your right hand and the other on your left'. — *Mt20:21; Mk10:37*
D Jesus answered 'Do you realize what you are asking? Are they able to drink of the cup that I shall drink of, or to be baptized with the baptism that I am baptized with'? — *Mt20:22; Mk10:38*
E They answered 'We are able'. — *Mt10:22; Mk10:39*
F Jesus then said 'You shall indeed drink of my cup, and be baptized with the baptism that I am baptized with. — *Mt20:23; Mk10:39*
G However, who sits on my right hand or on my left, is not mine to give. Those places will be given to those, who were prepared for it by my Father'. — *Mt20:23; Mk10:40*
H When the other ten heard of the incident, they were displeased with James and John. — *Mt20:24; Mk10:41; Lk22:24*
I Jesus called them to him and said 'The rulers of the Gentiles lord it over them, and the people consider them as benefactors. — *Mt20:25; Mk10:42; Lk22:25*
J 'This is not to be so with you, but who would be great among you, let him take care of other's needs, — *Mt20:26; Mk10:43; Lk22:26*
K 'and who desires to be the chief among you, let him be the servant, and he who wants to be the greatest shall be as the youngest. — *Mt20:27; Mk10:44; Lk22:26*
L 'For even I did not come to be attended to, but to help others and to give my life as a ransom for many'. — *Mt20:28; Mk10:45*

CHAPTER 114
The healing of two blind men

A As they were passing through Jericho, a great multitude followed him. — *Mt20:29; Mk10:46*
B There were also two blind men sitting by the roadside begging. — *Mt20:30; Lk18:35*
C When they heard that it was Jesus who was passing, one of them named Bartimaeus, the son of Timaeus, cried out 'Have mercy on us, Lord, Son of David'. — *Mt20:30; Mk10:46; 47; Lk18:36 ~ 38*
D The people around him told him to be quiet but he shouted out even more vigorously 'Son of David, have mercy on — *Mt20:31; Mk10:48; Lk18:39*

me'.
E Jesus stopped and asked that he be called. Someone said to the blind men 'Be glad. Arise and go for he calls for you'. | Mt20:32; Mk10:49 Lk18:40
F *Bartimaeus* flung away his shawl as they came to Jesus. | Mk10:50
G Jesus said to them 'What would you like me to do for you'? The blind men said 'Lord, grant that we should regain our sight'. | Mt20:32 ~ 33; Mk10:51; Lk18:41
H Jesus had compassion on them and he touched their eyes and said 'Because you trusted, you have been saved. Receive your sight'. They immediately regained their sight, and followed after him glorifying God. | Mt20:34; Mk10:52 Lk18:42~43
I When the people saw what had transpired, they praised God. | Lk18:43

CHAPTER 115
Jesus stays at Zacchaeus

A Jesus came to Jericho and was going through the town. | Lk19:1
B *Residing* there was a man named Zacchaeus, who was the highest ranking publican and very wealthy. | Lk19:2
C He wanted to see Jesus as he was passing, but he could not because he was short and the crowd obstructed him. | Lk19:3
D So he ran ahead and climbed up into a sycamore tree and waited to see Jesus when he came that way. | Lk19:4
E When Jesus reached that place, he looked up at him and said 'Zacchaeus, make haste and come down, for today I must stay at your house'. | Lk19:5
F Zacchaeus hastily scrambled down the tree and joyfully welcomed him to his home. | Lk19:6
G Those who were there grumbled among themselves saying 'Look he is going to be a guest of that man who is a sinner'. | Lk19:7
H Zacchaeus though stood before the Lord and said to him 'Lord, I pledge to give half of my goods to the poor, and whatsoever I have taken from any man by fraud, I will restore to him fourfold'. | Lk19:8
I Jesus said 'This day salvation is come to this house, for he also is a son of Abraham. | Lk19:9
J 'For I am come to find those that are lost and to save them'. | Lk19:10

The Harmonized Gospels — Apocalyptic Version

CHAPTER 116
Anticipation of Jesus's arrival in Jerusalem grips the nation

A Six days before the Passover, Jesus and his disciples came to Bethany, where he had restored Lazarus, who was dead, to life.	Jn12:1
B As the Jewish Passover was approaching, many from all over the country went up to Jerusalem to purify themselves, before the Passover started.	Jn6:4; Jn11:55
C They looked for Jesus, and spoke among themselves, as they stood in the temple saying 'What do you think? Will he come to the feast?'	Jn11:56
D The chief priests and the Pharisees also gave orders that if any man knew where Jesus was, they were to report it, so that he could be arrested.	Jn11:57

CHAPTER 117
Christ's tumultuous entry to Jerusalem

A On the way to Jerusalem, they arrived at Bethphage, which was close to Bethany and the Mount of Olives. Jesus sent out two of his disciples,	Mt21:1; Mk11:1 Lk19:28, 29
B and instructed them 'Go to the nearby village and you will immediately see an ass tied, with her colt next to her, which no one has ever ridden. Loose the colt and bring it to me.	Mt21:2; Mk11:2 Lk19:30
C 'If anyone would challenge you, tell them "The Lord has need of it," and they will let you alone.	Mt21:3; Mk11:3 Lk19:31
D The two disciples went and found the colt tied outside a building at a crossroad, and they untied it.	Mk11:4; Lk19:32
E The owners who were there said to them 'Why do you untie the colt?'	Mk11:5; Lk19:33
F They answered as Jesus had told them to, and they were allowed to leave.	Mk11:6; Lk19;34
G This occurred so that the prophecy given by the prophets would come to pass, which said,	Mt21:4
H 'Say to the daughter of Sion "Look, your King comes to you, meek and sitting upon an ass, even the foal of an ass [1]",	Mt21:5; Jn12:15
I The disciples brought the colt to Jesus and they also arranged some clothing on the ass, and put Jesus to sit on it.	Mt21:6, 7; Mk11:7

---

1 Zech 9:9

The Harmonized Gospels — Apocalyptic Version

J His disciples did not understand at that time but when Jesus was glorified, they remembered that these things were written of him, and that they had done these things with him. — Lk19:35; Jn12:14; Jn12:16

K The huge crowd that was there, who had come in advance of the *Passover* feast, heard that Jesus was coming. Those who were there when he called Lazarus from the grave witnessed of him and all the crowd came to see Jesus because of this miracle. They spread their garments before him, and some cut down branches and lay them on the road before him. — Mt21:8; Mk11:8; Lk19:36; Jn12:12, 13, 17 ~ 18

L The people around him kept up a continuous tumult saying 'Blessed is the heir of the kingdom of our father David, who comes in the name of the Lord. Hosanna to the highest'. — Mt21:9; Mk11:9, 10; Lk19:37 ~ 38; Jn12:13

M Some of the Pharisees who were in the crowd said to him 'Master, tell your disciples to stop'. — Lk19:39

N But he replied 'I tell you that even if they should be silent, the stones would immediately speak out'. — Lk19:40

O The Pharisees therefore said among themselves, 'See how we have no say. The whole world is gone after him'. — Jn12:19

P When he came near the city, he looked at it and wept, — Lk19:41

Q saying 'If only you knew today how your peace will come. But now it is hidden from you. — Lk19:42

R 'For the days shall come when your enemies will build a wall around you and surround you on every side to keep you in. — Lk19:43

S 'Then they shall level you to the ground, both you and your children, and they shall not leave one stone standing upon another, because you did not know that this is the time of your visitation'. — Lk19:44

T When he entered Jerusalem, all the city was in uproar and many were asking 'Who is this?' — Mt21:10

U The multitude replied 'This is Jesus, the prophet of Nazareth, which is in Galilee'. — Mt21:11

CHAPTER 118
Some Greeks ask to see Christ

A There were some Greeks there who had came up to worship at the feast. — Jn12:20

B They spoke to Philip, which was from Bethsaida in Galilee, and said 'Sir, we would like to see Jesus'. — Jn12:21

C Philip told Andrew, and together they went to Jesus and told him. — Jn12:22

CHAPTER 119
Jesus — Light of the World

A Jesus said 'The time has come for the Son of man to be glorified. — *Jn12:23*
B 'I tell you the truth, that except a grain of wheat falls to the ground and die, it stays alone. But if it dies, it produces much fruit. — *Jn12:24*
C 'He that loves his life shall lose it, but he that hates his life in this world shall gain eternal life. — *Jn12:25*
D 'If any man would serve me, let him follow me. Where I am, there also my servant will be. If any man serves me, he will be honored by my Father. — *Jn12:26*
E 'I am deeply troubled, but shall I say "Father, save me from this hour"? Is it not for this purpose that I came? — *Jn12:27*
F 'Father, let your name be magnified'. Then a voice was heard from heaven saying 'I have both magnified it, and will glorify it again'. — *Jn12:28*
G The people that stood by heard it and said that it was loud as thunder. Others said 'An angel spoke to him'. — *Jn12:29*
H Jesus said to them 'This voice is not for my sake but for yours. — *Jn12:30*
I 'A judgment is to be made of this world, and soon the prince of this world will be cast out. — *Jn12:31*
J 'And if the Son of man is raised up from the earth, He will draw all men unto me'. — *Jn12:32*
K This he said to indicate his coming death. — *Jn12:33*
L The people asked 'We have heard from the law that Christ lives for ever, yet you say "The Son of man must be raised up?" Who is this Son of man?' — *Jn12:34*
M Jesus continued 'For a little while longer, the light is with you. Walk while you have the light, lest darkness come upon you. For he that walks in darkness does not know where he is going. — *Jn12:35*
N 'While you have light, believe in the light that you may be the children of light. — *Jn12:36*
O 'He that believes on me, believes not just on me, but on him that sent me. — *Jn12:44*
P 'He that sees me sees him that sent me. — *Jn12:45*
Q 'I am come as a light into the world, so that whosoever believes on me should not dwell in darkness. — *Jn12:46*
R 'If any man hears my words and do not believe, I will not condemn him, for I did not come to judge the world, but to save it. — *Jn12:47*
S 'He that rejects me and does not receive my words, has one that judges him. The word that I have spoken, the same shall be used to judge him in the last day. — *Jn12:48*
T 'What I speak is not of myself, but the Father who sent me, he it is who told me what I should do and what I should speak. — *Jn12:49*
U 'And I know that his commands lead to everlasting life. Whatsoever I speak therefore, even as the Father has commanded me, so I — *Jn12:50*

speak'.
V Jesus said these things and departed, concealing himself from them. | *Jn12:36*

W Yet even though he had done so many miracles in their sight, they did not believe him. | *Jn12:37*

X This fulfilled the saying of Esaias the prophet which he spoke saying 'Lord, who has believed our report and to whom has the strength of the Lord been revealed[1]?' | *Jn12:38*

Y They could not believe because Esaias also said, | *Jn12:39*

Z 'He has blinded their eyes and hardened their hearts, so that they would not see with their eyes nor understand with their hearts and be converted, that I should heal them[2], | *Jn12:40*

AA These things said Esaias when he envisioned his glory and spoke of him. | *Jn12:41*

AB However, there were among the chief rulers, many who believed on him, but because of the Pharisees they did not say anything lest they should be put out of the synagogue. | *Jn12:42*

AC For they loved the praise of men more than the praise of God. | *Jn12:43*

AD This was how Jesus rode into Jerusalem to the temple. He observed what was going on and as evening was approaching, he left for Bethany with the twelve disciples. | *Mk11:11*

CHAPTER 120

The cursing of the fig tree

A In the morning, Jesus started out for Jerusalem and he was hungry. | *Mt21:18; Mk11:12*

B Seeing a fig tree with leaves in the distance, he came to it hoping to find some fruit. But when he came to it he found nothing but leaves, for it was not yet the season for fruit. | *Mt21:19; Mk11:13*

C Jesus said to it 'No man shall eat fruit from you ever again'. | *Mt21:19; Mk11:14*

---

1 Is 53:1
2 Is 6:9-10

CHAPTER 121

Christ expels the traders from the temple

A It was just prior to the Jewish Passover when they entered Jerusalem.	Jn2:13
B There they found on the temple grounds, traders who sold oxen, sheep and doves, as well as those who changed money.	Jn2:14
C On seeing these, Jesus made a scourge of small cords, with which he drove them all out of the temple, together with their sheep, doves and oxen. As for the money-changers, he scattered their money and threw out their tables.	Jn2:15; Mt21:12 Mk11:15; Lk19:45
D He told those who sold the doves 'Take these things from here and do not turn my Father's house into a market'.	Jn2:16
E He stopped people who were carrying their goods through the temple,	Mk11:16
F and said to them 'Is it not written "My house shall be called by all nations, the house of prayer?" but you have made it a den of thieves'.	Mt21:13; Mk11;17 Lk19:46
G When his disciples saw this they remembered that it was written 'The zeal of your house has eaten me up[1]'.	Jn2:17
H Then some of the Jews said to him 'What gives you the right to do these things? What sign of your authority can you show us?	Jn2:18
I Jesus replied 'Destroy this temple, and in three days I will raise it up'.	Jn2:19
J In response the Jews sneered 'It took forty-six years to build this temple in building, and you are going to build it in three days?'	Jn2:20
K They did not understand that he was speaking of the temple of his body.	Jn2:21
L (After he was resurrected, his disciples remembered that he had said this to them and they believed the scriptures, and all that Jesus had said.)	Jn2:22
M The scribes and chief priests heard what was going on and sought how they could destroy him, but they were afraid to act against him because the people were impressed with his doctrine.	Mk11:18

---

1 Ps 69:9

CHAPTER 122
Christ heals in the temple

A The blind and the infirm also came to him in the temple and he healed them all. — Mt21:14

B When the chief priests and scribes saw the wonderful things that he was doing, and how the people were chanting 'Praise to the Son of David,' they were upset, — Mt21:15

C and they asked him 'Do you hear what they are saying'? Jesus replied 'Yes, and have you not read the scripture that says "Out of the mouth of babes and sucklings you have perfected praise[1]"'? — Mt21:16

D At evening, Jesus went out of the city into Bethany, where he stayed for the night. — Mt21:17; Mk11:19

CHAPTER 123
The drying up of the fig tree

A The next morning as they passed by the fig tree, it was dried up from the roots. — Mk11:20

B Peter, remembering what had happened the previous morning, said 'Master, look. The fig tree which you cursed is withered away'. — Mt21:20; Mk11:21

C Jesus said to them 'Believe and trust in God'. — Mk11:22

D Jesus then said unto them 'I tell you with certainty, that if you trust in God, without any wavering, you will not only be able to do this to the fig tree, but if you even tell the mountain "Throw yourself into the sea" it will come to pass. — Mt21:21; Mk11:23

E 'Therefore I tell you, that if you desire anything, when ye pray, believe that you will receive it, and you will have it'. — Mt21:22; Mk11:24

---

1 Ps 8:2

CHAPTER 124
The temple authorities confront Jesus

A They entered Jerusalem and Jesus came to the temple and started teaching the people.	Mt21:23; Mk11:27 Lk20:1
B The chief priests and others in authority came to him and asked 'Who gave you the authority to do what you are doing here?'	Mt21:23; Mk11:28 Lk20:2
C Jesus replied 'I also have a question for you. If you can answer me, then I will tell you who gave me authority to do these things.	Mt21:24; Mk11:29 Lk20:3
D 'Tell me, when John baptized, was it ordained from heaven or by men'?	Mt21:25; Mk11:30 Lk20:4
E His questioners discussed among themselves, that if they answered 'From heaven,' that Jesus would tell them 'Why then do you not believe him'?	Mt21:25; Mk11:31 Lk20:5
F If they answered 'Of men', the people will be offended because they all considered John to be a prophet.	Mt21:26; Mk11:32 Lk20:6
G So they answered Jesus 'We cannot tell'. Jesus therefore told them 'Neither will I tell you who authorized me to do these things.	Mt21:27; Mk11:33 Lk20:7 ~ 8
H 'But answer me this. A certain man had two sons. To one of his sons he says "Son, go and work in the vineyard today".	Mt21:28
I The son answered and said 'I will not'. However, he repented afterwards and obeyed.	Mt21:29
J Coming to his next son, the man gave the same instruction. This son replied "I will go" but he did not.	Mt21:30
K 'Tell me, which of the two did his father's will'? They answered 'The first son'. Jesus then said to them 'I tell you with certainty, that the publicans and the prostitutes will be part of the new world order before you.	Mt21:31
L 'For when John came to you preaching righteousness, you did not believe him, but the publicans and the prostitutes did. Even after seeing all that happened afterwards, you did not repent or believe him'.	Mt21:32

The Harmonized Gospels — Apocalyptic Version

CHAPTER 125
The parable of the self-righteous Pharisee

A Jesus also told them a parable, because some of them felt they were more righteous than others and looked down on them.	Lk18:9
B He said 'Two men went to the temple to pray. One of them was a Pharisee and the other a publican.	Lk18:10
C 'The Pharisee stood and prayed "God, I give you thanks that I am not as other men, who are extortionists, unjust, adulterers or even as this publican.	Lk18:11
D '"I fast twice in the week and I give tithes of all that I possess".	Lk18:12
E 'The publican, on the other hand, stood behind everyone and would not even lift up his eyes to heaven, but smote his breast and said "God be merciful to me a sinner".	Lk18:13
F 'I tell you that this publican went down to his house justified rather than the other, for every one that exalts himself shall be abased and he that humbles himself shall be exalted'.	Lk18:14

CHAPTER 126
The parable of the landowner

A 'Listen to another parable. A certain landowner planted a vineyard. He secured it with a hedge and a watchtower and a pit for the winepress. Then he leased it to some farmers and went far away to another country.	Mt21:33; Mk12:1 Lk20:9
B 'When the time for reaping came, he sent his servants to the farmers, to get his share of the produce.	Mt21:34; Mk 12:2 Lk20:10
C 'But the farmers mishandled the servants of the landowner. They beat one, killed one, and stoned another.	Mt21:35; Lk20:10 Mk12:3 ~ 4
D 'The landowner sent more servants, but they suffered a similar fate.	Mt21:36; Mk12:5 Lk20:11 ~ 12
E 'Finally, the landowner sent his only son, whom he dearly loved, thinking "They will surely respect my son".	Mt21:37; Mk12:6 Lk20:13
F 'But when the farmers saw the son, they said among themselves, "This is the heir to the property. Let us kill him and take his inheritance".	Mt21:38; Mk12:7 Lk20:14
G 'So they seized the son, killed him and threw his body out of the vineyard.	Mt21:39; Mk12:8 Lk20:15
H 'When the landowner comes, what will he do unto those husbandmen'?	Mt21:40; Mk12:9 Lk20:15

The Harmonized Gospels — Apocalyptic Version

I The men replied 'He will mercilessly destroy those wicked men, and let out his vineyard to other farmers, who will give him his portion when it is due'.	Mt21:41; Mk12:9 Lk20:16
J Jesus then said 'Have you not read in the scriptures, that "The stone which the builders rejected, has become the cornerstone. This judgment is from the Lord, and wonderful to see[1]".	Mt21:42; Mk12:10, 11 Lk20:17
K 'I tell you that in like manner, your place in the new world order will be taken from you, and given to others who show fruits worthy of it.	Mt21:43
L 'Anyone who tries to break this stone shall be broken, but if this stone falls on anyone, it will grind him to powder'.	Mt21:44; Lk20:18
M When the chief priests and Pharisees heard these parables, they realized that Jesus was speaking about them.	Mt21:45; Mk12:12 Lk20:19
N They wanted to seize him and take him away, but they feared the people, who looked on him as a prophet. They left and went to plan what to do.	Mt21:46; Mk12:12 Lk20:19

CHAPTER 127
The parable of the marriage celebration

A Someone invited Jesus to dine and he said to the man 'When you want to invite others to a meal, do not invite your friends, or your brothers, or your relations, or your rich neighbors, for they will also invite you in return and you will be recompensed.	Lk14:12
B 'When you prepare a banquet, call the poor, the maimed, the lame, and the blind.	Lk14:13
C 'Then you shall be blessed, for they cannot invite you in return and you will receive your recompense at the resurrection of the just'.	Lk14:14
D Then one of them that was in the company said 'Blessed is he that shall eat bread in the kingdom of God'.	Lk14:15
E Jesus responded with a parable. He said,	Mt22:1
F 'The circumstances in God's coming worldwide government is like a king, who arranged a marriage celebration for his son.	Mt22:2; Lk14:16
G 'He sent out his servants to remind those invited to the wedding to come and that he was expecting them, but they all made excuses.	Mt22:3; Lk14:17, 18
H 'So he sent some more servants, with the instruction "Tell those who are invited that I have prepared a meal and al-	Mt22:4

---

1 Ps 118:22 ~ 23

The Harmonized Gospels — Apocalyptic Version

ready killed my oxen and calves. All things are ready. Please come to the marriage".

I 'But they ignored the kings' servants and went about their business.	*Mt22:5*
J 'One said "I have bought a piece of land and I am going to see it. Please have me excused".	*Lk14:18*
K 'Another said 'I have bought five teams of oxen, and I am going to match them. I beg you to have me excused".	*Mt22:5; Lk14:19*
L Another had to attend to his merchandise.	*Mt22:5*
M 'Another said "I have just now married and therefore I cannot come".	*Lk14:20*
N 'Others abused the servants, and even killed some of them.	*Mt22:6*
O 'When the servants told the king what transpired, he was very angry, so he sent his armies, which destroyed the murderers and burnt their city.	*Mt22:7; Lk14:21*
P 'Then the king said to his servants "The preparations for the wedding are made, but those invited were not worthy.	*Mt22:8*
Q '"Go therefore into the highways and invite as many as you find to the marriage, even though they are poor or crippled or blind".	*Mt22:9; Lk14:21*
R 'So his servants went to the highways, and invited all that they saw, whether they were bad or good.	*Mt22:10*
S 'Then a servant said "Lord, we have done as you instructed but there is still room".	*Lk14:22*
T 'The king said to his servants "Go out into the streets and alleys and bring them in till the wedding has its complement of guests.	*Lk14:23*
U '"But as for those who refused my invitation, none of them shall partake of my supper".	*Lk14:24*
V 'When the king came to see the guests, he saw one who did not dress for the wedding.	*Mt22:11*
W 'So the king asked him "Sir, how is it that you came here not dressed for the wedding"? But the person could say nothing.	*Mt22:12*
X 'Then the king instructed his servants "Bind his hand and feet. Take him away and shut him outside in the dark, where there shall be weeping and the gnashing of teeth.	*Mt22:13*
Y '"For many are called, but few are chosen"'.	*Mt22:14*

CHAPTER 128
The Herodians confront Jesus

A The Pharisees went away and met to scheme on how they might cause him to say something they could seize on. They sent spies who pretended to be disciples, so that they might use something Jesus said to report him to the governor. | Mt22:15; Mk12:12 Lk20:20

B Then they sent their disciples with some officers of Herod and said 'Master, we know that you speak the truth, and teach the way of God with boldness, without fear of men, or their office. | Mt22:16; Mk12:13, 14 Lk20:21

C 'What do you think? Is it lawful to give tribute to Caesar, or not'? | Mt22:17; Mk12:14 Lk20:22

D Jesus perceiving their subterfuge replied 'Why do you try to entrap me, you hypocrites? | Mt22:18; Mk12:15 Lk20:23

E 'Show me the tribute money'. At his request they produced a coin. | Mt22:19; Mk12:15 Lk20:24

F Then Jesus said 'Whose image is on this coin and whose writing'? | Mt22:20; Mk12:16 Lk20:24

G The Pharisees said 'Caesar's'. Then Jesus told them 'Give to Caesar the things which are Caesar's, and give to God the things that are God's'. | Mt22:21; Mk12:17 Lk20:24 ~ 25

H When they had heard these words, they could not respond so they went their way. | Mt22:22; Mk12:17 Lk20:26

CHAPTER 129
Jesus corrects the Sadducees on the resurrection

A That same day, some Sadducees, who believe that there is no resurrection, came to him and said, | Mt22:23; Mk12:18 Lk20:27

B 'Master, Moses said that if a man dies without having any children, his brother shall marry his brother's wife, and raise up children to inherit his brother's property. | Mt22:24; Mk12:19 Lk20:28

C 'Consider the situation where there are seven brothers. The first brother marries the widow, but dies before making any children, so leaving the widow to the next brother. | Mt22:25; Mk12:20 Lk20:29

D 'Likewise, the second brother married her and also died, leaving no children and the same thing happened to the third, as well as the rest of the seven brothers. | Mt22:26; Mk12:21 Lk20:30 ~ 31

E 'Last of all the woman also died? | Mt22:27; Mk12:22 Lk20:32

F 'In the resurrection, which of the seven brothers will she be wife to, since she was wife to all of them'? | Mt22:28; Mk12:23 Lk20:33

The Harmonized Gospels — Apocalyptic Version

G Jesus replied 'Your error is in not knowing the scriptures, or the power of God.	Mt22:29; Mk12:24
H 'Those in this world marry and are given in marriage.	Lk20:34
I 'But they who are deemed worthy to inherit the world to come and the resurrection from the dead do not marry, nor are given in marriage.	Lk20:35
J 'Neither can they die any more, for they are as the angels [1], being children of God who are born out of the resurrection.	Mt22:30; Mk12:25 Lk20:36
K 'The fact that there is a resurrection of the dead, was shown in the book written by Moses, where at the bush God said,	Mt22:31; Mk12:26 Lk20;37
L '"I am the God of Abraham, and the God of Isaac, and the God of Jacob".	Mt22:32; Mk12:26 Lk20:37
M 'God is not the God of the dead, but of the living[2]. In this matter therefore, you are sadly mistaken'.	Mt22:32; Mk12:27 Lk20:38
N When the people heard what Jesus said, they were all amazed,	Mt22:33
O and one of the scribes said 'Master, you have spoken well'.	Lk20:39
P After that they did not try to question him anymore.	Lk20:40
Q When the Pharisees saw that Jesus had also put the Sadducees to silence, they joined forces with them, seeking to destroy Jesus.	Mt22:34; Lk19:47
R But they did not know what to do, for all the people were eager to hear him.	Lk19:48

CHAPTER 130

Parable of the Good Samaritan

A A lawyer, trying to test him, stood up and asked 'Master, what shall I do to receive eternal life'?	Lk10:25
B Jesus responded 'What does the law say? What do you think'?	Lk10:26
C The lawyer answered 'You shall love the Lord your God with all your heart, with all your being, with all your strength, and with all your mind. You shall also love your neighbor as yourself'.	Lk10:27

---

1 The male/female state of humans is for the purpose of reproduction, which will no longer be necessary when the chosen are immortalized after the period of judgment (Ezek 37:1 ~ 14; Rev 21:4; John 6:58).

2 Though the patriarchs are dead, their resurrection is sure (Ex 3:6; Rev 20:4~5; Rev 21:4; ICor 15:52~53; IThess 4:15~17).

The Harmonized Gospels — Apocalyptic Version

D Jesus then said 'You have answered correctly. Follow this and you shall receive eternal life'.	*Lk10:28*
E Then one, seeking to justify himself, asked Jesus 'And who is my neighbor'?	*Lk10:29*
F Jesus replied 'A certain man went down from Jerusalem to Jericho, and was waylaid by robbers, who beat him up badly and stripped him of his clothes, leaving him half dead.	*Lk10:30*
G 'A certain priest happened to pass that way and when he saw the wounded man he crossed to the other side.	*Lk10:31*
H 'So too, a Levite passing the place saw the man and went on his way.	*Lk10:32*
I 'Then a Samaritan on his business came to where the man was and he had compassion on him.	*Lk10:33*
J 'He stopped and bandaged the man's wounds after applying oil and wine. He then put the man on his own beast and brought him to an inn to be attended to.	*Lk10:34*
K 'The next day, before he continued on his journey, he gave some money to the innkeeper and said to him "Take care of him, and if it costs more than this, I will pay you when I return this way'.	*Lk10:35*
L 'Now, tell me, which of these three would you say was a neighbor to the man that was beaten up by the thieves'?	*Lk10:36*
M The man answered 'The one that helped him'.	*Lk10:37*
N Jesus said 'Go, and do likewise'.	*Lk10:37*

CHAPTER 131
The lawyers confront Jesus

A One of them, a lawyer, asked,	*Mt22:35; Mk12:28*
B 'But Master, which is the greatest commandment in the law?'	*Mt22:36; Mk12:28*
C Jesus answered 'The most important commandment is this: "Pay close attention Israel. The Lord our God is the only God.	*Mk12:29*
D 'You shall love the Lord your God with all your heart, and with all your strength, and with all your mind.	*Mt22:37; Mk12:30*
E 'This is the first and greatest commandment.	*Mt22:38*
F 'The second to it is "You shall love your neighbor as yourself". There is no precepts greater than these.	*Mt22:39; Mk12:31*
G 'From these two commandments flow all that is written in the books of the law and the prophets'.	*Mt22:40*
H Then the scribe said 'Well said, Master. You have indeed spoken the truth, for there is one God and none but him.	*Mk12:32*
I 'To love him with all the heart, and with all the mind, and with all the being, and with all the strength, and to love his	*Mk12:33*

neighbor as himself, is more than all the burnt offerings and sacrifices'.
J When Jesus saw that the man had answered carefully he said 'This is not far from what the government of God is about'. | Mk12:34

CHAPTER 132
Jesus reveals his pre-incarnate existence

A Seeing that a group of Pharisees together before him, Jesus asked them, | Mt22:41

B 'What do you think of Christ? Whose son is he'? The Pharisees responded 'The Son of David'. | Mt22:42; Mk12:35

C Then Jesus asked them 'How is it then, that David, when inspired by God, called him Lord, saying | Mt22:43 Lk20:41

D '"The Eternal said unto my Lord, 'Sit here by my right hand, till I make your enemies your footstool[1]'"? | Mt22:44; Mk12:36 Lk20:42 ~ 43

E 'If David calls him Lord, how can he be his son'? | Mt22:45; Mk12:37 Lk20:44

F But there was no man who could answer him. From that day, no one came to challenge him with their questions. | Mt22:46; Mk12:34

CHAPTER 133
Jesus condemns the Scribes and Pharisees

A The Pharisees, who were covetous, heard what Jesus said and they derided him. | Lk16:14

B He said to them 'You are seeking to justify yourselves before men, but God knows your hearts. Indeed, those things that men highly esteem is abominable to God'. | Lk16:15

C Jesus then addressed the gathering in the presence of his disciples, | Mt23:1; Lk20:45

D saying 'The scribes and the Pharisees have authority handed down from Moses. | Mt23:2

E 'Therefore, do whatsoever they tell you to do, but do not emulate their actions, for they say what should be done, but they themselves do not practice it. | Mt23:3

F 'They put heavy burdens on men's shoulders that make life difficult, but they themselves will not lift one of their fingers to help. | Mt23:4

---

1 Ps 110:1

The Harmonized Gospels — Apocalyptic Version

G 'All that they do, they do to be noticed by others. They dress in long robes and make large wallets to carry the scriptures, and decorate its fringes.	*Mt23:5; Mk12:38 Lk20:46*
H 'At the feasts, they love to be at the table of the honored, and in the synagogues, they love the chief seats.	*Mt23:6; Mk12:39 Lk11:43; Lk20:46*
I 'They love to be hailed in public with the title "Rabbi, Rabbi".	*Mt23:7; Mk12:38 Lk11:43; Lk20:46*
J 'I tell you, do not let anyone call you "Rabbi", for there is one Teacher, even Christ, and you are all brethren.	*Mt23:8*
K 'Call no man your spiritual father upon the earth, for there is only one spiritual father, and He is in heaven.	*Mt23:9*
L 'Do not let yourself be called "Master", for there is one Master, even Christ.	*Mt23:10*
M 'If any would be great among you, let him serve.	*Mt23:11*
N 'For he who exalts himself shall be humiliated, and he that humbles himself shall be exalted.	*Mt23:12*
O 'Your punishment awaits you, Scribes and Pharisees, you hypocrites, for you have hidden the news of the coming world government from men. Not only do you not want to be part of it, but you would prevent others from being in it.	*Mt23:13*
P 'Your punishment awaits you, scribes and Pharisees, you hypocrites, for you cheat widows of their houses, and make long prayers to impress others. Therefore your judgment shall be the more severe.	*Mt23:14; Mk12:40 Lk20:47*
Q 'Your punishment awaits you, scribes and Pharisees, you hypocrites, for you scour the sea and land to find one disciple, and when you are done with him, you make him twice as evil as yourselves.	*Mt23:15*
R 'Your punishment awaits you, you blind guides, for you say, "If anyone makes an oath by the temple, they may be free of it, but if anyone makes an oath by the gold of the temple, he must keep it".	*Mt23:16*
S 'Can you not see which is greater? Is it the gold, or the temple that sanctifies the gold?	*Mt23:17*
T 'You say also "If anyone makes an oath by the altar, they may be free of it, but if anyone makes an oath by the gift that is upon it, he must keep it".	*Mt23:18*
U 'Can you not see which is greater? Is it the gift, or the altar that sanctifies the gift?	*Mt23:19*
V 'If anyone makes an oath by the altar, they do so by it, and by all things on it.	*Mt23:20*
W 'If anyone makes an oath by the temple, they do so by it, and by the one who dwells in it.	*Mt23:21*
X 'If anyone makes an oath by heaven, they do so by the throne of God, and by the one who sits on it.	*Mt23:22*
Y 'Your punishment awaits you, scribes and Pharisees, you	*Mt23:23; Lk11:42*

The Harmonized Gospels — Apocalyptic Version

hypocrites, for you pay tithe of mint, anise, cumin and other herbs, but have not kept the weightier matters of the law, which are justice, mercy and trust in God. Yes you have done what you should do in one instance, but you should not leave the other undone.

Z 'You are like blind guides, who strain a gnat out of your drink, but swallow a camel. | Mt23:24

AA 'Beware scribes and Pharisees, you hypocrites, for you clean the outside of the cup and plate, while the inside is full of greed, extortion and wickedness. | Mt23:25 Lk11:39

AB Foolish ones, do you not see that he who is displayed on the outside is the same as the one on the inside? | Lk11:40

AC 'You blind Pharisee, first clean the inside of the cup, so that the outside may be clean also. | Mt23:26

AD 'If instead you would give alms from what you have, then indeed you will be clean. | Lk11:41

AE 'Beware you scribes and Pharisees, hypocrites, for you are like white mausoleums, which look beautiful on the outside, but the inside are full of dead men's bones, and of other evil. | Mt23:27

AF 'Or like a flat grave, which men unknowingly walk over. You likewise appear righteous on the outside, but on the inside, you are full of hypocrisy and iniquity'. | Mt23:28 Lk11:44

AG Then one of the lawyers said 'Master, by saying this you fault us also'. | Lk11:45

AH Jesus replied 'Beware also you lawyers, for you put grievous burdens on men and you yourselves do nothing to ease them, not even with one of your fingers. | Lk11:46

AI 'Beware you lawyers, for you have hidden away all knowledge. You yourselves do not seek it yet you hinder those looking for it. | Lk11:52

AJ 'Beware you lawyers, scribes and Pharisees, hypocrites, because you build memorials for the prophets, and decorate the mausoleums of the righteous, | Mt23:29 Lk11:47

AK 'saying to yourselves "If we had been alive in the time of our fathers, we would not have killed the prophets, like they did". | Mt23:30

AL 'But you condemn yourselves, showing that you are indeed the children of those who killed the prophets, | Mt23:31

AM 'for you do worse than your fathers, | Mt23:32

AN 'and so show that you would do just as your fathers did. They indeed killed them, and you build their sepulchers. | Mt23:32 Lk11:48

AO 'As serpents, descended from vipers, how can you escape the final destruction? | Mt23:33

AP 'God in his wisdom said "I will send you preachers, teachers, apostles and writers. Some of them you will kill, | Mt23:34; Lk11:49

The Harmonized Gospels — Apocalyptic Version

some you will crucify, some you will savagely scourge in your synagogues, and others you will pursue from city to city, to destroy them.
AQ 'So that you may be partakers in all the righteous blood shed upon the earth, from the blood of righteous Abel to the blood of Zacharias, son of Barachias, who you killed in the temple before the altar. | *Mt23:35* *Lk11:50, 51*
AR 'I tell you with surety, that this generation shall do all these things and shall answer for it'. | *Mt23:36; Lk11:51*
AS Then some of the Pharisees said to him 'You should leave this place immediately for Herod will surely kill you'. | *Lk13:31*
AT Jesus replied 'Go and tell that fox "See, I will cast out devils and heal the sick today and tomorrow, and on the third day I will be perfected". | *Lk13:32*
AU 'Nevertheless, I must continue today and tomorrow and also the day following, for it cannot be that a prophet perish outside of Jerusalem. | *Lk13:33*
AV 'O Jerusalem, Jerusalem, you who have killed your prophets and stoned those sent to you. How many times did I send to bring you to me, even as a hen would gather her chicken under her wings, but you would not come. | *Mt23:37; Lk13:34*
AW 'Therefore, your house will be made desolate. | *Mt23:38; Lk13:35*
AX 'I tell you, that in time to come, you will not be permitted to come before me, unless you can say "Blessed is he that comes from the Lord"'. | *Mt23:39; Lk13:35*
AY When he said these things to them, the scribes and the Pharisees began to rail against him, trying to provoke him to say something rash, | *Lk11:53*
AZ so that they could use something he said, to lay an accusation against him. | *Lk11:54*

CHAPTER 134
The Widow's mite

A Jesus was sitting in view of the collection room and saw how the people were casting their money into the treasury. Many who were rich cast in much, | *Mk12:41* *Lk21:1*
B but a poor widow came and threw in two small coins. | *Mk12:42; Lk21:2*
C He called his disciples and said to them 'I tell you with certainty that this poor widow has cast more into the treasury than all the others, | *Mk12:43; Lk21:3*
D 'for they gave of their abundance, but she, in her want, gave all that she had, even all her lively-hood. | *Mk12:44; Lk21:4*

The Harmonized Gospels — Apocalyptic Version

CHAPTER 135
Prophecy of events preceding Christ's return

A Jesus was leaving the temple and one of his disciples said 'Master, are not these buildings wonderful with its precious stones and beautiful decorations?'	Mt24:1; Mk13:1 Lk21:5
B But Jesus told them 'Do you see these buildings? I tell you with certainty, that all these will be broken down, so that there will not be one stone left on another[1].	Mt24:2; Mk13;2 Lk21:6
C Jesus came to the mount of Olives, and when he was seated, Peter, James, John and Andrew came to him in private and asked him 'Tell us when these things will occur. What sign shall signal your return and the end of this era?'	Mt24:3; Mk13:3, 4 Lk21:7
D Jesus replied 'Do not let any man deceive you.	Mt24:4; Mk13:5
E 'Many will come, saying that I sent them and even quoting my words, and they will deceive the multitudes.	Mt24:5; Mk13:6 Lk21:8
F 'You will also hear of wars, near and far. Do not let it trouble you, for all these things must occur well before the end.	Mt24:6; Mk13:7 Lk21:9
G 'Nations and kingdoms shall be at war with one another, and there will be famines, diseases and earthquakes, all over the world.	Mt24:7; Mk13:8 Lk21:10 ~ 11
H 'But these are just the beginning of suffering.	Mt24:8; Mk13:8
I 'As for yourselves, they will take you to judges and the synagogues. You will be beaten and brought before rulers and kings for my sake, as a witness against them.	Mk13:9; Lk21:12 ~ 13
J 'They shall persecute you and kill you and you will be hated by all nations because you speak in my name.	Mt24:9; Mk13:13
K 'When they seize you and deliver you to the councils, do not be concerned about what to say, or even think about what to say. At that time, you will say the things given to you, for it is not you that speak, but God will inspire you. For I will give you the words to speak and wisdom, which all your adversaries shall not be able to withstand.	Mk13:11; Lk21:14 ~ 15
L 'At that time too, many of you will turn away and accuse one another to the authorities, till you come to hate one another.	Mt24:10
M 'For a brother will deliver his brother to death, and the father will deliver his son. Children will turn against their parents and cause them to be put to death.	Mk13:12; Lk21:16
N 'Though you shall be hated by all men for my name's sake, they will not be allowed to touch one hair of your head.	Lk21:17

---

1 The temple was destroyed in CE 70 by the Roman army under Titus. When Christ returns He will build a magnificent new temple (Ezek 41 & 42).

The Harmonized Gospels — Apocalyptic Version

O 'So be patient and fear not.	*Lk21:18*
P 'Many false preachers will also go about deceiving many.	*Lk21:19*
Q 'Because of the extent of wrong-doing, many will lose their love for one another .	*Mt24:11, 12*
R 'But if anyone endures to the end, they shall be saved.	*Mt24:13; Mk13:13*
S 'The good news of the coming worldwide government of God will be preached throughout the world as a witness to all nations, before the end comes.	*Mt24:14; Mk13:10*
T 'When you see Jerusalem surrounded by armies and the "abomination of desolation", described by Daniel the prophet, standing in the holy place, let the one who reads this know that it is time[1].	*Mt24:15; Mk13:14* *Lk21:20*
U 'For those are the days of vindication, when all the things which were written come to pass.	*Lk21:22*
V 'All who are in Judaea should flee with haste into the mountains and let those outside the country stay away.	*Mt24:16; Mk13:14* *Lk21:21*
W 'If anyone is on the rooftop porch, let him not stop inside to take anything on the way out.	*Mt24:17; Mk13:15* *Lk17:31*
X 'If anyone is in the field, let him not go back for his clothes.	*Mt24:18; Mk13:16* *Lk17:31*
Y 'Remember Lot's wife.	*Lk17:32*
Z 'It will be a difficult time for those who are pregnant or breast feeding.	*Mt24:19; Mk13:17* *Lk21:23*
AA 'Pray that you do not have to flee in winter, or on a Sabbath.	*Mt24:20; Mk13:18*
AB For there shall be great distress in the land, and wrath upon this people.	*Lk21:23*
AC 'Many shall fall by the edge of the sword, and others shall be led away as captives into all nations. Jerusalem shall be trodden down by the Gentiles, until the times of the Gentiles are fulfilled.	*Lk21:24*
AD 'For that will be a time of great tribulation, never before seen since the beginning of mankind, to that time, or ever again.	*Mt24:21; Mk13:19*
AE 'Unless the Lord intervenes In those days, no life would be saved. But for the sake of the elect, these excesses will be brought to an end.	*Mt24:22; Mk13:20*
AF 'So if anyone tells you "Look, here is Christ or, look, there he is", or that the kingdom is here already, do not believe them,	*Mt24:23; Mk13:21* *Lk17:21*
AG 'for imposters will come claiming to be the Christ. Other	*Mt24:24; Mk13:22*

---

1 Circa 167 BCE the 'abomination of desolation' spoken of by Daniel (Dan 11:31; Dan 12:11) was fulfilled by Antiochus Epiphanes who set up an image of Zeus in the Temple at Jerusalem and desecrated the altar by sacrificing pigs on it. Christ intimates that a similar event will again occur before His return.

The Harmonized Gospels — Apocalyptic Version

corrupt preachers will associate themselves with miraculous signs and events, to the extent that even the elect could be deceived, if it was possible.

AH 'The time will come when you shall yearn for my coming and not see it, — *Lk17:22*

AI 'but I say again, — *Mt24:25*

AJ 'If they tell you "He is in the desert," do not go there. If they say " He is hidden in a secret place," do not believe them. — *Mt24:26; Lk17:23*

AK 'For as a lightning strike in the east shines even to the west, so also will be the sign of my return, — *Mt24:27; Lk17:24*

AL 'So be warned for I have told you what to expect. — *Mk13:23*

AM 'Immediately after this time of tribulation, the sun shall be dark and the moon shall not give her light. The heavens shall be shaken with stars falling from the sky. — *Mt24:29; Mk13:24, 25*

AN 'Upon the earth the nations shall be in distress and perplexed, with the sea and the waves roaring. — *Lk21:11; Lk21:25 Lk21:25*

AO 'Men's hearts shall fail them from fear, when they see all these things happening on the earth and in the heavens. — *Lk21:26*

AP 'Then only will I appear in the sky. All the people of the earth will tremble with fear, when they see me coming through the clouds with power and great glory. — *Mt24:30; Mk13:26 Lk21:27*

AQ 'When you see these things happening, look up and lift up your heads, for your redemption is at hand. — *Lk21:28*

AR 'At that time, with the sound of the great trumpet, I will send my angels to gather my elect from the uttermost corner of the earth to the furthest reaches of the sky. — *Mt24:31; Mk13:27*

AS 'Learn from the fig tree. When it's young branches starts to sprout leaves, it is a sign that summer is close. — *Mt24:32; Mk13:28 Lk21:29 ~ 30*

AT 'So likewise, when you see these events unfolding, know that the time of God's government is close, even very close. — *Mt24:33; Mk13:29 Lk21:31*

AU 'For I tell you that the generation that witness these signs, shall live to see its fulfillment. — *Mt24:34; Mk13:30 Lk21:32*

AV 'Know that the heavens and the earth may pass away, but my words will not fail to come to pass. — *Mt24:35; Mk13:31 Lk21:33*

AW 'But of that day and hour, no man knows. The angels of heaven do not know when, neither does the Son. My Father, though, is the only one that knows. — *Mt24:36; Mk13:32 Lk17:20*

AX 'As it was in the days of Noe, so will it be at the time of my return. — *Mt24:37; Lk17:26*

AY 'For in the days just before the flood, people were eating, drinking and marrying, right up to the day that Noe entered into the ark, — *Mt24:38; Lk17:27*

AZ 'They were blissfully unaware of what was to happen, till the flood came, and swept them all away. The situation will be the same at my return. — *Mt24:39; Lk17:27*

The Harmonized Gospels — Apocalyptic Version

BA 'In the days of Lot, they ate and drank; they bought and sold; they planted and built.	Lk17:28
BB 'But on the day that Lot went out of Sodom, fire and brimstone rained down from heaven and destroyed them all.	Lk17:29
BC 'So too will it be when I am to be revealed.	Lk17:30
BD 'If it is at night and two men are asleep in bed, one shall be taken and the other left.	Lk17:34
BE 'If two people are in a field, one shall be taken and the other left.	Mt24:40; Lk17:36
BF 'If two women are grinding at the mill, one shall be taken and the other left'.	Mt24:41; Lk17:35
BG His disciples asked him 'Where to, Lord'? He replied 'Where the carcass is, there the eagles will gather.	Lk17:37; Mt24:28
BH 'Pay attention to yourselves, lest at any time you let your hearts be overcome with excess and drunkenness, and the cares of this life, so that day come upon you unawares.	Lk21:34
BI 'For it will be as a snare on all those that dwell on every corner of the earth.	Lk21:35
BJ 'Watch therefore, and pray always, that you may be counted worthy to escape all these things that shall come to pass, and to stand before the Son of man.	Lk21:36
BK 'Be diligent, for you do not know exactly when your Lord will come.	Mt24:42; Mk13:33
BL 'If the master of the house knew exactly when the thief would come, he would have waited for him and kept his house from being broken into.	Mt24:43; Lk12:39
BM 'Therefore, be always ready, for in the time you least expect, I may return'.	Mt24:44; Lk12:40
BO Peter asked 'Lord, do you speak this parable for us, or for everyone'?	Lk12:41
BN Christ continued 'It is as a man leaving for a long journey, who gave authority to his servants and assigned every man his work, and commanded the porter to watch'.	Mt24:45; Mk13:34 Lk12:35, 36
BP The Lord asked rhetorically 'Who is a faithful and wise servant?	Mt24:45; Lk12:42 Mt24:46;
BQ 'If his lord finds him doing his duty when he returns, that servant shall be blessed.	Lk12:37, 43
BR 'Truly I tell you, that servants so doing would be made chief over all that is the Lord's and the Lord himself will put on an apron and come and serve at the table.	Mt24:47; Lk12:44 Lk12:37
BS 'But if a servant is evil, he will think to himself "My lord will not be coming soon,"	Mt24:48; Lk12:45
BT 'and abuse his fellow-servants, while indulging himself with the drunkards.	Mt24:49; Lk12:45
BU 'When the lord of that servant comes back, in a day and	Mt24:50

time least expected, — *Lk12:46*
BV 'he shall remove him, and put him together with the hypocrites, where there shall be weeping and gnashing of teeth. — *Mt24:51; Lk12:46*
BW 'Be diligent therefore, for you do not know if the master of the house will come in the evening, or at midnight, or at the crowing of the cock or in the morning. Blessed are those servants if he finds them ready. — *Mk13:35; Lk12:38*
BX 'Beware lest he comes unexpectedly and find you sleeping. — *Mk13:36*
BY 'The servant who knows his lord's will, but did not apply himself to do what was required, will be beaten with many stripes. — *Lk12:47*
BZ 'The servant who did not know, but who did commit things worthy of stripes, shall be beaten with few stripes. For to whom much is given, much is required and to whom much is committed, more will be asked of him. — *Lk12:48*
CA 'I tell you again, be diligent'. — *Mk13:37*

CHAPTER 136
Parable of the ten virgins

A 'The coming of the new world order is like ten virgins, which took their oil lamps, and went to meet the bridegroom. — *Mt25:1*
B 'Five of them were wise, and the other five were foolish. — *Mt25:2*
C 'The foolish ones took their lamps, and no extra oil, — *Mt25:3*
D 'but the wise took along extra oil in vessels . — *Mt25:4*
E 'It came about that the bridegroom was delayed, so they all fell asleep. — *Mt25:5*
F 'At midnight, someone cried out " The bridegroom is coming. It is time to go and meet him". — *Mt25:6*
G 'All the virgins arose, and prepared their lamps. — *Mt25:7*
H 'The foolish ones then said to the wise "Give us some of your oil, for our lamps are gone out". — *Mt25:8*
I 'But the wise answered "Sorry, there is not enough for all of us. You must go and purchase your own oil from the vendors". — *Mt25:9*
J 'While the foolish went out to purchase their oil, the bridegroom arrived. Those that were ready, went in with him to the marriage, and the door was shut. — *Mt25:10*
K 'Afterwards, the other virgins came saying "Lord, Lord, let us in". — *Mt25:11*
L 'But he replied "I tell you with certainty, that I do not know you". — *Mt25:12*
M 'Be prepared therefore, for you do not know the day or the time of my return'. — *Mt25:13*
N All during the day time Jesus taught in the temple and at night, he went and stayed at the nearby mount, called the mount of Olives. — *Lk21:37*
O Early the next morning, all the people came to the temple to hear him speak. — *Lk21:38*

CHAPTER 137
Parable of the talents 1

A 'A man traveling to a far country called his servants and assigned to them portions to manage while he was away. | Mt25:14

B 'To one he delivered five portions, to another two, and to another one. Each was allotted according to his ability. The man then left on his journey. | Mt25:15

C 'The one who received the five portions went and traded with it, and made a profit of five portions. | Mt25:16

D 'Likewise, the one who received two portions gained an additional two portions. | Mt25:17

E 'But the one who received one portion, went and dug a hole in the earth, where he hid what his lord had given him. | Mt25:18

F 'After a long period of time, the lord returned and summoned his servants to give account. | Mt25:19

G 'The one who received five portions came and brought and additional five portions and said "Lord, you assigned me five portions, which I have used to gain five more portions". | Mt25:20

H 'His lord then said to him "Well done. You are a good and faithful servant. Since you have been faithful over a few things, I give you authority over many things. Rejoice in the approval of your lord". | Mt25:21

I 'The one who received the two portions came and said "Lord, you assigned me two portions, which I used to gain two more portions". | Mt25:22

J 'His lord said to him "Well done. You are a good and faithful servant. Since you have been faithful over a few things, I give you authority over many things. Rejoice in the approval of your lord". | Mt25:23

K 'Then the one who received one portion came and said "Lord, I knew you to be a demanding master, seeking to reap, even though you did not sow, and gathering even where you had not planted. | Mt25:24

L '"So I was afraid, and went and hid the portion you had given me in a pit. Here is the portion you assigned me". | Mt25:25

M 'His lord then said to him "You are a wicked and lazy servant. I will judge you by your own words, for you know that I reap what I did not sow, and gather what I have not planted. | Mt25:26

N 'You should have left my portion with the traders, so that on my return, I would have received my portion with interest. | Mt25:27

O 'Take now this portion from him, and give it to the one who has five portions. | Mt25:28

P 'I tell you that every one that has will be given more, so that he shall have an abundance, but the one that does not have much, shall lose even the little that he has. | Mt25:29

Q 'And also cast this unprofitable servant outside. There shall be weeping and gnashing of teeth'. | Mt25:30

CHAPTER 138
Parable of the talents 2

A Jesus spoke a parable to them because he was near Jerusalem and they expected that God's intervention in the world was imminent. He said, — Lk19:11

B He said 'A certain nobleman was going to a far country to be granted kingship over the territory, and to return to it. — Lk19:12

C 'So he called his ten servants and gave to each a pound, with the instruction to work with it till he returned. — Lk19:13

D 'Now the citizens hated him, and sent a message ahead of him to the king, saying "We will not have this man rule over us". — Lk19:14

E 'In spite of that, he was given the kingdom and returned. Then he commanded that the servants he had given the money be called, that he might know how much every man had gained by trading. — Lk19:15

F 'The first came and said "Lord, your pound has gained ten pounds". — Lk19:16

G 'The Lord said to him "Well done, you good servant. Because you have been faithful in a little, have authority over ten cities". — Lk19:17

H The second came, saying "Lord, your pound has gained five pounds". — Lk19:18

I 'The Lord said to him also "Be over five cities". — Lk19:19

J 'Another came and said "Lord, look, here is your pound which I have wrapped up and put away — Lk19:20

K '"For I was afraid, knowing that you are a hard man, who expects to get something that you did not work for, and reap from what you did not sow". — Lk19:21

L 'The Lord said to him "Out of your own mouth I will judge you, you wicked servant. You knew that I was a hard man, taking what I did not labor for, and reaping what I did not sow. — Lk19:22

M 'Why then did you not give my money to the bank, so that at my coming I might have received what I gave you with interest'? — Lk19:23

N 'The Lord then said to them that stood by "Take from him the pound and give it to him that has ten pounds". — Lk19:24

O 'They said to him "But Lord, he has ten pounds". — Lk19:25

P 'I tell you, that every one who has shall be given more, but they that do not have shall lose even what they have. — Lk19:26

Q 'As for these my enemies, who would not have me rule over them; bring them here and execute them before me'. — Lk19:27

CHAPTER 139
Parable of the Crooked Steward

A Jesus said to his disciples 'A certain rich man was brought a complaint that his steward was mismanaging his business.	Lk16:1
B 'So he sent a message to the steward saying "Is this true what I am hearing? Come and report on your handling of my business, for I am considering whether you are to continue as my steward".	Lk16:2
C 'The steward was in a quandary and thought "What am I do now that my lord is considering dismissing me as his steward? I cannot do hard work and I am ashamed to beg.	Lk16:3
D '"I know what I will do, so that if I am dismissed from this stewardship, others may provide me some favor at their houses".	Lk16:4
E 'So he summoned all those who owed his lord to come to him. To the first one he asked "How much do you owe my lord"?	Lk16:5
F 'The first debtor replied "A hundred measures of oil". The steward told him "Here is your note of indebtedness. Sit down and quickly change it to fifty".	Lk16:6
G 'To another the steward asked "How much do you owe"? That debtor replied "A hundred measures of wheat". The steward said to him "Here is your note of indebtedness. Change it to eighty".	Lk16:7
H The lord commended the crooked steward on his cleverness and said 'So it is that the children of this world are more clever *in achieving their goals* than the children of light *in theirs*.	Lk16:8
I 'I tell you therefore, use the fruits of unrighteousness to make friends with righteousness, so that when you fail, you may be received into eternal life[1].	Lk16:9
J 'He that is faithful in the least matter is faithful in much and he that is unjust in the least matter is unjust also in much.	Lk16:10
K 'If therefore you are not faithful with the unrighteous mammon, who will put into your hands the true riches?	Lk16:11
L 'If you are not faithful with another man's property, who will give you anything for yourself'?	Lk16:12

---

1 Jesus is not here applauding the wickedness of the crooked steward (Tit 2:9 ~ 10). His message to his disciples is to use their unrighteous lives (Rom 3:23) to seek favor with God, so that when they are dismissed from this life by death for their errors, God will receive them with favor and grant them eternal life.

CHAPTER 140
The judgment at the resurrection

A 'When I am glorified, I shall return with my holy angels, and shall sit upon my great throne. — Mt25:31

B 'Then all nations shall appear before me. At that time I will separate one from another, as a shepherd separates his sheep from the goats. — Mt25:32

C 'I will set the sheep on my right hand, but the goats on the left. — Mt25:33

D 'Then will the King say to those on his right hand "Come, you that have been blessed of my Father, enter the new world order that has been prepared for you from the foundation of the world. — Mt25:34

E '"For I was hungry, and you gave me food. I was thirsty, and you gave me a drink. I was homeless, and you took me in. — Mt25:35

F '"I was naked, and you clothed me. I was sick, and you visited me. I was in prison, and you came to see me". — Mt25:36

G 'At that time, the righteous will ask him "Lord, when did we see you hungry and feed you, or thirsty and gave you something to drink? — Mt25:37

H '"When did we see you homeless and take you in, or naked and gave you clothes? — Mt25:38

I '"When did we comfort you in the sick-bed or in prison"? — Mt25:39

J 'The King will then tell them "I tell you with certainty, that if you did it to the least of my brethren, you have done it to me". — Mt25:40

K 'But to those on his left hand, he shall say "Leave my presence, you who are cursed, and enter into the consuming fire, prepared for the devil and his angels. — Mt25:41

L '"For I was hungry and you gave me no food. I was thirsty and you gave me nothing to drink. — Mt25:42

M '"I was homeless and you did not take me in. I was naked and you gave me no clothes. I was sick and also in prison, but you did not visit me". — Mt25:43

N 'These shall also ask him "Lord, when did we see you hungry, or thirsty, or homeless, or naked, or sick, or in prison, and did not help you"? — Mt25:44

O 'Then he shall tell them "I tell you with certainty, that since you did not help the least of these my brethren, you did not help me". — Mt25:45

P 'These shall suffer complete destruction, but the righteous shall receive eternal life'. — Mt25:46

CHAPTER 141
Lazarus and the rich man

A 'There was a certain rich man who wore the finest clothes of purple and linen, and who dined sumptuously every day.   *Lk16:19*
B 'There also was a certain beggar named Lazarus, covered with sores, who waited at his gates,   *Lk16:20*
C 'yearning to be fed with the crumbs which fell from the rich man's table. The dogs too came and licked his sores.   *Lk16:21*
D 'Then the beggar died, and was carried by the angels to the place where Abraham was. The rich man also died, and was buried.   *Lk16:22*
E 'When he awoke from the grave, he found himself at the edge of the flaming pit and saw Abraham a good distance away with Lazarus next to him.   *Lk16:23*
F 'So he cried out "Father Abraham, have mercy on me, and send Lazarus, that he may dip the tip of his finger in water, and cool my tongue, for I am thirsty because of this flame".   *Lk16:24*
G 'But Abraham said to him "Son, you must remember that in your lifetime you enjoyed the good things, while Lazarus suffered in his. So now he is called to deliverance and you are about to be destroyed.   *Lk16:25*
H '"Besides this, there is a great gulf separating us from you, so that we cannot come to you, nor can those on your side come to us".   *Lk16:26*
I 'The rich man said "I beg you therefore, father, that you would send him to my father's house.   *Lk16:27*
J '"I have five brothers there and he can warn them so that they do not end up in this place of destruction".   *Lk16:28*
K 'Abraham replied "They have Moses and the prophets. Let them heed what they said".   *Lk16:29*
L 'The rich man said "Not so father Abraham. If however, someone went to them from the dead, they will repent".   *Lk16:30*
M 'But Abraham said "If they will not listen to Moses and the prophets, they will not be persuaded, even though one came to them who rose from death".'   *Lk16:31*

CHAPTER 142
The leaders of the Jews plot against Jesus

A Jesus said unto his disciples, — Mt26:1
B 'As you know, in two days time is the feast of the Passover, when I am to be betrayed and crucified'. — Mt26:2; Mk14:1; Lk22:1
C At that time, the chief priests, the scribes and the elders of the people, met in the palace of the high priest, who was called Caiaphas. — Mt26:3; Mk14:1; Lk22:2
D There they schemed how they could seize Jesus and have him killed. — Mt26:4
E They also agreed that it should not be on a Holy day of the Feast of Unleavened Bread[1], so as not to make a commotion among the people. — Mt26:5; Mk14:2

CHAPTER 143
Judas agrees to betray the Christ

A Satan came into Judas Iscariot, who was one of the twelve. He then went to the chief priests, intending to betray Jesus, — Mt26:14; Mk14:10; Lk22:3
B and asked them 'What will you give me to deliver him to you'? When the priests heard this they were pleased and they agreed to give him thirty pieces of silver. — Mt26:15; Mk14:11; Lk22:4 ~ 5
C From that time Judas sought an opportunity to betray Jesus when he was away from public view. — Mt26:16; Mk14:11; Lk22:6

CHAPTER 144
Jesus' response to the accolade

A At that Passover season, while Jesus was in Jerusalem, many believed in his name when they saw all the great things that he did. — Jn2:23
B Jesus however, was not carried away by their response for he knew all men. — Jn2:24
C He did not seek the testimony of man for he knew what was in man. — Jn2:25

---

1 The Feast of Unleavened Bread had two High Days or Holy Day Sabbaths (Lev 23:7 ~8), which very often did not coincide with the weekly Sabbath.

CHAPTER 145
Jesus anointed for burial

A Two days before the Passover, Jesus and his disciples were in Bethany at the house of Simon the leper having supper. Martha served, but Lazarus was one of them that sat at the table.	Mt26:2; Mt26:6; Mk14:3; Jn12:2
B Then Mary came to Jesus with an alabaster box of very precious ointment. She anointed his head and feet, and proceeded to wipe his feet with her hair. The house was filled with the odor of the fragrance.	Mt26:7; Mk14:3 Jn12:3
C On seeing this, his disciples were upset and Judas Iscariot, Simon's son, who was the one who betrayed him, said 'What is the purpose of this waste?	Mt26:8; Mk14:4 Jn12:4
D 'This ointment could have been sold for quite a sum, and given to the poor'.	Mt26:9; Mk14:5 Jn12:5
E He said this, not that he cared for the poor, but because he was a thief. He was the one who kept the purse with all that was donated.	Jn12:6
F When Jesus understood what transpired, he said 'Why do you censure the woman? Let her alone, for she has done a good work on me.	Mt26:10; Mk14:6 Jn12:7
G 'The poor will always be with you, but you will not always have me.	Mt26:11; Mk14:7 Jn12:8
H 'When she poured this ointment, she has anointed my body in advance of my burial.	Mt26:12; Mk14:8 Jn12:7
I 'I tell you with certainty, that when my work and message is preached to the whole world, what this woman did will be told as a memorial for her'.	Mt26:13; Mk14:9
J Many of the Jews knew that he was there and wanted to see him as well as Lazarus, who he restored to life.	Jn12:9
K Because of Lazarus, many of the Jews had come to believe Jesus.	Jn12:11
L The chief priests, knowing this, even consulted on how they might put Lazarus to death also.	Jn12:10

CHAPTER 146

Jesus and his disciples celebrate the Passover

A Before the feast of unleavened bread, and the killing of the Passover, the disciples came to Jesus and asked him 'Where should we prepare for you to eat the Passover'?	Mt26:17; Mk14:12 Lk22:7
B Jesus appointed Peter and John and told them 'Go into the city and you will see a man carrying a pitcher of water. Follow him.	Mt26:18: Mk14:13 Lk22:8 ~ 10
C 'When you come to the house he enters, say to the owner "The Master says, where is the guest chamber for him to keep the Passover with his disciples".	Mt26:18; Mk14:14 Lk22:11
D He will show you a large upper room furnished and prepared'.	Mk14:15; Lk22:12
E The disciples did as Jesus instructed and made the arrangements for the Passover.	Mt26:19; Mk14:16 Lk22:13
F At evening, Jesus knew that the Father had given all things into his hands and that the time had come that he should depart out of this world to go to the Father. Having loved his own which were in the world right to the end, Jesus sat down to eat with the twelve disciples.	Mt26:20; Mk14:17 Lk22:14; Jn13:1, 3
G During the meal, Jesus took a piece of bread, and after he blessed it, he broke it and gave to the disciples saying 'Take this and eat it. This is as my body which is given for you'.	Mt26:26; Mk14:22 Lk22:19
H He then took the cup, and giving thanks to God, he gave it to them and said 'Share this among you, drinking all of it.	Mt26:27; Mk14:23 Lk22:17
I 'For this is as my blood of the new covenant, which is to be shed, so that many can have their sins forgiven.	Mt26:28; Mk14:24 Lk22:19 ~ 20
J 'Do this in remembrance of me.	Lk22:19
K 'I have looked forward to eating this Passover with you before I suffer.	Lk22:15
L 'I tell you, that after today, the next time I drink of this fruit of the vine with you again, I will be glorified and in my Father's new world order'.	Mt26:29; Mk14:25 Lk22:16; Lk22:18
M This reignited the strife among them as to who should be greatest.	Lk22:24
N After supper was eaten and the devil had put into the heart of Judas Iscariot, Simon's son, to betray him,	Jn13:2
O Jesus got up, laid aside his garments and took a towel with him.	Jn13:4
P He then poured water into a basin, and began to wash the disciples' feet, and wipe them with the towel he carried.	Jn13:5
Q When he came to Simon Peter, Peter said to him 'Lord, do you mean to wash my feet'?	Jn13:6
R Jesus answered 'What I do, you will not understand now,	Jn13:7

The Harmonized Gospels — Apocalyptic Version

but you shall understand later'.

S Peter said 'You shall never wash my feet'. Jesus replied 'If I do not wash you, you have no part in me'. | *Jn13:8*

T Simon Peter said 'Lord, why my feet only? Why not my hands and my head'? | *Jn13:9*

U Jesus said 'He that has bathed needs only to wash his feet to be clean throughout, and you are clean, but not all'. | *Jn13:10*

V He knew who would betray him, which was why he said 'You are not all clean'. | *Jn13:11*

W After he had washed their feet and put back on his garments, he sat down again and said to them 'Do you know what I have just done to you? | *Jn13:12*

X 'You call me Master and Lord, and you are correct, for so I am. | *Lk22:27; Jn13:13*

Y 'If I then, your Lord and Master, have washed your feet, you also ought to wash one another's feet. | *Jn13:14*

Z 'For I have given you an example, that you should do as I have done to you. | *Jn13:15*

AA 'In truth I tell you that the servant is not greater than his lord, neither is he that is sent greater than he that sent him. | *Jn13:16*

AB 'If you know these things, happy are you if you do them. | *Jn13:17*

AC 'I speak this not to all of you. I know who I have chosen, but so that scripture may be fulfilled, he that eats bread with me has lifted up his heel against me. | *Jn13:18*

AD 'I tell you this before it occurs, so that when it comes to pass, you may believe that I am the one. | *Jn13:19*

AE 'I say to you that he that receives whomsoever I send, receives me and he that receives me receives him that sent me'. | *Jn13:20*

AF Jesus was troubled in his heart and said 'In truth I tell to you that one of you with his hand on this table and eating with me shall betray me'. | *Mt26:21; Mk14:18 Lk22:21; Jn13:21*

AG When they heard this they were despondent and began to discuss among themselves who would do such a thing. They each asked 'Lord, is it I'? Judas, who was the one who was to betray him, also asked 'Master, is it I?' | *Mt26:22, 25; Mk14:19 Lk22:23; Jn13:22*

AH Jesus answered 'It is as I said. One of the twelve, who is eating this meal with me, will betray me. | *Mt26:23, 25; Mk14:20*

AI 'I must suffer the things that are written of me, but the man that betrays me had better beware, for it would be better for him that he was not born'. | *Mt26:24; Mk14:21 Lk22:22*

AJ Reclining next to Jesus was one of his disciples, who he had great affection for. | *Jn13:23*

AK Simon Peter beckoned to this disciple, signaling that he should ask who it was that Jesus spoke about. | *Jn13:24*

AL The disciple leaned towards Jesus and asked 'Lord, who | *Jn13:25*

The Harmonized Gospels — Apocalyptic Version

is it'?

AM Jesus answered, 'It is he to whom I shall give this morsel of bread after I have dipped it'. Jesus then dipped the morsel and gave it to Judas Iscariot, the son of Simon. *Jn13:26*

AN After Jesus gave Judas the morsel, Satan entered into him and Jesus said to him 'What you must do, do it quickly'. *Jn13:27*

AO None at the table knew why he said this to him. *Jn13:28*

AP Some of them thought that it was because Judas had the purse and that Jesus was directing him to buy the necessities for the feast, or even that he should give something to the poor. *Jn13:29*

AQ Judas, having taken the morsel, went out immediately into the night. *Jn13:30*

AR When Judas had left Jesus said 'Now is the Son of man magnified and God is glorified in him. *Jn13:31*

AS 'If God is glorified in him, God shall also glorify him in himself and shall not delay in glorifying him. *Jn13:32*

AT 'Little children, I am with you for a little while longer. You shall seek me and as I said to the Jews, where I go, you cannot come. So I now say the same thing to you. *Jn13:33*

AU 'A new commandment I give to you, that you love one another as I have loved you. So also must you love one another. *Jn13:34*

AV 'By this shall all men know that you are my disciples, if you have love one to another. *Jn13:35*

AW 'You have remained with me all the while. *Lk22:28*

AX 'I appoint you a part in my kingdom, as my Father has appointed me. *Lk22:29*

AY 'So that you may eat and drink at my table in my kingdom, and sit on thrones judging the twelve tribes of Israel'. *Lk22:30*

AZ Then the Lord said to Simon, 'Simon, know that Satan wanted you, so that he may sift you as wheat. *Lk22:31*

BA 'But I have prayed for you that your faith does not fail. When you are converted, strengthen your brethren'. *Lk22:32*

BB Jesus warned them 'You will all stumble tonight because of me, for it is written "I will smite the shepherd and all the flock shall be scattered[1]". *Mt26:31; Mk14:27*

BC 'However, I will be resurrected and I will go before you to Galilee. *Mt26:32; Mk14:28*

BD Simon Peter said 'Lord, where are you going?' Jesus answered 'Where I go you cannot follow me now, but you shall follow me afterwards'. *Jn13:36*

BE Peter said to him 'Lord, why can I not follow you now? I *Jn13:37*

---

1 Zech 13:7

The Harmonized Gospels — Apocalyptic Version

will lay down my life for your sake.

BF Jesus said 'Will you lay down your life for my sake? In truth I say to you that the cock shall not crow, till you have denied me three times'. | Jn13:38

BG Peter then said to him 'Though all others may be offended because of you, I will never be offended. I am ready to go to prison and to death with you'. | Mt26:33; Mk14:29 Lk22:33

BH Jesus replied 'I tell you with certainty, that on this very night, before the cock crows twice, you will deny three times that you know me '. | Mt26:34; Mk14:30 Lk22:34

BI But Peter insisted 'Even though I have to die with you, I will not deny that I am with you'. All the other disciples also said likewise. | Mt26:35; Mk14:31

BJ Jesus asked them 'When I sent you out previously without money or food or extra shoes, did you want for anything'? They said 'No'. | Lk22:35

BK He continued 'From now onwards, take with you your money and your food. | Lk22:36

BL 'If you do not have a sword, sell some of your clothes and buy one. | Lk22:36

BM 'For I tell you, that it is written "And he was counted among the lawbreakers" and this is yet to take place, for all the things written about me will come to pass[1]'. | Lk22:37

BN They said 'Lord, look, here are two swords', to which he said 'It is enough'. | Lk22:38

---

1 Is 53:12

CHAPTER 147
Jesus' last sermon to his disciples (1)

A 'Let not your heart be troubled. You believe in God, believe also in me.	Jn14:1
B 'In my Father's house are many offices. If this was not so I would have told you. I go to prepare a place for you.	Jn14:2
C 'And if I go and prepare a place for you, I will come again, and receive you unto myself, so that where I am, there you may be also.	Jn14:3
D 'So you know where I am going and the way you also know'.	Jn14:4
E Thomas said 'Lord, we do not know where you are going. How can we know the way'?	Jn14:5
F Jesus said to him 'I am the way, the truth, and the life. No man can come to the Father, but by me.	Jn14:6
G 'If you had known me, you would have known my Father also. So from now on you know him, and have seen him'.	Jn14:7
H Philip said 'Lord, show us the Father and it will be enough for us'.	Jn14:8
I Jesus said 'This long I have been with you and do you not know me Philip? He that has seen me has seen the Father. How can you say then, Show us the Father?	Jn14:9
J 'Do you not believe that I am in the Father and the Father is in me? The words that I speak to you, I do not speak of myself, but the Father that dwells in me, it is he that does it.	Jn14:10
K 'Believe me that I am in the Father, and the Father in me, or else believe me for the very works' sake.	Jn14:11
L 'In truth I tell you that he that believes on me, shall do the same works that I do and he shall do even greater works than these because I go to my Father.	Jn14:12
M 'Whatsoever you shall ask in my name, I will do, that the Father may be glorified in the Son.	Jn14:13
N 'If you ask any thing in my name, I will do it.	Jn14:14
O 'If you love me, keep my commandments.	Jn14:15
P 'I will ask the Father and he shall give you a helper in my place[1], that he may abide with you forever.	Jn14:16
Q 'This is even the Spirit of truth, which the world cannot receive, because it cannot perceive him or know him. But you know him, for he is with you and shall be in you[2].	Jn14:17
R 'I will not leave you comfortless, but I will come to you.	Jn14:18
S 'In a little while, the world will see me no more, but you see me, and because I live you shall also live.	Jn14:19

---

1 The Godly Nature, which was given to the disciples later (Acts 2:3,4), is the presence of the resurrected Jesus and the Father.
2 Jesus is referring to God's nature. (John 14:11)

The Harmonized Gospels — Apocalyptic Version

T 'At that day you shall know that I am in my Father, and you in me, and I in you.	Jn14:20
U 'He that hears my commandments and keeps them, is he that loves me. He that loves me shall be loved of my Father, and I will love him and will manifest myself to him'.	Jn14:21
V Judas, not Iscariot, said 'Lord, how is it that you will manifest yourself to us and not unto the world'?	Jn14:22
W Jesus replied 'If a man loves me, he will keep my words and my Father will love him, and we will come to him and make our abode with him.	Jn14:23
X 'He that does not love me will not keep my sayings. These words which you hear is not mine but the Father's which sent me.	Jn14:24
Y 'These things I have spoken to you while yet present with you.	Jn14:25
Z 'The help of the Godly Nature which the Father will send to you because of me, shall teach you all things and bring all things to your remembrance that I have said unto you.	Jn14:26
AA 'Peace I leave with you. My peace I give to you, unlike anything the world can give. This I give to you. Let not your heart be troubled, neither let it be afraid.	Jn14:27
AB 'You have heard how I said to you that I am going away and will come again to you. If you loved me, you would rejoice, because I said that I go to the Father. For my Father is greater than I.	Jn14:28
AC 'And now I have told you before it has occurred, so that when it comes to pass, you might believe.	Jn14:29
AD 'Hereafter I will not talk much with you, for the prince of this world[1] comes, and he has nothing in me.	Jn14:30
AE 'So that the world may know that I love the Father, I do all as the Father commanded'.	Jn14:31

---

1 Christ was referring to Satan. (Matt 4:8; Eph 2:2; Rev 12:9)

The Harmonized Gospels — Apocalyptic Version

CHAPTER 148
Jesus' last sermon to his disciples (II)

A 'I am the true vine and my Father is the vinedresser.	Jn15:1
B 'If a branch in me does not bear fruit, he will take it away, but if a branch bears fruit, he will prune it so that it bears more fruit.	Jn15:2
C 'Your heart is now right because of the words which I have spoken to you.	Jn15:3
D 'Stay with me and I will be with you. The branch cannot bear fruit by itself without being attached to the vine. So too you cannot bear fruit except you are in me.	Jn15:4
E 'I am the vine and you are the branches. He that lives in me and I in him, will bear much fruit, for without me you can do nothing.	Jn15:5
F 'If a man is not in me, he will dry up as a withered branch and men will gather it to throw into the fire, where it is burnt up.	Jn15:6
G 'If you live in me and my words remain in you, you will ask whatever you like and it will be done for you.	Jn15:7
H 'How will my Father be greatly honored and praised? Only if you bear much fruit. Then only will you be my disciples.	Jn15:8
I 'As the Father has loved me, so have I loved you. Stay in my love.	Jn15:9
J 'If you follow my instructions, you will stay in my love, even as I have kept my Father's instructions and retain his love.	Jn15:10
K 'I have told you these things so that my joy might be in you and that your joy might abound.	Jn15:11
L 'This is my commandment. You should love one another as I have loved you.	Jn15:12
M 'What is the greatest love that a man can have? It is that he lay down his life for his friends.	Jn15:13
N 'You are my friends if you do whatsoever I command you.	Jn15:14
O 'From now on I do not call you servants for the servant does not know what his lord is planning, but I call you friends, because all that I have heard of my Father, I have told you.	Jn15:15
P 'You have not chosen me, but I chose you so that you should go out and bear fruit. Your fruit is sure, for whatsoever you shall ask of the Father in my name, he will give it to you.	Jn15:16
Q 'I command you again that you love one another.	Jn15:17
R 'If the world hates you, know that it hated me before it hated you.	Jn15:18
S 'If you were of the world, the world would love its own. But you are not of the world, because I have chosen you to come out of the world. Therefore the world hates you.	Jn15:19
T 'Remember what I said to you, that the servant is not greater than his lord. If they persecuted me, they will also persecute you. If they accepted my teaching, they will also accept yours.	Jn15:20
U 'But they will do all kinds of things to you because of me, because they do not know the one that sent me.	Jn15:21

The Harmonized Gospels — Apocalyptic Version

V 'If I had not come and spoken to them, they would not be accountable for their sin, but now they have no excuse for their sin. | Jn15:22

W 'He that hates me hates my Father also. | Jn15:23

X 'If I had not done among them works that were never done before by any other man, they would not be accountable for their sin, but they saw and hated both me and my Father. | Jn15:24

Y 'But this must take place so that the word might be fulfilled that is written in their books of the law "They hated me without a cause[1]". | Jn15:25

Z 'When the Helper comes, which I will send to you from the Father, even that Spirit of truth which originates from the Father, that will be proof of me. | Jn15:26

AA 'And you also shall bear witness of me, because you have been with me from the beginning'. | Jn15:27

CHAPTER 149
Jesus' last sermon to his disciples (III)

A 'I tell you these things so that you should not lose heart. | Jn16:1

B 'They shall expel you from the synagogues, and indeed the time will come when whosoever kills you will think that he is doing it for God. | Jn16:2

C 'All these things they will do to you, because they do not know the Father or me. | Jn16:3

D 'I am telling you these things now, so that when the time comes, you will remember that I told you of them. I did not tell you these things before because I was with you. | Jn16:4

E 'But now I go to him who sent me. You have asked me "Where are you going"? | Jn16:5

F 'and because I have said these things to you, your heart is overcome with sorrow. | Jn16:6

G 'Nevertheless I am telling you the truth when I say it is expedient for you that I go away. For if I do not go away, the Helper will not come to you, but if I leave, I will send it to you. | Jn16:7

H 'When it has come, it will show the world what sin is and what is righteousness and justice. | Jn16:8

I 'The sin is that they did not believe me. | Jn16:9

J 'Righteousness is that I go to my Father, and you will no longer see me. | Jn16:10

K 'Justice is that the prince of this world is judged. | Jn16:11

L 'I have many more things to tell you, but you cannot cope with them now. | Jn16:12

M 'However, when the Spirit of truth comes, it will guide you into all | Jn16:13

---

1 Ps 35:19; Ps 69:4

truth, for it does not speak by itself but of what it has been directed to say, and it will reveal to you the things to come.

N 'It will honor me, for all that it is directed by me to do, it will reveal you. | Jn16:14

O 'All the things that the Father has, are given to me, which is why I said that it shall take whatever I direct and reveal it to you. | Jn16:15

P 'In a little while you will not see me, but after a little while longer, you shall see me, because I go to the Father'. | Jn16:16

Q His disciples were puzzled by his statement 'In a little while you will not see me, but after a little while longer, you shall see me, because I go to the Father'? | Jn16:17

R One voiced 'What does he mean when he says " A little while?" we don't understand what he is saying'. | Jn16:18

S Jesus knew that they wanted to ask him, so he said 'Are you talking about what I mean when I say "A little while, and you shall not see me, but in a little while longer you shall see me"? | Jn16:19

T 'In truth I tell you that you shall weep and lament, but the world shall rejoice. You shall be sorrowful, but your sorrow shall be turned into joy. | Jn16:20

U 'A woman is in pain at the time of her childbirth, but as soon as she delivers, she thinks no more of her anguish, for the joy of bringing a child into the world. | Jn16:21

V 'You likewise are now sorrowful, but I will see you again, and then your heart shall rejoice. That joy no man can take from you. | Jn16:22

W 'At that time you will no longer need for me to explain. In truth I tell you that whatsoever you shall ask the Father in my name, he will give it you. | Jn16:23

X 'Up to now you have not asked anything in my name, but henceforth ask in my name and you shall receive, so that your joy may be full. | Jn16:24

Y 'Some things that I have spoken to you are unclear, but the time is coming when I shall no longer speak to you obtusely, but I shall tell you plainly of the Father. | Jn16:25

Z 'In that day you shall ask in my name, and as I said to you before, I will pray the Father for you. | Jn16:26

AA 'For the Father himself loves you, because you have loved me and have believed that I came out from God. | Jn16:27

AB 'I came out from the Father and came into the world. Now I leave the world and go back to the Father'. | Jn16:28

AC His disciples said 'Indeed you are now speaking plainly and not in riddles. | Jn16:29

AD 'We are now sure that you know all things, and this need not be questioned by any man. We believe that you came out from God'. | Jn16:30

AE Jesus said 'Do you think you now believe? | Jn16:31

AF 'I tell you that the hour is coming, and is now close at hand, when you shall be scattered, every man to himself, and shall leave me | Jn16:32

alone. Yet I am not alone because the Father is with me.
AG 'I have told you these things so that, in me, you might have peace. In the world you shall have tribulation. But be of good cheer, for I have overcome the world'. | Jn16:33

CHAPTER 150
Jesus' prayer for his disciples.

A After Jesus had said these things, he looked up to heaven and said 'Father, the time has come. Glorify your Son, that your Son also may show your majesty. | Jn17:1

B 'For you have given him power over all flesh, that he should give immortality to as many as you have given him. | Jn17:2

C 'And for what use is immortality? It is that they might know you, the only true God, and Jesus Christ, whom you have sent. | Jn17:3

D 'I have shown your majesty on the earth. I have finished the work which you gave me to do. | Jn17:4

E 'And now, O Father, glorify me with your own Spirit, which I had with you before the world was made. | Jn17:5

F 'I have shown who you are to the men which you gave me out of the world. They were yours and you gave them to me, and they have cherished your word. | Jn17:6

G 'They know now, that all that you empowered me to do, came from you. | Jn17:7

H 'For I have told them the words which you directed me and they have received them. They surely know that I came out from you and they have believed that you did indeed send me. | Jn17:8

I 'I pray for them. I do not pray for the world, but for these which you have given me, for they are yours. | Jn17:9

J 'All that are mine are yours and all that are yours are mine, and I am honored in them. | Jn17:10

K 'From now on, I shall be no more in the world, but these are in the world, for I come to you. Holy Father, keep by your power, those who you have given me, that they may be one, as we are. | Jn17:11

L 'While I was with them in the world, I kept them faithful to you. All those that you gave me I have kept, and none of them is lost, but for the son of perdition, that the scripture might be fulfilled. | Jn17:12

M 'Now I come to you and I tell them these things while I am in the world, that they too might share in my joy. | Jn17:13

N 'I have told them your words and the world has rejected them, because they are not of the world, even as I am not of the world. | Jn17:14

O 'I do not pray that you should take them out of the world but that you should keep them from the evil. | Jn17:15

P 'They are not of the world even as I am not of the world. | Jn17:16

Q 'Sanctify them by your truth. Your word is truth. | Jn17:17

The Harmonized Gospels — Apocalyptic Version

R 'As you have sent me into the world, even so have I also sent them into the world.	Jn17:18
S 'And for their sake I give myself, that they also might be sanctified through the truth.	Jn17:19
T 'I do not pray for these alone, but for all those who shall believe on me through their witness.	Jn17:20
U 'I pray that they may all be one, as you Father are in me and I in you, that they may also be one in us, so that the world may believe that you have sent me.	Jn17:21
V 'The honor which you gave me, I have given them, so that they may be one, even as we are one.	Jn17:22
W 'I in them, and you in me, that they may be made perfect in oneness and that the world may know that you have sent me, and have loved them, as you have loved me.	Jn17:23
X 'Father, I ask also that those who you have given me, be with me always, that they may see my glory, which you have given me, for you loved me before the foundation of the world.	Jn17:24
Y 'O righteous Father, the world has not known you, but I have known you, and these have known that you have sent me.	Jn17:25
Z 'I have declared to them your majesty and will continue to declare it, that the love with which you loved me may be in them, and I in them'.	Jn17:26
AA They ended the observance with an hymn and then went out to the Mount of Olives.	Mt26:30; Mk14:26 Lk22:39

CHAPTER 151
Jesus prays at Gethsemane

A Jesus led them to a place called Gethsemane, which was a garden across the brook called Cedron. There he said to the disciples 'Wait here, while I go and pray,'	Mt26:36; Mk14:32 Lk22:39; Jn18:1
B and taking with him Peter and the two sons of Zebedee, James and John, he went about a stone's throw away. As his coming trial started to weigh down on him,	Mt26:37; Mk14:33 Lk22:41
C he said to them 'I am sorrowful, for my death comes. Stay here and wait with me. Pray too that you do not fail when trials come'.	Mt26:38; Mk14:34 Lk22:40
D Jesus then went a little further and falling on his face, he prayed that this trial be taken from him if possible.	Mt26:39; Mk14:35
E He prayed 'O my Father, all things are possible for you. Make this cup pass from me. Nevertheless, let it be, not as I would, but according to your will'.	Mt26:39; Mk14:36 Lk22:42
F An angel from heaven also came to strengthen him.	Lk22:43
G He was in deep distress and prayed with such feeling that sweat was dripping from him as great drops of blood falling to the ground.	Lk22:44
H He come back to where the disciples were, and saw that they were asleep. He woke them and said to Peter 'Could you not stay awake with me for one hour?	Mt26:40; Mk14:37 Lk22:45
I 'Be alert and pray that you do not falter, for the mind indeed is willing, but the body is weak'.	Mt26:41; Mk14:38 Lk22:46
J Jesus went back a second time and prayed 'My Father, if this cup cannot pass me and I must drink of it, your will be done'.	Mt26:42; Mk14:39
K Coming back to the disciples, he found them all asleep again, for their eyes were heavy. When he woke them they were at loss for words.	Mt26:43; Mk14:40
L He left them a third time to pray, saying much the same words.	Mt26:44; Mk14:41
M He came back to find his disciples asleep again. He woke them and said 'Is this the time to sleep or let down your guard? Look, the time has come for me to be delivered into the hands of sinners.	Mt26:45; Mk14:41
N 'Get up, let us get going, for the one who is to betray me is here'.	Mt26:46; Mk14:42

CHAPTER 152
Jesus arrested

A Judas, who betrayed Jesus, knew the place where he frequented with his disciples.	Jn18:2
B Just as Jesus finished speaking, Judas, one of the twelve *disciples*, came accompanied with a large group of men, armed with lanterns, torches, swords and sticks. These were sent by the chief priests, the scribes and the civil leaders of the people.	Mt26:47; Mk14:43 Lk22:47; Jn18:3
C Now the betrayer of Jesus had said to them 'The one that I kiss, is the one. Secure him quickly'.	Mt26:48; Mk14:44
D So he came to straight to Jesus and after greeting Jesus with the words, 'Hello, master', he kissed him.	Mt26:49; Mk14:45
E Jesus asked him 'Friend, do you betray me with a kiss'?	Mt26:50; Mk14:46 Lk22:48
F Jesus, who knew what was about to happen, stepped forward and asked 'Who do you seek'?	Jn18:4
G They replied 'Jesus of Nazareth'. Jesus said 'I am he'.	Jn18:5
H As soon as he said this to them, they went backward, and fell to the ground.	Jn18:6
I He again asked 'Whom do you seek'? They said again 'Jesus of Nazareth'.	Jn18:7
J Jesus replied 'I have told you that I am he. If therefore you seek me, let these go their way'.	Jn18:8
K He did this that the statement he made might be fulfilled, when he said 'Of those who you gave me, I have lost none'.	Jn18:9
L When his companions saw what was transpiring, one said 'Lord, shall we attack them with the sword'?	Lk22:49
M Then Simon Peter drew out his sword and struck at a servant of the high priest, named Malchus, cutting off his ear.	Mt26:51; Mk14:47 Lk22:50; Jn18:10
N Jesus said to Peter 'Put away your sword in its sheath, for all who use the sword, will perish by the sword'. Jesus then touched the man's ear and healed it.	Mt26:52; Lk22:51
O Jesus continued 'The cup which my Father has given me, shall I not drink it?	Jn18:11
P 'Do you not know that even now, I can pray to my Father, and he will immediately send me more than twelve legions of angels?	Mt26:53
Q 'But how then will the scriptures be fulfilled? It must indeed be this way'.	Mt26:54
R Then Jesus addressed the senior Priests, captains and elders who had come with the multitude saying 'Have you come with swords and staves to take me, as if I were a	Mt26:55; Mk14:48 Lk22:52

The Harmonized Gospels — Apocalyptic Version

thief?
S I sat in the temple, and taught day after day, but you did not seize me then, but this is your hour, when darkness reigns. | *Mt26:55; Mk14:49*
Lk22:53

T 'You have done this though, to fulfill the scriptures given by the prophets'. | *Mt26:56; Mk14:49*

U The band and the captain and officers of the Jews took Jesus, and bound him. All the disciples deserted him, and ran away, | *Jn18:12*
Mt26:56; Mk14:50

V except for a certain young man who wore a linen wrap, However, when the band of men sought to seize him, | *Mk14:51*

W he also left the linen cloth in their hands and fled from them naked. | *Mk14:52*

X Those that had seized Jesus, led him away to Annas first, for he was the father-in-law of Caiaphas, who was the high priest that year. | *Jn18:13*

Y This was the same Caiaphas who gave counsel to the Jews, that it was expedient that one man should die for the people[1]. | *Jn18:14*

Z Afterwards they took him to Caiaphas the high priest, who was waiting with an assembly of the scribes and the civic leaders. | *Mt26:57; Mk14:53*
Lk22:54; Jn18:24

CHAPTER 153
The trial before Caiaphas

A Simon Peter, together with another disciple, followed Jesus some distance behind. That disciple was known to the high priest, and went in with the group into the palace of the high priest. | *Mt26:58; Mk14:54*
Lk22:54, 55
Jn18:15

B Peter, however, stood outside the door. The other disciple went and spoke to the woman who was at the door, and she let Peter in. | *Jn18:16*

C The servants and officials stood together around a fire they had made, because it was cold. They warmed themselves and Peter stood with them to warm himself. | *Jn18:18*

D The high priest asked Jesus of his disciples, and of his doctrine. | *Jn18:19*

E Jesus answered 'I spoke openly in public. I taught in synagogues and in the temple, where the Jews were always present. I have said nothing in secret. | *Jn18:20*

F 'Why do you ask me? Ask those who heard me about what | *Jn18:21*

---

1 John 11:40

The Harmonized Gospels — Apocalyptic Version

I said to them. Look, they know what I said'.

G When he said this, one of the officers who stood nearby struck Jesus with the palm of his hand and said 'How dare you answer the high priest in this manner'? | Jn18:22

H Jesus answered 'If I have spoken lies, tell of it, but if the truth, why do you smite me'? | Jn18:23

I The chief priests and all the men on the council were looking for anyone willing to give false evidence against Jesus, so they could put him to death. | Mt26:59; Mk14:55

J Many false witnesses came forward, but their testimony was contradictory. | Mt26:60; Mk14:56
Mk14:59

K Eventually, two came forward, | Mt26:60; Mk14:57

L and said 'We heard this man say, "I am able to destroy this temple made by hand, and to build another in three days without hands".' | Mt26:61; Mk14:58

M As the day dawned, the high priest got up and said to Jesus 'What do you have to say about these accusations against you'? | Mt26:62; Mk14:60
Lk22:66, 67

N But Jesus said nothing. Then the high priest said to him 'I ask you in the name of the living God, that you tell us whether you are the Christ, the Son of God'. | Mt26:63; Mk16:61

O Jesus the said to him 'If I tell you, you will not believe and if I were to question you, you will not answer me, nor let me go. I tell you, that the next time you see me, I will be appointed to the right hand of the Almighty, and coming from the clouds in the heavens'. | Mt26:64; Mk16:62
Lk22:68, 69

P They asked him again 'Tell us. Are you the Son of God'? He said to them 'It is as you say'. | Lk22:70

Q The high priest then tore his clothes and said 'He has blasphemed. We have no need for any more witnesses. You have heard his blasphemy. | Mt26:65; Mk14:63
Lk22:71

R 'What now is your judgment'? The council replied 'He is guilty and deserving of the death penalty'. | Mt26:66; Mk14:64

S Then some spat on him and ridiculed him. They blindfolded him and slapped him | Mt26:67; Mk14:65
Lk22:63

T saying 'Prophesy to us, if you are the Christ. Tell us who just slapped you'? | Mt26:68; Mk14:65
Lk22:64

U They did many other things to him and blasphemed him. | Lk22:65

CHAPTER 154
Peter denies Christ

A Peter was in a lower chamber of the palace when these events were taking place. A maid of the high priest	*Mt26:69; Mk14:66*
B saw Peter warming himself and said 'Were you not with Jesus in Galilee?	*Mt26:69; Mk14:67 Lk22:56; Jn18:17*
C In front of all who were there, Peter denied knowing Christ saying 'I do not know what you are talking about'. He went out into the porch just as the cock crew.	*Mt26:70; Mk14:68 Lk22:57; Jn18:17*
D Another woman saw him and said to those that were there 'This man was with Jesus of Nazareth'.	*Mt26:71; Mk14:69 Lk22:58; Jn18:25*
E Again Peter denied the accusation. This time he swore and said 'I do not know the man'.	*Mt26:72; Mk14:70 Lk22:58*
F After a while, one of the servants of the high priest, who was a kinsman of the one whose ear was cut off said 'Did I not see you in the garden with him? Surely you must be one of them, for you are a Galilean and your speech betrays you'.	*Mt26:73; Mk14:70 Lk22:59; Jn18:26*
G Peter vehemently began to curse and he again swore saying 'I do not know the man'.	*Mt26:74; Mk14:71 Lk22:60*
H The cock crew a second time and the Lord turned and looked at Peter. Peter then remembered that Jesus had said to him 'Before the cock crow twice, you shall deny me thrice'[1]. Peter went outside and wept bitterly.	*Mt26:75; Mk14:72 Lk22:60 ~ 62 Jn18:27*

---

1 John 13:38

CHAPTER 155
Judas repents

A Judas, who had betrayed Jesus, was filled with remorse when he saw that Christ was condemned. He took the thirty pieces of silver, which he had received and went back to the chief priests and leaders of the people and told them,	Mt27:3
B 'I have sinned for I have betrayed the innocent'. They replied to him 'So, what does that have to do with us? That is your business'.	Mt27:4
C Judas then threw down the pieces of silver in the temple, and went away and hanged himself[1].	Mt27:5
D The chief priests considered what to do with the silver pieces, and one said 'It is not lawful to return the money to the treasury, because it is the price of blood'.	Mt27:6
E So they decided to take the money and buy a field from a potter, and use it for burying strangers.	Mt27:7
F That is why, *even to the date of this writing*, that field is called 'The field of blood'.	Mt27:8
G All of this fulfilled the prophecy given by Jeremy the prophet, that says 'They took the thirty pieces of silver, which was the price that the children of Israel valued him at,	Mt27:9
H 'and bought the field of a potter. This was the lot the Lord appointed to me[2]'.	Mt27:10

CHAPTER 156
Jesus taken before Pontius Pilate

A Early in the morning the whole council, which included the chief priests, the scribes and the civic leaders, met to determine how they may put Jesus to death.	Mt27:1; Mk15:1 Jn18:28
B They shackled him, and followed by a large crowd, they took him from Caiaphas to the hall of judgment of Pontius Pilate, the governor.	Mt27:2; Mk15:1 Lk23:1; Jn18:28
C They themselves did not go into the judgment hall, as that would cause them to be defiled and keep them from eating the Passover.	Jn18:28
D Pilate went out to them and asked 'What accusation do you bring against this man'?	Jn18:29

---

1 Judas went about this act so energetically that his body tore away at the noose and fell some distance, spilling out his intestines (Acts 1:18).
2 Zech 11:13

The Harmonized Gospels — Apocalyptic Version

E The chief priests and leaders presented their accusations against him, claiming that he was perverting the nation, and telling others not to give tribute to Caesar saying that he himself is Christ the King.	Mt27:12; Mk15:3 Lk23:2
F Pilate asked 'Why do you not take him and judge him according to your law'? The Jews replied 'It is not lawful for us to put any man to death'.	Jn18:31
G This was so that the saying of Jesus might come to pass, for he had spoken of how he should die.	Jn18:32
H Pilate went back in the judgment hall and asked Jesus 'Are you the King of the Jews'?	Mt27:11; Mk15:2 Jn18:33
I Jesus asked 'Did you ask this on your own or did someone tell this to you'?	Jn18:34
J Pilate replied 'Am I a Jew? Your own nation and the chief priests have delivered you to me. What have you done'?	Jn18:35
K Jesus answered 'My kingdom is not of this world. If my kingdom was of this world, then my servants would fight so that I not be delivered to the Jews. But my kingdom is not from now'.	Jn18:36
L Pilate asked again 'Art you a king then'? Jesus answered 'You ask if I am a king. For this purpose I was born, and for this reason I came into the world, so that I should witness to the truth. Every one that is true hears my voice'.	Lk23:3; Jn18:37
M Pilate said to him 'What is truth'? Then he went back out to the Jews and said 'I find no fault in him at all'.	Lk23:4; Jn18:38
N They answered 'If he was not a malefactor, we would not have brought him to you'.	Jn18:30
O Pilate went again to Jesus and said 'Have you nothing to say. Look how many accusations they heap against you'?	Mt27:13; Mk15:4
P But Jesus did not respond. The governor saw this and was greatly impressed.	Mt27:12, 14; Mk15:5; Lk23:5
Q The accusers on the other hand were all the more adamant saying 'He is stirring up the people throughout Judah starting from Galilee and all up to this place'.	Lk23:5
R When Pilate heard them mention Galilee, he asked whether the man were a Galilaean.	Lk23:6
S When Pilate ascertained that Jesus came from Herod's jurisdiction, he sent him over to Herod, who was at Jerusalem at that time.	Lk23:7

CHAPTER 157
Jesus taken before Herod

A Herod the tetrarch had heard of the fame of Jesus.   Mt14:1; Mk6:14
B He said to his servants 'This is John the Baptist, who is risen from the dead, which is why he can do such mighty works'.   Mt14:2; Mk6:14; Lk9:7
C Some disputed and claimed that he was Elias while others said 'He is like one of the ancient prophets'.   Mk6:15; Lk9:8
D But Herod insisted 'It is John, whom I beheaded and who is risen from the dead', and he desired to see him.   Mk6:16; Lk9:9
E Thus when Herod saw Jesus, he was very excited, for he had heard many things about him and wanted to see him for a long time. He was even hoping to see Jesus do some miracle before him.   Lk23:8
F Herod questioned Jesus about many things, but Jesus did not say a word to him.   Lk23:9
G All the while the chief priests and scribes stood and leveled accusations against him.   Lk23:10
H Finally Herod and his soldiers began to ridicule and mock him. They put on him a fine robe of scarlet and purple and sent him back to Pilate.   Mt27:28; Mk15:17; Lk23:11; Jn19:2
I That same day Pilate and Herod became friends, for there had previous been some antagonism between them.   Lk23:12

CHAPTER 158
Jesus taken back to Pilate

A The soldiers of the governor took Jesus into the hall, called the Praetorium, and a band of them gathered around Jesus.   Mt27:27; Mk15:16
B They plaited a crown of thorns, which they put on his head, and they put a staff in his right hand.   Mt27:29; Mk15:17; Jn19:2
C Then they knelt before him, and mocked him, saying 'Hail, King of the Jews!'   Mt27:29; Mk15:18; Jn19:3
D Pilate met again with the chief priests and the rulers in the presence of the people and said 'Look I am bringing him out to you that you may know that I find no fault in him'.   Lk23:13; Jn19:4
E 'You have brought this man to me, saying that he is fomenting rebellion among the people. I have examined him in front of you and have found no fault in this man about those things which you accuse him of.   Lk23:14
F 'So too has Herod, when I sent you to him. This man has done nothing for which he should be put to death.   Lk23:15

The Harmonized Gospels — Apocalyptic Version

G 'I will therefore scourge him and let him go'.	*Lk23:16*
H Then Jesus was brought out wearing the crown of thorns, and the purple robe. Pilate said to them 'Look, here is the man!'	*Jn19:5*
I When the chief priests and officers saw him like this, they shouted out 'Crucify him, crucify him'. Pilate said to them 'You take him and crucify him, for I find no fault in him'.	*Jn19:6*
J The Jews replied 'We have a law, and by our law he ought to die, because he made himself the Son of God'.	*Jn19:7*
K When Pilate heard this he was all the more afraid.	*Jn19:8*
L He went back into the judgment hall with Jesus and said to him 'Where are you from'? Jesus, however, did not answer him.	*Jn19:9*
M Then Pilate said to him 'Do you refuse to speak to me? Do you not know that I have the power to crucify you, and I have the power to release you'?	*Jn19:10*
N Jesus replied 'You could have no power at all against me, except it were given to you from above. Therefore, he that delivered me to you bears the greater responsibility'.	*Jn19:11*
O From then Pilate sought for a way to release Jesus.	*Jn19:12*
P The soldiers meanwhile spat upon Jesus, and took the staff from his hand and beat him on his head with it.	*Mt27:30; Mk15:19*
Q When they had their fill of mocking him, they took off the robe of scarlet and purple and put back his own clothes on him.	*Mt27:31; Mk15:20*
R It was close to the time of the feast days, when it was customary for the governor to release a prisoner, who was chosen by the people.	*Mt27:15; Mk15:6; Lk23:17*
S The crowd which had gathered, started to clamor for Pilate to follow this tradition.	*Mk15:8*
T At that time a well known prisoner, called Barabbas, was in custody. He was a robber and had committed murder during an insurrection.	*Mt27:16; Mk15:7; Lk23:19; Jn18:40*
U Pilate asked them 'Who would you like me to release to you? Would you prefer Barabbas, or Jesus which is called the Christ'?	*Mt27:17; Mk15:9; Jn18:39*
V Pilate did this for he knew that Jesus was being accused because the chief priests envied him.	*Mt27:18; Mk15:10*
W (His wife had also sent him a message when he sat down to judge saying 'Have nothing to do with that righteous man, for I have had visions of him in my dreams').	*Mt27:19*
X The chief priests and leaders however, stirred up the multitude to ask for Barabbas to be released and for Jesus to be killed.	*Mt27:20; Mk15:11*
Y So when the governor asked them 'Which of them should I release to you?' They said 'Barabbas'.	*Mt27:21; Lk23:18*

The Harmonized Gospels — Apocalyptic Version

Z The killing of the Passover was about six hours away[1]. Pilate, wanting to release Jesus said to the Jews. What shall I do with this Jesus, whom you call the King of the Jews'?	Jn18:40 Mt27:22; Mk15:12 Lk23:20; Jn19:14
AA They shouted 'Take him away, take him and crucify him'. Pilate asked 'Shall I crucify your King'? The chief priests answered 'We have no king but Caesar'.	Mt27:22; Mk15;13 Lk23:21
AB The governor said to them a third time 'Why, what evil has he done? I have found no cause that he should be put to death. I will therefore scourge him and let him go'.	Mt27:23; Mk15:14 Lk23:22, 23
AC The But they shouted even more vigorously 'Take him away and crucify him. If you let this man go, you are not Caesar's friend, for whosoever makes himself a king speaks against Caesar'.	Mt27:23; Mk15:14 Jn19:12; 15
AD When Pilate heard this and saw that he could not do otherwise if he did not want a riot to break out, he brought Jesus out and sat down in the judgment seat in a place that is called the Pavement, but in the Hebrew, Gabbatha.	Mt27:24; Jn19:13
AE He sent for water, and washing his hands before the crowd, he said 'I am innocent of the blood of this righteous man. It is now up to you'.	Mt27:24
AF Then all the people said 'Let his blood be on us, and on our children'.	Mt27:25
AG So the governor released Barabbas and delivered Jesus to be scourged and crucified. They took Jesus, and led him away.	Mt27:26; Mk15:15 Lk23:24, 25 Jn19:1, 16

CHAPTER 159
The crucifixion

A Jesus carrying his cross, started out for the place of the skull, which is called Golgotha in Hebrew.	Jn19:17
B On the way to the crucifixion site, the soldiers ordered a man named Simon to carry the cross. Simon, the father of Alexander and Rufus, had come from the district of Cyrene and was going about his business at the time.	Mt27:32; Mk15:21 Lk23:26
C Following him was a great crowd of people and women, which who were weeping and lamenting.	Lk23:27
D Jesus turned to them and said 'Daughters of Jerusalem, do not weep for me, but weep for yourselves and for your children.	Lk23:28
E 'For the days are coming, when they shall say, "Blessed are the barren and the wombs that never bore child, or the	Lk23:29

---

1 P. Ramsundar, 'Dating Christ's Crucifixion' American Journal of Biblical Theology 2010, 9(52).

The Harmonized Gospels — Apocalyptic Version

breasts that never gave suck".

F 'Then they shall say to the mountains "Fall on us". and to the hills "Cover us". — *Lk23:30*

G 'For if they do these things to a green tree, what will they do to the dry'? — *Lk23:31*

H They arrived in Calvary at the place called Golgotha, which means 'place of the skull'. — *Mt27:33; Mk15:22*

I There they gave him a drink of vinegar mixed with myrrh, but when he had tasted it, he refused it. — *Mt27:34; Mk15:23*

J At the third hour they crucified him. — *Mt27:35; Mk15:25; Mt27:35; Mk15:24*

K Jesus said then 'Father, forgive them, for they do not know what they are doing'. — *Lk23:34*

L After the soldiers crucified him, they divided his garments into four parts, to distribute among themselves, but when they got to his coat they found it was without seam and woven in one piece. — *Mt27:36; Jn19:23*

M One said 'Let us not cut it, but cast lots for it' and the rest agreed. This fulfilled the scripture which said 'They parted my clothes among them, and for my coat they cast lots'[1]. The soldiers then sat down to watch. — *Jn19:24*

N Pilate had a sign made and put it on the cross. The writing was in Greek, Latin and Hebrew and said 'THIS IS JESUS OF NAZARETH, THE KING OF THE JEWS'. — *Mt27:37; Mk15:26; Lk23:38; Jn19:19*

O This sign was seen by many of the Jews, for the place where Jesus was crucified was near the city. — *Jn19:20*

P The chief priests of the Jews went to Pilate and said 'Do not write 'The King of the Jews', but that he said, I am King of the Jews'. — *Jn19:21*

Q Pilate replied 'What I have written I have written'. — *Jn19:22*

R Standing at the cross of Jesus were his mother, her sister Mary of Cleophas, and Mary Magdalene. Some distance away was Mary mother of James the less and Joses, and Salome the mother of the sons of Zebedee. — *Jn19:25; Mt27:56; Mk15:40*

S When Jesus saw his mother standing nearby with the disciple whom he loved, he said to his mother 'Mother, look at your son!' — *Jn19:26*

T Looking at the disciple he said 'Look at your mother'. (From then onwards the disciple would take care of her and she would dwell in his house). — *Jn19:27*

U Two thieves were also crucified at the same time with him. One was on his right hand, and the other on the left. — *Mt27:38; Mk15:27; Lk23:32, 33; Jn19:18*

---

1 Psalm 22:18

The Harmonized Gospels — Apocalyptic Version

V This fulfilled the scripture that said 'He was numbered with the lawbreakers[1]'.	Mk15:28
W The people that were there, insulted and mocked him	Mt27:39; Mk15:29
X saying 'You who say that you will destroy the temple and rebuild it in three days, why don't you save yourself. If you are the Son of God, come down from the cross'.	Mt27:40; Mk15:30
Y The chief priests, the scribes and leaders also mocked him saying,	Mt27:41; Mk15:31
Z 'He saved others, but he cannot save himself. If he truly is the Christ, the King of Israel, let him come down from the cross, and we will believe him.	Mt27:42; Mk15:32 Lk23:35
AA 'He claimed to know God. Let God deliver him now, if he wants him. Did he not say "I am the Son of God".'	Mt27:43
AB The soldiers offered him vinegar,	Lk23:36
AC and also mocked him saying 'If you are the king of the Jews, save yourself'.	Lk23:37
AD One of the criminals who was crucified with him also upbraided him, saying 'If you are the Christ, save yourself and us'.	Mt27:44; Mk15:32 Lk23:39
AE But the other one rebuked him saying 'Do you not fear God. We all received the same condemnation.	Lk23:40
AF 'We are justly condemned for we have received a fair recompense for our deeds, but this man has done nothing amiss'.	Lk23:41
AG To Jesus he said 'Lord, remember me when you inherit your kingdom'.	Lk23:42
AH Jesus said to him 'I tell you now with certainty that you shall join me in paradise'.	Lk23:43
AI When it was noon, a darkness came over all the land until the ninth hour.	Mt27:45; Mk15:33 Lk23:44, 45
AJ Jesus cried out 'Eli, Eli, lama sabachthani' which means 'My God, my God, why have you forsaken me[2]?'	Mt27:46; Mk15:34
AK When those standing nearby heard him, one said 'He is calling for Elias'.	Mt27:47; Mk15:35
AL After this, Jesus knowing that everything was accomplished to fulfill the scripture said 'I thirst'.	Jn19:28
AM A vessel of vinegar was set nearby and one ran and soaking a sponge with vinegar, he stuck it on a stick and raised it for him to drink.	Mt27:48; Mk15:36 Jn19:29
AN After Jesus drank of the vinegar someone said 'Leave him alone. Let us see whether Elias will come and save him'.	Mt27:49; Mk15:36
AO But another took a spear and thrust it into his side, releasing a gush of blood and water[3].	(Mt27:49); Jn19:34

---

1 Is 53:12
2 Psalm 22:1.
3 Fenton and Moffatt translations.

The Harmonized Gospels — Apocalyptic Version

AP Jesus cried out and said 'It is finished. Father, into your hands I entrust my spirit'. After saying this he died.	Mt27:50; Mk15:37 Lk23:46; Jn19:30
AQ At the same time, the veil of the temple was split in two from the top to the bottom and there was also an earthquake. Rocks were split apart	Mt27:51; Mk15:38 Lk23:45
AR and the graves of many of the righteous were broken open and they came back to life[1].	Mt27:52
AS These came out of their graves after being brought back to life, and went into the city, where many can witness of it.	Mt27:53
AT It was the preparation day and since the bodies were not to remain on the cross on the Sabbath day, this Sabbath also being a high day, the Jews went to Pilate and asked for the legs of the crucified be broken, so that they could be taken down.	Jn19:31
AU The soldiers came and broke the legs of the two lawbreakers crucified with Jesus,	Jn19:32
AV but when they came to Jesus and saw that he was already dead, they did not break his legs.	Jn19:33
AW (For one of the soldiers had pierced his side with a spear, and blood and water had issued out of the wound).	Jn19:34
AX One that saw it reported it and his report is reliable and can be trusted.	Jn19:35
AY All these things happened to fulfill the scripture 'A bone of him shall not be broken[2]'	Jn19:36
AZ and also 'They shall look on him whom they pierced[3]'.	Jn19:37
BA A centurion was with those standing guard over Jesus. When they saw the earthquake, and the other things that transpired, they were fearful and the centurion said 'Truly this was a righteous man and the Son of God'.	Mt27:54; Mk15:39 Lk23:47
BB All the people who were there, and who witnessed what happened, beat on their breasts and returned home.	Lk23:48
BC Many of the women who had been helpers of Jesus and others who knew him, were also looking on from a distance	Mt27:55; Mk15:41 Lk23:49

---

1 2Kings 13:21.
2 Psalm 34:20.
3 Psalm 12:10.

CHAPTER 160
The burial

A As the evening approached, a rich man of Arimathaea, named Joseph, who was also a disciple of Jesus, but did not publicize it for fear of the Jews,	Mt27:57; Mk15:43 Lk23:50; Jn19:38
B went to Pilate, and begged him for Jesus' body.	Mt27:58; Mk15:43 Lk23:52
C This man was a counselor and he was a good and fair-minded man, who waited on the God's government. He had not agreed with sentence of the council and their deeds.	Lk23:51
D Pilate wanted confirmation that Jesus was dead, so he called the centurion and asked him whether it was so.	Mk15:44
E The centurion confirmed the matter so Pilate commanded that the body be delivered to Joseph.	Mt27:58; Mk15:45 Jn19:38
F Nicodemus, who had previously visited Jesus by night, brought a mixture of myrrh and aloes, totaling about a hundred pounds.	Jn19:39
G They took the body of Jesus and wrapped it in linen clothes together with the spices, as was the burial custom of the Jews.	Mt27:59; Mk15:46 Jn19:40
H In the place where Jesus was crucified there was a garden nearby, where Joseph had built a new tomb in the rock.	Mt27:60; Mk14:46 Lk23:53; Jn19:41
I There they laid Jesus, because the preparation day[1] before the Jew's Holy Day Sabbath was coming to an end and the sepulcher was nearby.	Mk15:42; Lk23:54 Jn19:42
J They rolled a large stone to seal the sepulcher, and returned home.	Mt27:60; Mk14:46 Lk23:53, 56
K Mary Magdalene and Mary, *the mother* of Joses, were also there at the sepulcher when the body was laid.	Mt27:61; Mk15:47 Lk23:55
L *After the Holy Day Sabbath of the first day of Unleavened Bread was over*, they prepared spices and ointments and then rested on the *weekly* Sabbath day according to the commandment[2].	Lk23:56

---

1 During the days of unleavened bread, four convocations were required by law, viz. Passover, first day of unleavened bread, last day of unleavened bread and the Sabbath (Lev 23:3 ~ 8). Each celebration was preceded by a preparation period. The Pharisees conflated Passover and the first day of unleavened bread, so that one preparation period sufficed for both.

2 Christ was crucified on Wednesday (a preparation day) followed by the first day of unleavened bread Holy Day Sabbath ending on Thursday evening. The women prepared the spices on the Friday, the preparation day for the weekly Sabbath. (see P. Ramsundar, 'Dating Christ's Crucifixion' American Journal of Biblical Theology 2010, 9(52)).

The Harmonized Gospels — Apocalyptic Version

CHAPTER 161
The sealing of the tomb

A The day following *the first day of unleavened bread* was the day of preparation *for the Sabbath*[1], and the chief priests and the Pharisees came as a group to Pilate,	Mt27:62
B and said to him 'Sir, we remember that when that deceiver was alive, he said "After three days I will rise again".	Mt27:63
C 'Order therefore that the sepulcher be guarded for three days, in case his disciples come at night to steal him away and tell the people, "He is risen from the dead," in which case we will end up with a worse situation'.	Mt27:64
D Pilate replied 'I will give you a watch. Take them and secure it as best as you can'.	Mt27:65
E So they went and secured the sepulcher, by putting a seal on the stone and posting guards.	Mt27:66

CHAPTER 162
Mary Magdalene and the women visit the tomb

A After the Sabbath and just before daybreak on the first day of the week[2],	Mt28:1; Mk16:2 Lk24:1
B Mary Magdalene, from whom *Jesus* had cast seven devils, together with Joanna, Salome and Mary, mother of the other James, went to the sepulcher with the fragrant spices to prepare the body.	Mt28:1; Mk16:1 Mk16:9; Lk24:10 Jn20:1
C While on the way, they talked among themselves about getting someone to roll away the stone from the door of the sepulcher. However, this was already done by two angels of the Lord who had come down from the sky and rolled away the stone at the entrance with a loud commotion.	Mt28:2; Mk16:3, 4 Lk24:2,4 Jn20:1
D When the ladies arrived, they saw one of the angels sitting on the stone on the right side of the entrance.	Mk16:5
E The faces of the angels were bright like lightning, and their clothing was as white as snow.	Mt28:3; Mk16:5
F The guards were so afraid that they stood shaking, but otherwise immobile as if they were dead. The women were also afraid and prostrated themselves before the angels.	Mt28:4; Mk16:6
G One of the angels said to the women 'Do not be afraid. I know that you have come to see Jesus, who was crucified.	Mt28:5; Mk16:6; Lk24:5

---

1 See note 2 of Chapter 160.
2 Christ was resurrected before Sunday morning.

The Harmonized Gospels — Apocalyptic Version

H 'However, he is not here. Come and see where the Lord was laid'.	Mt28:6; Mk16:6
I They entered in and saw that the body of the Lord Jesus was not in the tomb.	Lk24:3
J The angel then told them 'Why do you seek the living from among the dead? He has been resurrected as he told you. Remember what he said to you when he was in Galilee,	Lk24:5,6
K that the Son of man must be delivered into the hands of sinful men to be crucified, and that he would be resurrected the third day'?	Lk24:7
L They remembered that Jesus had indeed said these words.	Lk24:8
M The angel continued 'Now go quickly to Peter and the disciples and tell them that he is resurrected, and that he goes before you into Galilee, where you shall see him. It is indeed as I have told you'.	Mt28:7; Mk16:7
N Though they were afraid, they were overjoyed, and hurried from the sepulcher to tell his disciples.	Mt28:8; Mk16:8
O Mary Magdalene said to Simon Peter, who was with the disciple who Jesus had affection for, 'They have taken away the Lord out of the sepulcher and we do not know not where they have taken him'.	Jn20:2; Lk24:9
P Peter and that other disciple immediately left for the sepulcher.	Lk24:12; Jn20:3
Q They both were running but the other disciple arrived at the sepulcher first.	Jn20:4
R He bent down and looked in and saw the linen clothes, but he did not go in.	Jn20:5
S Simon Peter then arrived and he went into the sepulcher and saw the linen clothes folded.	Lk24:12; Jn20:6
T The wrap that was tied around Jesus' head was not together with the linen clothes, but was folded and placed in a separate pile.	Lk24:12; Jn20:7
U The other disciple, who had reached the sepulcher first, saw and understood.	Jn20:8
V For before then they did not understand what the scripture meant by 'he must rise from the dead'.	Jn20:9
W They went back to their lodging wondering at what had happened,	Lk24:12; Jn20:10
X but Mary and the women who had returned with them, stayed at the sepulcher. Mary weeping and in tears, bent down and looked into the sepulcher,	Jn20:11
Y and saw two angels in white sitting. One was at the head and the other at the feet, of where the body of Jesus had lain.	Jn20:12
Z They said to her 'Woman, why are you weeping? She replied 'Because they have taken away my Lord, and I do not	Jn20:13

The Harmonized Gospels — Apocalyptic Version

know where they have carried him'.

AA When she had said this she turned around and saw Jesus standing, but did not know that it was he. — *Jn20:14*

AB Jesus said to her 'Woman, why are you weeping? Who are you looking for'? She, thinking that he may be the gardener said 'Sir, if you have taken him away, tell me where, so that I can get him back'. — *Jn20:15*

AC Jesus said 'Mary'. She looked closely and said 'Rabboni', which is translated 'Master' and held him by his feet. The other women too held his feet and worshipped him. — *Jn20:16; Matt 28:9*

AD Jesus said to them 'Let me go, for I have not yet gone up to my Father. Go to my brethren and tell them that I am going up to my Father, and your Father, and to my God and your God. — *Jn20:17*

AE 'Do not be afraid. Go and tell my brethren that they should go to Galilee, where they shall see me'. — *Mt28:10*

AF Mary Magdalene went and told the disciples that she had seen the Lord, and related all that he had said to her. The other ladies too spoke of what had transpired, — *Mk16:10; Jn20:18*

AG but to the disciples, their words seemed like a fantasy, so they did not believe them. — *Mk16:11; Lk24:11*

CHAPTER 163

Jesus manifests himself to Cleopas

A Later on that day, two of the disciples were walking to a village called Emmaus, which was about eight miles from Jerusalem. — *Lk24:13*

B They were talking about all the things which had taken place recently — *Lk24:14*

C and as they reasoned among themselves, Jesus himself came and walked with them. — *Mk16:12; Lk24:15*

D However, their minds were clouded so that they did not recognize that it was him. — *Lk24:16*

E Jesus asked them 'What matters are you speaking to one another about that make you so sad'? — *Lk24:17*

F One of them, whose name was Cleopas, replied 'Are you a newcomer in Jerusalem, so that you do not know the things that has transpired here in these last few days'? — *Lk24:18*

G Jesus said 'What things'? They answered 'Things about Jesus of Nazareth, a prophet who was mighty in deed and in word, before God and all the people. — *Lk24:19*

H 'And how the chief priests and our rulers have condemned him to death and crucified him. — *Lk24:20*

The Harmonized Gospels — Apocalyptic Version

I 'We had hoped that he would be the one who would redeem Israel. This all took place more than three days ago. — *Lk24:21*

J 'Also some women of our fellowship told us some astonishing things, about how they went at daybreak to the sepulcher, — *Lk24:22*

K 'and did not find his body. They said that they saw angels, who told them that he was alive. — *Lk24:23*

L 'Some of our fellowship then went to the sepulcher and did indeed find it as the women had said, that he was not in the tomb'. — *Lk24:24*

M Then Jesus said to them 'Are you doubters, reluctant to believe all that the prophets have written? — *Lk24:25*

N 'Did not Christ have to suffer all these things to enter into his glory'? — *Lk24:26*

O Then starting with the books of Moses and then expounding the books of the prophets, he explained all the scriptures that pointed to the things concerning himself. — *Lk24:27*

P As they drew close to the village which was their destination, Jesus acted as if he was going further on. — *Lk24:28*

Q They tried to change his mind saying 'Stay with us, for it is getting late and it would be dark soon'. Jesus consented and went in with them. — *Lk24:29*

R As they sat to eat, Jesus took the bread and blessed it and broke off pieces and gave it to them. — *Lk24:30*

S Then their understanding was opened and they realized that it was him. But he straightaway vanished out of their sight. — *Lk24:31*

T One said to the other 'Did not our hearts burn within us on the journey, while he was speaking to us of the scriptures'? — *Lk24:32*

U They got up and promptly returned to Jerusalem, where the eleven were staying with other disciples[1]. — *Lk24:33*

CHAPTER 164

Jesus manifests himself to the Disciples

A Late on that first day of the week, the disciples had shut themselves in for fear of the Jews. — *Jn20:19*

B The two disciples from Emmaus arrived and said 'The Lord is risen indeed and was seen *of us*'[2]. The disciples listened to them with skepticism, — *Mk16:12, 13; Lk24:34*

C as they recounted the events that took place on their journey and how they only realized that it was Jesus when he was break- — *Lk24:35*

---

1 John 20:24 shows that Thomas was not among the group at the time. The use of the term 'eleven' conveys that Thomas was staying at the location with the rest, but had temporarily left on some chore.

2 P. Ramsundar (2015) 'Resolving difficulties in the translation of Luke 24:34'.

The Harmonized Gospels — Apocalyptic Version

ing the bread.

D Even as they were speaking, Jesus himself appeared among them and said 'All hail. Peace be on you'.	Mk16:14; Lk24:36 Jn20:19
E The disciples were terrified, thinking that they were seeing an apparition.	Lk24:37
F But Jesus said to them 'Why are you so afraid and what are you imagining in your hearts'? He upbraided them for their unbelief and stubbornness, because they did not believe those who had seen him after he was risen.	Mk16:14; Lk24:38
G 'Look, here are my hands and my feet. It is me in person. Touch me, and see, for a spirit being does not have flesh and bones, yet as you can see, I do'.	Lk24:39; Jn20:20
H As he spoke he showed them his hands and his feet. They came to him and held on to his feet, worshipping him, though some did not know what to believe.	Mt28:9, 17; Lk24:40; Jn20:20
I While they were still trying to grasp the situation and to rejoice, Jesus said to them 'Do you have anything to eat?'	Lk24:41
J They offered him a piece of a broiled fish and a honeycomb, which he took it and ate before them.	Lk24:42,43
K Then he said 'This is what I spoke to you about when I was with you, that all things must be fulfilled, which were written in the books of Moses and the prophets and in the psalms about me'.	Lk24:44
L Then he expounded the scriptures to them so that they could understand.	Lk24:45
M He said 'It is written, and thus it is fit that the Christ had to suffer and to rise from the dead the third day,	Lk24:46
N 'so that repentance and the forgiveness of sins should be preached in his name to all nations, starting at Jerusalem.	Lk24:47
O 'You are the witnesses of these things'.	Lk24:48
P Jesus led them out to Bethany, where he lifted up his hands and blessed them saying,	Lk24:50; Jn20:22
Q 'I will send what was promised by my Father to you, even the Godly Nature, but you must wait in Jerusalem until you receive this power from above[1]'.	Lk24:49; Jn20:22
R Even as he blessed them, he departed from them, and was carried up into heaven and sat at the right hand of God.	Mk16:19; Lk24:51
S They worshipped him and returned to Jerusalem with great rejoicing.	Lk24:52
T There they continually gathered at the temple, praising and blessing God.	Lk24:53
U Thomas, one of the twelve, who was called Didymus, was not with them at the time Jesus visited.	Jn20:24

---

1 The presence of the God's Nature was bestowed on them on the day of Pentecost nearly fifty days later (Acts 2:1 ~ 4).

V The other disciples told him 'We have seen the Lord'. But he replied 'Except I shall see in his hands the print of the nails, and put my finger into the print of the nails, and thrust my hand into his side, I will not believe'. | *Jn20:25*

CHAPTER 165
The chief priests bribe the guards to lie

A The guards went to the city and told the chief priests all that had transpired. | *Mt28:11*

B The chief priests called the other leaders and after discussing the matter, they gave a large sum of money to the soldiers, | *Mt28:12*

C and told them 'Say that his disciples came in the night and stole him away while we slept. | *Mt28:13*

D 'If this matter comes to the attention of the governor, we will speak to him and protect you'. | *Mt28:14*

E The guardsmen took the money and did as they were instructed. This is why, *even to the day of this writing*, this story is commonly reported among the Jews. | *Mt28:15*

CHAPTER 166
Jesus meets the disciples with Thomas present

A Eight days after Jesus first manifested himself to the disciples, they were again inside and this time Thomas was with them. Jesus appeared among them, though the doors were shut, and said 'Peace be unto you'. | *Jn20:26*

B To Thomas he said 'Look at my hands and feel them with your fingers. Put your hand at my side and do not be faithless but believe'. | *Jn20:27*

C Thomas answered 'My Lord and my God'. | *Jn20:28*

D Jesus then said 'Thomas, because you have seen me, you have believed. Blessed are those who have not seen, and yet believe'. | *Jn20:29*

The Harmonized Gospels — Apocalyptic Version

CHAPTER 167
Jesus visits the disciples at the sea of Tiberias

A Jesus next manifested himself to the disciples at the sea of Tiberias. This is how that event transpired.	Jn21:1
B Simon Peter was with Thomas, called Didymus, Nathanael of Cana in Galilee, the sons of Zebedee, and two other disciples.	Jn21:2
C Simon Peter said to them 'I am going to fish'. They others said 'We will also go with you'. They straightaway boarded a ship and went fishing. All that night they caught nothing.	Jn21:3
D When it was morning, Jesus stood on the shore, but the disciples did not know it was him.	Jn21:4
E Jesus said to them 'Children, have you any fish'? They answered 'No'.	Jn21:5
F Jesus replied 'Cast the net on the right side of the ship, and you shall find some'. They cast in the place Jesus said and found that they were not able to bring in the net because of the multitude of fishes.	Jn21:6
G The disciple who Jesus had affection for said to Peter 'It is the Lord'. When Simon Peter heard that it was the Lord, he put on his fisherman's coat, for he was naked, and dived into the sea.	Jn21:7
H The other disciples came in the boat dragging the net with fishes, for they were just about one hundred yards from shore.	Jn21:8
I When they landed, they saw a fire of coals, with fish baking and bread at hand.	Jn21:9
J Jesus said to them 'Bring some of the fish which you have just caught'.	Jn21:10
K Simon Peter went and helped them pull the net to land. It was full of good sized fishes, numbering a hundred and fifty-three, yet in spite of the quantity of fishes, the net was not torn apart.	Jn21:11
L Jesus said 'Come and eat'. All this time none of the disciples dared to ask him 'Who are you'?, because they knew it was the Lord	Jn21:12
M Jesus took of bread and gave them, and did with the fish likewise.	Jn21:13
N This was the *fifth*[1] time that Jesus showed himself to his disciples, after he had risen from the dead.	Jn21:14
O After they had eaten, Jesus said to Simon Peter 'Simon, son of Jonas, do you love me more than these'? Simon said 'Yes, Lord. You know that I love you'. Jesus said to him 'Feed my lambs'.	Jn21:15
P Jesus said to Simon a second time 'Simon, son of Jonas, do you love me'? Peter replied 'Yes, Lord. You know that I love you'. Jesus said 'Feed my sheep'.	Jn21:16
Q Jesus said to Simon a third time 'Simon, son of Jonas, do you love me'? Peter was hurt because Christ asked him three times 'Do you	Jn21:17

---

1 John relates four separate appearances of the resurrected Christ including this one, but did not include the appearance to the women. There were also subsequent appearances (ICor 15:5—9).

love me'? So he said 'Lord, you know all things. You know that I love you'. Jesus said to him 'Feed my sheep.

R 'I tell you in truth that when you were young, you dressed yourself, and walked wherever you wanted. When you are old, you shall stretch out your hands, and another shall clothe you and carry you where you do not want to go'. | *Jn21:18*

S This Jesus said to indicated how Peter would die and so glorify God. After Jesus said this he said to another disciple 'Come with me'. | *Jn21:19*

T Peter looked and saw the disciple who Jesus had great affection for, following. This was the disciple and who had also leaned on Jesus' breast at supper, and had asked 'Lord, who is he that betrays you'? | *Jn21:20*

U Peter looked at the disciple and asked Jesus 'Lord, and where are you going with this man'? | *Jn21:21*

V Jesus said to him 'If it is my will that he waits for me till I come, what is that to you? You follow me'. | *Jn21:22*

W Thus there was this saying spread among the brethren, that that disciple should not die. Yet Jesus did not say to him, that he will not die, but 'If it is my will that he waits for me till I come, what is that to you'? | *Jn21:23*

CHAPTER 168

Jesus meets with his disciples in Galilee

A The eleven disciples went into Galilee, to the mountain that Jesus had told them about[1]. | *Mt28:16*

B They saw Jesus and worshipped him, but some still did not fully understand. | *Mt28:17*

C Jesus comforted them and left them with these instructions 'I have been granted all authority, both in the heavens and in earth[2]. | *Mt28:18*

---

1 This was forty days after Christ's resurrection (Acts 1:3).

2 John 1:1 ~ 4, 10 & 14, shows that the entity that is God consisted of two beings, one called the 'Father' and the other called the 'Word', though which God interfaced with his creation. The Word manifested himself in the human child, Jesus Christ, as the memories and experiences of the 'Word' was selectively passed to him. Thus the human Jesus became the residence of this being called the 'Word', and he could speak authoritatively of his experiences prior to his birth.

When the human Jesus died, God created a new non-physical body and infused it with the knowledge and experiences of Jesus Christ, including the prior experiences of the 'Word'. This resurrected Jesus is the one who has been granted all authority, who is on the right hand of God and shares a collective mind with God, making him 'at one' with God. This glorification of Jesus is typical of what God promises to all of mankind who chooses to follow God's way as typified by Christ's example (Mt1:23; Col 1:16 ~18; John 8:58, Rom 8:29; John 10:30; John 17:22; ICor 12:12 ~ 14).

The Harmonized Gospels — Apocalyptic Version

D 'As my Father has sent me, even so I send you'.	*Jn20:21*
E 'Go therefore, and teach all nations, baptizing them into the family of the Father, and of the Son, with the Nature of God. Preach the good news to everyone.	*Mt28:19; Mk16:15*
F 'He that believes and is baptized shall be saved, but he that does not believe shall be judged.	*Mk16:16*
G 'Whose sins you put aside, their sin will be put aside and whose sins you leave, their sin remains.	*Jn20:23*
H 'Teach them to live by all that I have taught you. Know this, I will always be with you, even to the end of the world.	*Mt28:20*
I 'By these signs you shall know the faithful. In my name they shall cast out devils and they shall be able to speak other languages.	*Mk16:17*
J 'If they inadvertently drink any noxious substance, it shall not hurt them, but they shall lay hands on the sick, and the sick will recover'.	*Mk16:18*

CHAPTER 169
Conclusion

A In the presence of his disciples, Jesus did many other notable acts that witness of him, which are not written in this book, for even the world itself could not contain all the books that could be written.	*Jn20:30* *Jn21:25*
B His disciples who witnessed of these things, wrote these words, and we know that their testimony is true.	*Jn21:24*
C But what is written, is written so that you might believe that Jesus is the Christ, the Son of God and that in believing you might have life through him.	*Jn20:31*
D The disciples went and preached everywhere. The Lord worked with them and confirmed their words with many signs. Amen.	*Mk16:20*

The Harmonized Gospels — Apocalyptic Version

Unassigned scriptures (KJV)

Luke 1:1 Forasmuch as many have taken in hand to set forth in order a declaration of those things which are most surely believed among us,

Luke 1:2 Even as they delivered them unto us, which from the beginning were eyewitnesses, and ministers of the word;

Luke 1:3 It seemed good to me also, having had perfect understanding of all things from the very first, to write unto thee in order, most excellent Theophilus,

Luke 1:4 That thou mightest know the certainty of those things, wherein thou hast been instructed.

The Harmonized Gospels — Apocalyptic Version

Chapter listing (Numeric)

Chapter 1	The origin of Jesus Christ.	pg 1
Chapter 2	The miraculous conception of John the Baptist.	pg 2
Chapter 3	Gabriel visits Mary.	pg 3
Chapter 4	Mary visits Elizabeth.	pg 4
Chapter 5	Joseph marries Mary.	pg 4
Chapter 6	The birth of John the Baptist.	pg 5
Chapter 7	The birth of Jesus.	pg 6
Chapter 8	The Genealogies.	pg 8
Chapter 9	Visit of the men from the East and the sojourn in Egypt.	pg 10
Chapter 10	Jesus at twelve in the temple.	pg 12
Chapter 11	The ministry of John the Baptist and his Baptism of Christ.	pg 13
Chapter 12	The temptation of Jesus.	pg 15
Chapter 13	Jesus' first disciples.	pg 16
Chapter 14	Jesus' first public miracle.	pg 18
Chapter 15	Jesus' second significant encounter with Peter, Andrew, James and John.	pg 18
Chapter 16	Jesus heals at the sheep market pool in Jerusalem.	pg 19
Chapter 17	Mary and Martha.	pg 22
Chapter 18	Jesus heals the man who was blind from birth.	pg 22
Chapter 19	Parable of the true shepherd.	pg 24
Chapter 20	Incident at the Feast of Dedication.	pg 25
Chapter 21	The visit of Nicodemus.	pg 26
Chapter 22	Jesus' disciples baptize.	pg 27
Chapter 23	Jesus preaches to the Samaritans.	pg 28
Chapter 24	Jesus heals the nobleman's son at Cana.	pg 30
Chapter 25	The forgiveness of the sinful woman.	pg 31
Chapter 26	Jesus attends the Feast of Tabernacles.	pg 32
Chapter 27	The woman taken in adultery.	pg 34
Chapter 28	Jesus — the light of the world.	pg 35
Chapter 29	The resurrection of Lazarus.	pg 37
Chapter 30	The imprisonment of John.	pg 40
Chapter 31	Christ begins his closing Ministry.	pg 40
Chapter 32	The calling of Simon Peter, Andrew, James and John to full time service.	pg 41
Chapter 33	Jesus casts out a demon in Capernaum.	pg 41
Chapter 34	Jesus heals Simon's mother-in-law.	pg 42
Chapter 35	Jesus heals following the Sabbath.	pg 42
Chapter 36	Jesus prays in a solitary place.	pg 42
Chapter 37	Christ ministers in Galilee.	pg 43
Chapter 38	The Sermon on the mount - Part I:The Beatitudes.	pg 43

The Harmonized Gospels — Apocalyptic Version

Chapter listing (Numeric) ctd.

Chapter 39	The Sermon on the mount - Part II: Charge to his disciples.	pg 44
Chapter 40	The Sermon on the mount - Part III: The spiritual intent of the law.	pg 45
Chapter 41	The Sermon on the mount - Part IV: Warning on seeking the praise of men.	pg 48
Chapter 42	The Sermon on the mount - Part V: On praying.	pg 49
Chapter 43	The Sermon on the mount - Part VI: On material concerns.	pg 50
Chapter 44	The Sermon on the mount - Part VII: On judging others.	pg 52
Chapter 45	The Sermon on the mount - Part VIII: How to be part of God's new world order.	pg 53
Chapter 46	Healing of a leper.	pg 54
Chapter 47	Healing of the Centurion's servant.	pg 55
Chapter 48	Resurrecting the Widow's dead son.	pg 56
Chapter 49	Commitment required of Jesus' followers.	pg 56
Chapter 50	Jesus calms the sea.	pg 57
Chapter 51	Casting out the demons at Gergesenes.	pg 57
Chapter 52	Healing of the bed-ridden man.	pg 59
Chapter 53	The calling of Matthew	pg 60
Chapter 54	The need for a new way of thinking.	pg 60
Chapter 55	The healing of the woman with the bleeding.	pg 61
Chapter 56	Restoring Jairus' daughter to life.	pg 62
Chapter 57	Healing of two blind men.	pg 62
Chapter 58	Jesus teaches throughout the region.	pg 63
Chapter 59	Jesus selects twelve apostles.	pg 64
Chapter 60	Jesus speaks of John the Baptist.	pg 67
Chapter 61	Jesus rebukes the cities of Judah.	pg 69
Chapter 62	Jesus' invitation.	pg 69
Chapter 63	Jesus on keeping the Sabbath.	pg 70
Chapter 64	Parable on seeking the place of honor.	pg 72
Chapter 65	Jesus ministers at the seaside.	pg 72
Chapter 66	The Pharisees accuse Jesus of working miracles by the power of Beelzebub.	pg 73
Chapter 67	Jesus tells of the sign of his authenticity.	pg 74
Chapter 68	Salvation is by obedience, not association.	pg 75
Chapter 69	The parable of the sower and the seed.	pg 75
Chapter 70	The parable of the wheat and the tares.	pg 77
Chapter 71	The parable of the sprouting seed.	pg 78

Chapter listing (Numeric) ctd.

Chapter 72	The parable of the mustard seed.	pg 78
Chapter 73	The parable of the leaven.	pg 78
Chapter 74	The parables of the treasure and the pearls.	pg 79
Chapter 75	The parable on casting the net.	pg 79
Chapter 76	Jesus finds skepticism in his hometown.	pg 80
Chapter 77	The beheading of John the Baptist.	pg 81
Chapter 78	Feeding of the five thousand.	pg 82
Chapter 79	Jesus walks on the sea.	pg 84
Chapter 80	On eating his flesh and drinking His blood.	pg 85
Chapter 81	Jesus heals in the district of Gennesaret.	pg 87
Chapter 82	Jesus on the washings of the Pharisees.	pg 87
Chapter 83	The Canaanite woman in Tyre/Sidon.	pg 89
Chapter 84	Healing the deaf and dumb man.	pg 90
Chapter 85	Feeding the four thousand.	pg 90
Chapter 86	The Pharisees and Sadducees ask for a sign.	pg 91
Chapter 87	The leaven of the Pharisees and Sadducees.	pg 92
Chapter 88	On accidental destruction.	pg 92
Chapter 89	The parable of the unfruitful fig tree.	pg 93
Chapter 90	Healing of the blind man at Bathsaida.	pg 93
Chapter 91	Jesus confirms that he is the Christ.	pg 94
Chapter 92	Jesus tells of his coming martyrdom.	pg 94
Chapter 93	Commitment required of disciples.	pg 95
Chapter 94	The transfiguration.	pg 95
Chapter 95	The prophecy of Elias.	pg 96
Chapter 96	The healing of the lunatic.	pg 97
Chapter 97	Jesus again tells of his coming martyrdom.	pg 98
Chapter 98	God's view on greatness.	pg 98
Chapter 99	Jesus pays tax.	pg 99
Chapter 100	On forbidding others to preach Christ.	pg 99
Chapter 101	Warning on offending Christ's disciples.	pg 99
Chapter 102	How to respond when offended.	pg 100
Chapter 103	God's delight on the repentance of sinners.	pg 101
Chapter 104	The parable of the unforgiving servant.	pg 101
Chapter 105	Parable of the prodigal son.	pg 102
Chapter 106	On Divorce	pg 103
Chapter 107	Blessing of the children.	pg 104
Chapter 108	The young man who couldn't.	pg 105
Chapter 109	The reward of his disciples.	pg 106
Chapter 110	The healing of the ten lepers.	pg 107

Chapter listing (Numeric) ctd.

Chapter 111	Jesus warns yet again of his coming sufferings.	pg 108
Chapter 112	The Zebedee brothers want to destroy Samaritans.	pg 108
Chapter 113	The sons of Zebedee seek preeminence.	pg 109
Chapter 114	The healing of two blind men.	pg 109
Chapter 115	Jesus stays at Zacchaeus.	pg 110
Chapter 116	Anticipation of Jesus's arrival in Jerusalem grips the nation.	pg 111
Chapter 117	Christ's tumultuous entry to Jerusalem.	pg 111
Chapter 118	Some Greeks ask to see Christ.	pg 112
Chapter 119	Jesus — Light of the World.	pg 113
Chapter 120	The cursing of the fig tree.	pg 114
Chapter 121	Christ expels the traders from the temple.	pg 115
Chapter 122	Christ heals in the temple.	pg 116
Chapter 123	The drying up of the fig tree.	pg 116
Chapter 124	The temple authorities confront Jesus.	pg 117
Chapter 125	The parable of the self-righteous Pharisee.	pg 118
Chapter 126	The parable of the landowner.	pg 118
Chapter 127	The parable of the marriage celebration.	pg 119
Chapter 128	The Herodians confront Jesus.	pg 121
Chapter 129	Jesus corrects the Sadducees on the resurrection.	pg 121
Chapter 130	Parable of the Good Samaritan.	pg 122
Chapter 131	The lawyers confront Jesus.	pg 123
Chapter 132	Jesus reveals his pre-incarnate existence.	pg 124
Chapter 133	Jesus condemns the Scribes and Pharisees.	pg 124
Chapter 134	The Widow's mite.	pg 127
Chapter 135	Prophecy of events preceding Christ's return.	pg 128
Chapter 136	Parable of the ten virgins.	pg 132
Chapter 137	Parable of the talents 1.	pg 133
Chapter 138	Parable of the talents 2.	pg 134
Chapter 139	Parable of the Crooked Steward.	pg 135
Chapter 140	The judgment at the resurrection.	pg 136
Chapter 141	Lazarus and the rich man.	pg 137
Chapter 142	The leaders of the Jews plot against Jesus.	pg 138
Chapter 143	Judas agrees to betray the Christ.	pg 138
Chapter 144	Jesus' response to the accolade.	pg 138
Chapter 145	Jesus anointed for burial.	pg 139

Chapter Listing (Numeric) ctd.

Chapter 146	Jesus and his disciples celebrate the Passover.	pg 140
Chapter 147	Jesus' last sermon to his disciples (I).	pg 144
Chapter 148	Jesus' last sermon to his disciples (II).	pg 146
Chapter 149	Jesus' last sermon to his disciples (III).	pg 147
Chapter 150	Jesus' prayer for his disciples.	pg 149
Chapter 151	Jesus prays at Gethsemane.	pg 151
Chapter 152	Jesus arrested.	pg 152
Chapter 153	The trial before Caiaphas.	pg 153
Chapter 154	Peter denies Christ.	pg 155
Chapter 155	Judas repents.	pg 156
Chapter 156	Jesus taken before Pontius Pilate.	pg 156
Chapter 157	Jesus taken before Herod.	pg 158
Chapter 158	Jesus taken back to Pilate.	pg 158
Chapter 159	The crucifixion.	pg 160
Chapter 160	The burial.	pg 164
Chapter 161	The sealing of the tomb.	pg 165
Chapter 162	Mary Magdalene and the women visit the tomb.	pg 165
Chapter 163	Jesus manifests himself to Cleopas.	pg 167
Chapter 164	Jesus manifests himself to the Disciples.	pg 168
Chapter 165	The chief priests bribe the guards to lie.	pg 170
Chapter 166	Jesus meets the disciples with Thomas present.	pg 170
Chapter 167	Jesus visits the disciples at the sea of Tiberias.	pg 171
Chapter 168	Jesus meets with his disciples in Galilee.	pg 172
Chapter 169	Conclusion.	pg 173

Chapter listing (Alphabetic)

Anticipation of Jesus's arrival in Jerusalem grips the nation.	Chapter 116	pg 111
The beheading of John the Baptist.	Chapter 77	pg 81
The birth of Jesus.	Chapter 7	pg 6
The birth of John the Baptist.	Chapter 6	pg 5
Blessing of the children.	Chapter 107	pg 104
The burial.	Chapter 160	pg 164
The calling of Matthew	Chapter 53	pg 60
The calling of Simon Peter, Andrew, James and John to full time service.	Chapter 32	pg 41
The Canaanite woman in Tyre/Sidon.	Chapter 83	pg 89
Casting out the demons at Gergesenes.	Chapter 51	pg 57
The chief priests bribe the guards to lie.	Chapter 165	pg 170
Christ begins his closing Ministry.	Chapter 31	pg 40
Christ expels the traders from the temple.	Chapter 121	pg 115
Christ heals in the temple.	Chapter 122	pg 116
Christ ministers in Galilee.	Chapter 37	pg 43
Christ's tumultuous entry to Jerusalem.	Chapter 117	pg 111
Commitment required of disciples.	Chapter 93	pg 95
Commitment required of Jesus' followers.	Chapter 49	pg 56
Conclusion.	Chapter 169	pg 173
The crucifixion.	Chapter 159	pg 160
The cursing of the fig tree.	Chapter 120	pg 114
The drying up of the fig tree.	Chapter 123	pg 116
Feeding of the five thousand.	Chapter 78	pg 82
Feeding the four thousand.	Chapter 85	pg 90
The forgiveness of the sinful woman.	Chapter 25	pg 31
Gabriel visits Mary.	Chapter 3	pg 3
The Genealogies.	Chapter 8	pg 8
God's delight on the repentance of sinners.	Chapter 103	pg 101
God's view on greatness.	Chapter 98	pg 98
Healing of a leper.	Chapter 46	pg 54
Healing of the bed-ridden man.	Chapter 52	pg 59
Healing of the blind man at Bathsaida.	Chapter 90	pg 93
Healing of the Centurion's servant.	Chapter 47	pg 55
The healing of the lunatic.	Chapter 96	pg 97
The healing of the ten lepers.	Chapter 110	pg 107
The healing of the woman with the bleeding.	Chapter 55	pg 61

Chapter Listing (Alphabetic) ctd.

Healing of two blind men.	Chapter 57	pg 62
The healing of two blind men.	Chapter 114	pg 109
Healing the deaf and dumb man.	Chapter 84	pg 90
The Herodians confront Jesus.	Chapter 128	pg 121
How to respond when offended.	Chapter 102	pg 100
The imprisonment of John.	Chapter 30	pg 40
Incident at the Feast of Dedication.	Chapter 20	pg 25
Jesus — Light of the World.	Chapter 119	pg 113
Jesus — the light of the world.	Chapter 28	pg 35
Jesus again tells of his coming martyrdom.	Chapter 97	pg 98
Jesus and his disciples celebrate the Passover.	Chapter 146	pg 140
Jesus anointed for burial.	Chapter 145	pg 139
Jesus arrested.	Chapter 152	pg 152
Jesus at twelve in the temple.	Chapter 10	pg 12
Jesus attends the Feast of Tabernacles.	Chapter 26	pg 32
Jesus calms the sea.	Chapter 50	pg 57
Jesus casts out a demon in Capernaum.	Chapter 33	pg 41
Jesus condemns the Scribes and Pharisees.	Chapter 133	pg 124
Jesus confirms that he is the Christ.	Chapter 91	pg 94
Jesus corrects the Sadducees on the resurrection.	Chapter 129	pg 121
Jesus finds skepticism in his hometown.	Chapter 76	pg 80
Jesus heals at the sheep market pool in Jerusalem.	Chapter 16	pg 19
Jesus heals following the Sabbath.	Chapter 35	pg 42
Jesus heals in the district of Gennesaret.	Chapter 81	pg 87
Jesus heals Simon's mother-in-law.	Chapter 34	pg 42
Jesus heals the man who was blind from birth.	Chapter 18	pg 22
Jesus heals the nobleman's son at Cana.	Chapter 24	pg 30
Jesus manifests himself to Cleopas.	Chapter 163	pg 167
Jesus manifests himself to the Disciples.	Chapter 164	pg 168
Jesus meets the disciples with Thomas present.	Chapter 166	pg 170
Jesus meets with his disciples in Galilee.	Chapter 168	pg 172
Jesus ministers at the seaside.	Chapter 65	pg 72
Jesus on keeping the Sabbath.	Chapter 63	pg 70
Jesus on the washings of the Pharisees.	Chapter 82	pg 87

The Harmonized Gospels — Apocalyptic Version

Chapter Listing (Alphabetic) ctd.

Jesus pays tax.	Chapter 99	pg 99
Jesus prays at Gethsemane.	Chapter 151	pg 151
Jesus prays in a solitary place.	Chapter 36	pg 42
Jesus preaches to the Samaritans.	Chapter 23	pg 28
Jesus rebukes the cities of Judah.	Chapter 61	pg 69
Jesus reveals his pre-incarnate existence.	Chapter 132	pg 124
Jesus selects twelve apostles.	Chapter 59	pg 64
Jesus speaks of John the Baptist.	Chapter 60	pg 67
Jesus stays at Zacchaeus.	Chapter 115	pg 110
Jesus taken back to Pilate.	Chapter 158	pg 158
Jesus taken before Herod.	Chapter 157	pg 158
Jesus taken before Pontius Pilate.	Chapter 156	pg 156
Jesus teaches throughout the region.	Chapter 58	pg 63
Jesus tells of his coming martyrdom.	Chapter 92	pg 94
Jesus tells of the sign of his authenticity.	Chapter 67	pg 74
Jesus visits the disciples at the sea of Tiberias.	Chapter 167	pg 171
Jesus walks on the sea.	Chapter 79	pg 84
Jesus warns yet again of his coming sufferings.	Chapter 111	pg 108
Jesus' disciples baptize.	Chapter 22	pg 27
Jesus' first disciples.	Chapter 13	pg 16
Jesus' first public miracle.	Chapter 14	pg 18
Jesus' invitation.	Chapter 62	pg 69
Jesus' last sermon to his disciples (I).	Chapter 147	pg 144
Jesus' last sermon to his disciples (II).	Chapter 148	pg 146
Jesus' last sermon to his disciples (III).	Chapter 149	pg 147
Jesus' prayer for his disciples.	Chapter 150	pg 149
Jesus' response to the accolade.	Chapter 144	pg 138
Jesus' second significant encounter with Peter, Andrew, James and John.	Chapter 15	pg 18
Joseph marries Mary.	Chapter 5	pg 4
Judas agrees to betray the Christ.	Chapter 143	pg 138
Judas repents.	Chapter 155	pg 156
The judgment at the resurrection.	Chapter 140	pg 136
The lawyers confront Jesus.	Chapter 131	pg 123
Lazarus and the rich man.	Chapter 141	pg 137
The leaders of the Jews plot against Jesus.	Chapter 142	pg 138

Chapter listing (Alphabetic) ctd.

The leaven of the Pharisees and Sadducees.	Chapter 87	pg 92
Mary and Martha.	Chapter 17	pg 22
Mary Magdalene and the women visit the tomb.	Chapter 162	pg 165
Mary visits Elizabeth.	Chapter 4	pg 4
The ministry of John the Baptist and his Baptism of Christ.	Chapter 11	pg 13
The miraculous conception of John the Baptist.	Chapter 2	pg 2
The need for a new way of thinking.	Chapter 54	pg 60
On accidental destruction.	Chapter 88	pg 92
On Divorce	Chapter 106	pg 103
On eating his flesh and drinking His blood.	Chapter 80	pg 85
On forbidding others to preach Christ.	Chapter 100	pg 99
The origin of Jesus Christ.	Chapter 1	pg 1
Parable of the Crooked Steward.	Chapter 139	pg 135
Parable of the Good Samaritan.	Chapter 130	pg 122
The parable of the landowner.	Chapter 126	pg 118
The parable of the leaven.	Chapter 73	pg 78
The parable of the marriage celebration.	Chapter 127	pg 119
The parable of the mustard seed.	Chapter 72	pg 78
Parable of the prodigal son.	Chapter 105	pg 102
The parable of the self-righteous Pharisee.	Chapter 125	pg 118
The parable of the sower and the seed.	Chapter 69	pg 75
The parable of the sprouting seed.	Chapter 71	pg 78
Parable of the talents 1.	Chapter 137	pg 133
Parable of the talents 2.	Chapter 138	pg 134
Parable of the ten virgins.	Chapter 136	pg 132
Parable of the true shepherd.	Chapter 19	pg 24
The parable of the unforgiving servant.	Chapter 104	pg 101
The parable of the unfruitful fig tree.	Chapter 89	pg 93
The parable of the wheat and the tares.	Chapter 70	pg 77
The parable on casting the net.	Chapter 75	pg 79
Parable on seeking the place of honor.	Chapter 64	pg 72
The parables of the treasure and the pearls.	Chapter 74	pg 79

Chapter Listing (Alphabetic) ctd.

Peter denies Christ.	Chapter 154	pg 155
The Pharisees accuse Jesus of working miracles by the power of Beelzebub.	Chapter 66	pg 73
The Pharisees and Sadducees ask for a sign.	Chapter 86	pg 91
The prophecy of Elias.	Chapter 95	pg 96
Prophecy of events preceding Christ's return.	Chapter 135	pg 128
Restoring Jairus' daughter to life.	Chapter 56	pg 62
Resurrecting the Widow's dead son.	Chapter 48	pg 56
The resurrection of Lazarus.	Chapter 29	pg 37
The reward of his disciples.	Chapter 109	pg 106
Salvation is by obedience, not association.	Chapter 68	pg 75
The sealing of the tomb.	Chapter 161	pg 165
The Sermon on the mount - Part I: The Beatitudes.	Chapter 38	pg 43
The Sermon on the mount - Part II: Charge to his disciples.	Chapter 39	pg 44
The Sermon on the mount - Part III: The spiritual intent of the law.	Chapter 40	pg 45
The Sermon on the mount - Part IV: Warning on seeking the praise of men.	Chapter 41	pg 48
The Sermon on the mount - Part V: On praying.	Chapter 42	pg 49
The Sermon on the mount - Part VI: On material concerns.	Chapter 43	pg 50
The Sermon on the mount - Part VII: On judging	Chapter 44	pg 52
The Sermon on the mount - Part VIII: How to be	Chapter 45	pg 53
Some Greeks ask to see Christ.	Chapter 118	pg 112
The sons of Zebedee seek preeminence.	Chapter 113	pg 109
The temple authorities confront Jesus.	Chapter 124	pg 117
The temptation of Jesus.	Chapter 12	pg 15
The transfiguration.	Chapter 94	pg 95
The trial before Caiaphas.	Chapter 153	pg 153
The visit of Nicodemus.	Chapter 21	pg 26
Visit of the men from the East and the sojourn in Egypt.	Chapter 9	pg 10

Chapter Listing (Alphabetic) ctd.

Warning on offending Christ's disciples.	Chapter 101	pg 99
The Widow's mite.	Chapter 134	pg 127
The woman taken in adultery.	Chapter 27	pg 34
The young man who couldn't.	Chapter 108	pg 105
The Zebedee brothers want to destroy Samaritans.	Chapter 112	pg 108

The Harmonized Gospels — Apocalyptic Version

Verse Finder Index

MATTHEW			MATTHEW			MATTHEW		
CH	VERSE	PAGE	CH	VERSE	PAGE	CH	VERSE	PAGE
1	1 ~ 8	8	9	1 ~ 8	59	16	1 ~ 4	91
	9 ~ 17	9		9 ~ 17	60		5 ~ 12	92
	18 ~ 20	4		18 ~ 22	61		13 ~ 23	94
	21 ~ 25	5		23 ~ 31	62		24 ~ 28	95
				32 ~ 34	73			
				35 ~ 38	63	17	1 ~ 2	95
2	1 ~ 3	10					3 ~ 13	96
	4 ~ 16	11	10	1 ~ 13	64		14 ~ 19	97
	17 ~ 23	12		14 ~ 26	65		20 ~ 23	98
				27 ~ 40	66		24 ~ 27	99
3	1 ~ 2	13		41 ~ 42	67			
	3	13, 14				18	1 ~ 5	98
	4 ~ 10	13	11	1 ~ 5	67		6 ~ 7	99
	11	14		6 ~ 19	68		8 ~ 10	100
	12 ~ 17	15		20 ~ 24	69		9	46, 100
				25 ~ 26	67		10	100
4	1 ~ 4	15		27 ~ 30	69		11 ~ 14	101
	5 ~ 11	16					15 ~ 20	100
	12 ~ 17	40	12	1 ~ 11	70		21 ~ 22	101
	18 ~ 22	41		12 ~ 14	71		23 ~ 35	102
	23 ~ 25	43		15	71, 72			
				16 ~ 20	72	19	1 ~ 5	103
5	1 ~ 5	43		21 ~ 33	73		6 ~ 15	104
	6 ~ 12	44		34 ~ 45	74		16 ~ 26	105
	13	44, 100		46 ~ 50	75		27 ~ 30	106
	14 ~ 16	44						
	17 ~ 27	45	13	1 ~ 6	75	20	1 ~ 11	106
	28 ~ 38	46		7 ~ 21	76		12 ~ 16	107
	39 ~ 43	47		22	76, 77		17 ~ 19	108
	44	46, 47		23 ~ 30	77		20 ~ 31	109
	45 ~ 48	47		31 ~ 34	78		32 ~ 34	110
				35	79			
6	1 ~ 6	48		36 ~ 42	77	21	1 ~ 7	111
	7 ~ 15	49		43	78		8 ~ 11	112
	16 ~ 18	48		44 ~ 52	79		12 ~ 13	115
	19 ~ 30	51		53 ~ 57	80		14 ~ 17	116
	31	51, 82		58	81		18 ~ 19	114
	32 ~ 34	52					20 ~ 22	116
			14	1 ~ 2	158		23 ~ 32	117
7	1 ~ 6	52		3	40, 81		33 ~ 40	118
	7 ~ 10	49		4	40, 81		41 ~ 46	119
	11	50		5 ~ 7	81			
	12	52		8 ~ 16	82	22	1 ~ 4	119
	13 ~ 25	53		17 ~ 22	83		5 ~ 14	120
	26 ~ 29	54		23 ~ 33	84		15 ~ 28	121
				34	84, 87		29 ~ 34	122
				35 ~ 36	87		35 ~ 40	123
8	1 ~ 4	54					41 ~ 46	124
	5 ~ 13	55	15	1	87			
	14 ~ 18	42		2 ~ 15	88	23	1 ~ 4	124
	19 ~ 22	56		16 ~ 28	89		5 ~ 23	125
	23 ~ 28	57		29 ~ 37	90		24 ~ 34	126
	29 ~ 34	58		38 ~ 39	91		35 ~ 39	127

Verse Finder Index (ctd.)

MATTHEW			MARK			MARK		
CH	VERSE	PAGE	CH	VERSE	PAGE	CH	VERSE	PAGE
24	1 ~ 10	128	1	1	1	7	1 ~ 4	87
	11 ~ 24	129		2 ~ 3	14		5 ~ 17	88
	25 ~ 27	130		4 ~ 6	13		18 ~ 30	89
	28	131		7 ~ 8	14		31 ~ 37	90
	29 ~ 39	130		9 ~ 12	15			
	40 ~ 50	131		13	16	8	1 ~ 8	90
	51	132		14 ~ 15	40		9 ~ 13	91
				16 ~ 28	41		14 ~ 21	92
				29 ~ 38	42		22 ~ 26	93
25	1 ~ 13	133		39	43		27 ~ 33	94
	14 ~ 30	134		40 ~ 45	54		34 ~ 38	95
	31 ~ 46	136						
			2	1 ~ 12	59	9	1 ~ 3	95
26	1	138		13 ~ 22	60		4 ~ 13	96
	2	138, 139		23 ~ 28	70		14 ~ 28	97
	3 ~ 5	138					29 ~ 37	98
	6 ~ 13	139	3	1 ~ 4	70		38 ~ 42	99
	14 ~ 16	138		5 ~ 6	71		43	46, 100
	17 ~ 20	140		7 ~ 12	72		44	100
	21 ~ 25	141		13 ~ 19	64		45	46, 100
	26 ~ 29	140		20 ~ 21	63		46	100
	30	150		22 ~ 30	73		47	46, 100
	31 ~ 32	142		31 ~ 35	75		48	100
	33 ~ 35	143					49 ~ 50	101
	36 ~ 46	151	4	1 ~ 6	75			
	47 ~ 54	152		7 ~ 18	76	10	1 ~ 2	103
	55	152, 153		19 ~ 20	77		3 ~ 5	104
	56 ~ 58	153		21	44		6 ~ 7	103
	59 ~ 68	154		22	65		8 ~ 12	104
	69 ~ 75	155		23	44		13 ~ 16	104
				24	52		17 ~ 27	105
				25	76		28 ~ 31	106
				26 ~ 34	78		32 ~ 34	108
27	1 ~ 10	156		35 ~ 41	57		35 ~ 48	109
	11 ~ 14	157					49 ~ 52	110
	15 ~ 21	159	5	1 ~ 8	57			
	22 ~ 26	160		9 ~ 20	58			
	27 ~ 29	158		21 ~ 34	61	11	1 ~ 7	111
	30 ~ 31	159		35 ~ 43	62		8 ~ 10	112
	32	160					11 ~ 14	114
	33 ~ 38	161	6	1 ~ 4	80		15 ~ 18	115
	39 ~ 49	162		5 ~ 6	81		19 ~ 24	116
	50 ~ 55	163		7 ~ 10	64		25 ~ 26	49
	56	161		11	65		27 ~ 33	117
	57 ~ 61	164		12 ~ 13	67			
	62 ~ 66	165		14 ~ 16	158	12	1 ~ 8	118
				17 ~ 18	40, 81		9	118, 119
				19 ~ 24	81		10 ~ 11	119
				25 ~ 29	82		12	119, 121
28	1 ~ 5	165		30	67		13 ~ 23	121
	6 ~ 8	166		31 ~ 37	82		24 ~ 27	122
	9 ~ 10	167		38 ~ 45	83		28 ~ 33	123
	11 ~ 15	170		46 ~ 52	84		34 ~ 37	124
	16 ~ 18	172		53	84, 87		38 ~ 40	125
	19 ~ 20	173		54 ~ 56	87		41 ~ 44	127

The Harmonized Gospels — Apocalyptic Version

Verse Finder Index (ctd.)

MARK			LUKE			LUKE		
CH	VERSE	PAGE	CH	VERSE	PAGE	CH	VERSE	PAGE
13	1 ~ 9	128	1	1 ~ 4	175	6	41 ~ 42	52
	10	129		5 ~ 22	2		43 ~ 44	53
	11 ~ 12	128		23 ~ 38	3		45	74
	13	128, 129		39 ~ 56	4		46 ~ 48	53
	14 ~ 22	129		57 ~ 64	5		49	54
	23 ~ 32	130		65 ~ 66	6			
	33 ~ 34	131		67 ~ 74	5	7	1 ~ 10	55
	35 ~ 37	132		75 ~ 80	6		11 ~ 17	56
							18 ~ 22	67
			2	1 ~ 11	6		23 ~ 35	68
14	1 ~ 2	138		12 ~ 31	7		36 ~ 50	31
	3 ~ 9	139		32 ~ 40	8			
	10 ~ 11	138		41 ~ 49	12	8	1 ~ 6	75
	12 ~ 17	140		50 ~ 52	13		7 ~ 13	76
	18 ~ 21	141					14 ~ 15	77
	22 ~ 25	140	3	1 ~ 3	13		16	44
	26	150		4 ~ 6	14		17	65
	27 ~ 28	142		7 ~ 9	13		18	76
	29 ~ 31	143		10 ~ 16	14		19 ~ 21	75
	32 ~ 42	151		17 ~ 18	15		22	57
	43 ~ 48	152		19 ~ 20	40		23 ~ 29	57
	49 ~ 54	153		21 ~ 22	15		30 ~ 39	58
	55 ~ 65	154		23	9, 15		40 ~ 48	61
	66 ~ 72	155		24 ~ 26	9		49 ~ 55	62
				27 ~ 38	10			
						9	1 ~ 4	64
			4	1 ~ 4	15		5	65
15	1	156		5 ~ 13	16		6	67
	2 ~ 5	157		14 ~ 25	80		7 ~ 9	158
	6 ~ 11	159		26 ~ 30	81		10	67, 82
	12 ~ 15	160		31 ~ 37	41		11 ~ 12	82
	16 ~ 18	158		38 ~ 43	42		13	82, 83
	19 ~ 20	159		44	43		14 ~ 17	83
	21	160					18 ~ 22	94
	22 ~ 27	161	5	1 ~ 4	18		23 ~ 29	95
	28 ~ 36	162		5 ~ 11	19		30 ~ 36	96
	37 ~ 39	163		12 ~ 16	54		37 ~ 43	97
	40	161		17 ~ 26	59		44 ~ 48	98
	41	163		27 ~ 39	60		49 ~ 50	99
	42 ~ 47	164					51 ~ 56	108
			6	1 ~ 9	70		57 ~ 62	56
				10 ~ 11	71			
16	1 ~ 5	165		12 ~ 16	64	10	1	64
	6	165, 166		17 ~ 19	72		2	63
	7 ~ 8	166		20 ~ 21	43		3	65
	9	165		22 ~ 26	44		4 ~ 9	64
	10 ~ 11	167		27	46		10 ~ 12	65
	12	167, 168		28 ~ 30	47		13 ~ 15	69
	13	168		31	52		16 ~ 21	67
	14	169		32 ~ 36	51		22	67, 69
	15 ~ 18	173		37	52		23 ~ 24	76
	19	169		38	47		25 ~ 27	122
	20	173		39	88		28 ~ 37	123
				40	65		38 ~ 42	22

The Harmonized Gospels — Apocalyptic Version

Verse Finder Index (ctd.)

LUKE			LUKE			LUKE		
CH	VERSE	PAGE	CH	VERSE	PAGE	CH	VERSE	PAGE
11	1 ~ 11	49	15	1 ~ 10	101	21	1 ~ 4	127
	12 ~ 13	50		11 ~ 17	102		5 ~ 10	128
	14 ~ 15	73		18 ~ 32	103		11	128, 130
	16	74					6 ~ 17	128
	17 ~ 23	73	16	1 ~ 12	135		18 ~ 24	129
	24 ~ 26	74		13	51		25 ~ 33	130
	27 ~ 28	75		14 ~ 15	124		34 ~ 36	131
	29 ~ 32	74		16	68		37 ~ 38	132
	33	44		17	45			
	34 ~ 36	51		18	46, 104	22	1 ~ 6	138
	37 ~ 38	87		19 ~ 31	137		7 ~ 20	140
	39 ~ 41	126					21 ~ 23	141
	42 ~ 43	125	17	1 ~ 2	99		24	109, 140
	44 ~ 49	126		3	100		25 ~26	109
	50 ~ 51	127		4	101		27	141
	52	126		5 ~ 6	98		28 ~ 32	142
	53 ~ 54	127		7 ~ 19	107		33 ~ 38	143
				20	130		39	150, 151
12	1	92		21	129		40 ~ 46	151
	2 ~ 3	65		22 ~ 24	130		47 ~ 52	152
	4 ~ 9	66		25	94		53 ~ 55	153
	10	73		26 ~ 27	130		56 ~ 62	155
	11 ~ 12	65		28 ~ 30	131		63 ~ 71	154
	13 ~ 20	50		31 ~ 32	129			
	21 ~ 29	51		33	95			
	30 ~ 32	52		34 ~ 37	131	23	1	156
	33 ~ 34	51					2 ~ 7	157
	35 ~ 36	131	18	1 ~ 8	50		8 ~ 15	158
	37	131		9 ~ 14	118		16 ~ 19	159
	38	132		15 ~ 17	104		20 ~ 29	160
	39 ~ 45	131		18 ~ 27	105		30 ~ 34	161
	46 ~ 48	132		28 ~ 30	106		35 ~ 37	162
	49 ~ 53	66		31 ~ 34	108		38	161
	54 ~ 57	91		35 ~ 39	109		39 ~ 44	162
	58 ~ 59	45		40 ~ 43	110		45	162, 163
							46 ~ 49	163
13	1 ~ 5	92	19	1 ~ 10	110		50 ~ 56	164
	6 ~ 9	93		11 ~ 27	134			
	10 ~ 17	71		28 ~ 34	111	24	1 ~ 2	165
	18 ~ 21	78		35 ~ 44	112		3	166
	22	63		45 ~ 46	115		4	165
	23 ~ 27	53		47 ~ 48	122		5	165, 166
	28 ~ 29	55					6 ~ 9	166
	30	107	20	1 ~ 8	117		10	165
	31 ~ 35	127		9 ~ 15	118		11	167
				16 ~ 19	119		12	166
14	1 ~ 6	71		20 ~ 33	121		13 ~ 20	167
	7 ~ 11	72		34 ~ 40	122		21 ~ 35	168
	12 ~ 17	119		41 ~ 45	124		36 ~ 53	169
	18	119, 120		46 ~ 47	125			
	19 ~ 24	120						
	25	95						
	26	66						
	27 ~ 33	95						
	34 ~ 35	100						

Verse Finder Index (ctd.)

JOHN

CH	VERSE	PAGE
1	1~5	1
	6~7	6
	8	14
	9~14	1
	15	14
	16~17	1
	18	69
	19~27	14
	28	14, 15
	29~31	16
	32	15, 16
	33	16
	34~51	17
2	1~11	18
	12	80
	13~22	115
	23~25	138
3	1~9	26
	10~28	27
	29~36	28
4	1~11	28
	12~35	29
	36~43	30
	44	80
	45~54	30
5	1~9	19
	10~29	20
	30~47	21
6	1~3	82
	4	111
	5~6	82
	7~14	83
	15~21	84
	22~39	85
	40~62	86
	63~71	87
7	1~19	32
	20~41	33
	42~53	34
8	1~11	34
	12~31	35
	32~53	36
	54~59	37

JOHN

CH	VERSE	PAGE
9	1~14	22
	15~37	23
	38~41	24
10	1~16	24
	17~36	25
	37~42	26
11	1~11	37
	12~35	38
	36~54	39
	55~57	111
12	1	111
	2~11	139
	12~14	112
	15	111
	16~22	112
	23~35	113
	36	113, 114
	37~43	114
	44~50	113
13	1~7	140
	8~25	141
	26~37	142
	38	143
14	1~19	144
	20~31	145
15	1~21	146
	22~27	147
16	1~13	147
	14~32	148
	33	149
17	1~17	149
	18~26	150
18	1	151
	2~11	152
	12~16	153
	17	155
	18~21	153
	22~23	154
	24	153
	25~27	155
	28~29	156
	30~38	157
	39	159
	40	159, 160

JOHN

CH	VERSE	PAGE
19	1	160
	2~4	158
	5~11	159
	12	159, 160
	13~17	160
	18~27	161
	28~29	162
	30~33	163
	34	162, 163
	35~37	163
	38~42	164
20	1	165
	2~13	166
	14~18	167
	19	168, 169
	20	169
	21	173
	22	169
	23~24	173
	25	170, 173
	26~29	170
	30~31	173
21	1~17	171
	18~23	172
	24~25	173

www.ingramcontent.com/pod-product-compliance
Lightning Source LLC
Chambersburg PA
CBHW050636300426
44112CB00012B/1821